THE BIBLE'S AUTHORITY

THE BIBLE'S AUTHORITY

*A Portrait Gallery of Thinkers
from Lessing to Bultmann*

J. C. O'Neill

T&T CLARK
EDINBURGH

T&T CLARK
59 GEORGE STREET
EDINBURGH EH2 2LQ
SCOTLAND

First published 1991

British Library Cataloguing in Publication Data
O'Neill, J. C.
The Bible's authority: a portrait gallery of thinkers
from Lessing to Bultmann
1. Germany. Christianity. Philosophy
I. Title
209.22

ISBN   0 567 29189 8

Typeset by Barbers Highlands Ltd, Fort William
Printed and bound in Great Britain by Billing & Sons Ltd,
Worcester

To my daughters

Rachel Catherine and Philippa

... eine Geschichte der Wissenschaften, insofern diese durch Menschen behandelt worden [sind], zeigt ein ganz anderes und höchst belehrendes Ansehen, als wenn bloss Entdeckungen und Meinungen aneinander gereiht werden.

Goethe, Geschichte der Farbenlehre, Einleitung.

... a history of the sciences and scholarly disciplines from the point of view of the men who were engaged in them shows a completely different aspect and is much more instructive than a mere list of discoveries and theories.

Contents

Preface

This book began as a course of lectures in the University of Cambridge on Biblical Criticism and Authority in the Nineteenth Century. I am grateful to the Senatus of Westminster College who encouraged me to give these university lectures outside my normal teaching; to the United Reformed Church which allowed me two sabbatical terms largely devoted to writing some of these chapters; to the Alexander von Humboldt Stiftung in the Federal Republic of Germany which generously paid for me and my wife to spend the second of these sabbatical terms at the University of Göttingen; to Frau Margret Schünemann who checked a large number of my translations from the German; to Ernest Nicholson and Frank Kermode for encouragement; and to many friends who helped me to understand the people I am writing about a little better: Ernst Bammel, Wilfried Barner, Michael Black, Gerd Buchdahl, Christoph Burchard, Robert Morgan, Michael Mulligan, Berndt Schaller, Rudolf Smend, Francis Watson, George Wells, and above all Nicholas Boyle, who helped me more than anyone else and also suggested the motto from Goethe.

I could not have written this book without the loving support of my wife Judith.

J. C. O'Neill
Edinburgh, 1989

Introduction

Anyone who looks dispassionately at English-speaking culture in the forty years that have elapsed since the end of World War II has to explain two very surprising phenomena, both quite unexpected after the defeat of a Germany that had, after all, begun that conflict. The first surprising phenomenon concerns the widest cultural scene; the second relates to the subject of this book, the authority of the Bible.

Since the defeat of the Third German Empire, English-speaking thought has been deeply influenced by German writers and thinkers. So many new impulses have come from them. In philosophy Ludwig Wittgenstein, an Austrian who settled in Cambridge, has dominated the subject. When his influence waned, Frege's influence took over. In politics, Karl Marx's writings fascinated the first post-war generation and then seemed to pass away. Astonishingly enough, when his thought had all but been consigned to obscurity, his name burst out once more, with renewed brilliance, and surrounded by a new galaxy of German thinkers: Ernst Bloch, Herbert Marcuse and the Frankfurt School. The works and teaching and ideas of Sigmund Freud have been never so alive and so widely disseminated as in the post-war world. In literature, the most influential book of criticism has been Erich Auerbach's *Mimesis*, the work of a German who has provided critics from other European cultures, above all English-speaking critics, with the Ariadne thread for understanding their own realistic heritage. This intellectual dominance exists not just at a fashionable level or at a popular level. Behind Wittgenstein and Marx and Freud stand Kant and Hegel. It is as though the very defeat of Germany – and for a second time – confirmed the intellectual pre-eminence of German thinkers.

If at the level of culture attempts to deny my thesis by citing names such as Satre or Bertrand Russell or Leavis or Keynes might raise more than a smile, the attempt to deny my thesis in theology can encounter nothing but dismay. I shall never forget the look on Donald MacKinnon's face when the name of William Temple was mentioned in attempted refutation of the suggestion that no theologian of stature had been born since Bultmann (1884) and Barth (1886). Barth was the hero of all young theologians in the first post-war generation. Bonhoeffer, his younger disciple, had a period of fashion, but the decisive voice in theology in the 1960s became that of Rudolf Bultmann, and Bultmann still reigns. Perhaps Reinhold Niebuhr and C. H. Dodd could be cited against this, but nothing they said is not to be found in nineteenth-century German theology, however great their credit for persisting in piping away each at his own single tune: 'moral man and immoral society' on the one hand, and 'realized eschatology' on the other.

The second surprising phenomenon an observer of English-speaking culture would have to explain is the persistence of the authority of the Bible. This despite secularization. Educated writers in English fairly safely now assert that everyone knows that we have to do without belief in God, and that the key events of the Christian faith are 'mythical', that is, they did not happen in the ordinary sense of happen. Whether or not God exists, he is, they assume, to all intents and purposes 'dead'. The more perceptive critics, like Jean Paul long ago, mourn that event. Erich Heller, in his classic collection of essays entitled *The Disinherited Mind* inscribed Hölderlin's lines in the preface as a sort of motto for the book:

> Warum zeichnet, wie sonst, die Stirne des
>   Mannes ein Gott nicht,
> Drückt den Stempel, wie sonst, nicht dem
>   Getroffenen auf?

> Why does a god no more inscribe the
> brow of a mortal,
> Setting his seal, as of old, on the
> victim chosen above?

Like Hölderlin, he was sad.

Yet the phenomenon that persists is the continued authority of the Bible. I don't just mean that more commentaries on the Bible, monographs about Biblical questions, encyclopaedias of the Bible and its interpretation, popular books about the Bible are published than ever before. I don't just mean the revival of fundamentalism, with the astonishing rise of pentecostalist fellowships throughout the English-speaking world. I am pointing to something much deeper, which I know produces the scholarly and semi-scholarly books on the Bible and which I suspect underpins the rise of pentecostalism. This is the indissoluble connection, at the very heart of our culture, of the belief that 'God is dead' and the belief that the Bible represents and embodies and carries within it the secret of history. The shrewd pentecostalist preacher who commands his millions of devoted followers might insist it is his continued supernaturalist theology that does it, but what keeps the show on the road is the belief he imbibed from his Bible College teachers, which they in turn got from conservative German scholarship, that knew to drink at the same fountain as their radical colleagues, that the Bible gives anyone who reads it the clue to the history of the world, that the private religion of the Bible is indestructible.

Even the German theologians who openly or covertly accepted that God was dead and the crucial events 'mythical' – Semler, Eichhorn, David Friedrich Strauss, Ferdinand Christian Baur, above all Bultmann – showed that the Bible retained its authority by devoting the enormous scholarly energy of their lives to expounding it. All the secular German thinkers – and this is even more significant – grounded their own systems in the system provided by their reading of the Bible. Kant, in resolutely espousing a religion within the bounds of reason alone, drew all his key terms from the Bible. His thought consists of a way of living with the Fall, according to the Law, in the Hope of attaining the Kingdom of Freedom. Hegel unashamedly drew his view of history from the periodising of history provided in the Bible and he said the goal and the starting-point of history was marked by the Biblical statement, 'When the fulness of the time was come, God sent his Son'. Hegel's pupil Karl Marx secularized the history of salvation taught in the Bible. Freud's analysis of the human condition is a secularised version of the struggle in the soul of every Bible believer between Freedom and the Law.

If any dispassionate observer of English-speaking culture since World War II has to explain two phenomena, the triumph of German thought and the continuing authority of the Bible, what possible explanation can lie to hand? I have already suggested the second phenomenon is part of the first, that the continued authority of the Bible is part of the triumph of German thinkers. But why the triumph of German thinkers when the embodiment of their pride, the German Empire, had been humbled, not once but twice?

The answer is simple. The German thinkers triumphed in the humiliation of their national symbol because that is what they had room in their thought to accept. Their very thought expected history to move from triumph to defeat and to find triumph in defeat. History moved forward through blood and tears and struggle; but history always moved forward. They could build in ruins, because history always built in ruins. The deeper the humiliation of pride the better, for history would triumph.

Whence did this view of history derive? Without doubt, from the German reading of the Bible. Anyone who tries to understand where this English-speaking generation has got to must undoubtedly try to understand the German thinkers who still dominate us. The thesis of my book is that such an attempt to understand German thinkers will be at a loss to know what to make of them unless it is prepared to ask, How did they see the Bible?

This book began as a series of lectures on 'Criticism and Biblical Authority from Lessing to Käsemann' first delivered in the Divinity School in Cambridge on Wednesdays and

Saturdays at 9 a.m. in Michaelmas term 1974. I started to turn the lectures into a book in 1978, and since then I have worked hard on the subject almost every vacation, as well as in two sabbatical terms. Although I have been wrestling with the writings of Barth and Nietzsche since beginning to take an interest in them in 1948 or 1949, I have not been able to keep abreast of all 'the literature', let alone what has been written on each of the other nineteen thinkers. On those terms, no one could deal with more than two or three of the figures I speak of, even with a lifetime to give; and my steady occupation in all these years has not been this book but rather the close and detailed exegesis of the text of the New Testament. My only hope has been to read as widely as I could in the authors I chose, and to study with microscopic attention those crucial passages where they allow us to glimpse their deeper and most characteristic thoughts on the authority of the Bible. I never say that such-and-such a thinker espoused such-and-such a position without having found in his writings a clear statement to that effect.

The book revives a classical approach to the study of ideas, which in today's academic climate may perhaps appear startling and new – the expository approach, by way of intellectual biography. Bruno Bauer, whose portrait is in this collection, was master of the genre; Eichhorn and Albert Schweitzer were practitioners; while Basil Willey in our century can stand as a more recent example. The approach demands of the reader a more than usual active exercise of sympathy and discernment, but the great advantage over the usual technical discussion of issues like the Bible's authority is that the best work is made available to the general reader, who is not debarred by esoteric language or by detailed discussion of the arguments scholars have deployed against other scholars who have pronounced on the subject. Both the teacher and the student for their part can go further than the general reader; they are offered direct access to the text, and are given long and full extracts upon which to work for themselves. The book seeks to draw active sympathy from the readers; time to turn over in solitude what is to be seen in each of the portraits.

My method has been first to sketch in the life of the thinker before moving on to his ideas. This I have found a most delightful way to approach the great question of their thought. Everyone's lives are interesting, but especially when one's own life touches theirs at some point or other. I am a teacher who loves listening to other people's lectures and watching how students' minds develop. What more delightful an occupation than to get to know the history of fellow-teachers who themselves were once students, to observe them at home, in the lecture theatre, talking to students, writing their books, trying to get them published, fighting their battles.

I have a further reason to delight. I am a professional Biblical critic, and the thinkers whose work I am exploring were either themselves professional Biblical critics or they based their thought on the study of the work of great professional critics of their day. Although I often find their conclusions questionable, I have to admit that as critics they are superb. Their attacks on conservative positions are almost invariably well mounted. No ignorant iconoclasts here; they are among the best thinkers of their age who saw the evidence more clearly and more comprehensively, who could write more clearly and briefly and persuasively than their opponents. They were able to think: that is, to propose cool hypothesis after cool hypothesis, based on a comprehensive knowledge of the evidence; and they had the tact and the insight to arrive very often at the historical truth of the matter where their opponents floundered. They usually beat the so-called defenders of the Bible's authority at their own game. Unless we see that, we miss some of the seriousness and importance of the subject.

Only when I have done that (tried to understand their lives and the way they developed, and tried to follow sympathetically their particular contribution to the critical study of the Bible) do I move finally to an estimate of their views about the authority of the Bible. By then I am in a position to judge.

Although I believe great issues are at stake, including the authority of God and the authority of the Bible, I make no claim this book will solve them. I don't think the study of history gives the clue to history, unlike almost all the men whose thought appears between these covers. Histories should simply say what is the case, and so clear the way for reasonable creatures to make sound judgements and to do what they ought to do.

The Biblical critics and thinkers I deal with rather surprisingly argue for (or at least bear witness to) the authority of the Bible. That is very interesting. As historian, I want to show why. As historian, I shall try to show the reasoning wasn't very good. As a reasonable person, I can no longer follow their reasons. And I have to confess, as a reasonable historian, that the Bible's authority looks to me greater than ever, a theme this book can only hint at, for the theme of this book is the story of how Biblical criticism in its heyday, in Germany from Lessing (and his forerunners) to Bultmann, supplanted the Bible's true authority in favour of a new sort of authority for the Bible. The Bible's authority if anything was strengthened and made more widely accepted, but it was a different authority.

There are similarities between this thesis and the central thesis of Hans Frei's book *The Eclipse of Biblical Narrative: A Study in Eighteenth and Nineteenth Century Hermeneutics.*[1] He argues that the great revolutionary discovery of the eighteenth-century theologians was that the Bible was a collection of realistic narratives. Yet they could do nothing with that revolutionary recognition, since they imagined that 'history-like' stories had to possess 'historical likelihood' if they were to retain their authority. That led them to attempt to locate that authority elsewhere, for example (with Schleiermacher) in the consciousness of the author of the narrative and in the consciousness of Jesus, the chief character in the narrative. Hence 'the eclipse of Biblical narrative' of which the title speaks, an eclipse that did not pass over until Karl Barth (according to Frei) was able to show that the theologically most significant biblical narratives could be read 'realistically' without making history the test of meaning.

[1] (New Haven and London: Yale University Press, 1974).

I am close to Frei's thesis in arguing that eighteenth and nineteenth-century German interpreters of the Bible and philosophers retained the authority of scripture by putting a new substitute authority in place of the old authority. However, Hans Frei believes that by taking up a position close to Barth's he can detect the errors of Barth's great forerunners and show the solution to the problems they failed to solve. I venture to doubt whether Barth is very different from his predecessors, and have simply given him his own chapter alongside the other twenty thinkers whose lives contribute to our story.

Frei boasts that his book contains no actual examples of the examination of a single Biblical text. I have tried to approach the problem of the authority of the Bible by seeing how men, who as professionals or as passionate amateurs gave the most serious attention to close examination of Biblical passages, actually dealt with their texts. Frei's approach is necessarily abstract, and runs the risk of suggesting that 'The Bible' was the problem. In truth, all the thinkers we are concerned with still lived in a world in which the very words of the Bible, its great texts and the events of the Exodus, the Exile, and the Incarnation were living moments in their imaginative existence. Their problem was not 'The Bible' as such but how to come to terms with the words and images that had shaped their lives.

Whatever consequences we may draw from these twenty-one stories, they are good stories in their own right. Yet we cannot avoid drawing consequences, and my own conclusion is this. The continued authority given to the Bible by Christians and non-Christians who had ceased to believe that the authority comes from Almighty God who makes promises and gives gifts to his creatures is hard to justify, and can lead to strange and terrible consequences. The Bible, instead of being a book giving information about God and containing his promises, was seen as the record of how humanity came to understand itself and history. All the religious emotion rightly attached to the worship of God, instead of being renounced (which is the logical thing to do it there is no God), was attached to the history of humanity interpreted according to Biblical patterns, as having one single meaning to which those who understood history had to submit. In Christendom barbarous things known to be wrong had been done in defiance of God. Now barbarous things known to be wrong were contemplated and done in obedience to history. The idea history was a coherent force which had to be obeyed was drawn from the Bible by profound and subtle thinkers who maintained the Bible's authority while denying the existence and authority of the God of whom the Bible spoke.

This is not an anti-German book. There are plenty of Germans, from Michaelis to Wolfhart Pannenberg in our own day, who have ventured criticisms of their fellow Germans similar to the criticisms I shall put forward. But they are minor figures criticising the giants who have made all the running. It is a pro-German book in that I silently assume that no one who wrote in French or English in the period is worthy of a place.

The great scholars and thinkers who appear represent a coherent German tradition. These men are heirs of a particular heritage of medieval mysticism and Augustinianism, and they are heirs of Luther. They drew on the astonishing intellectual awakening of the Enlightenment and they all belong to the language group that produced romanticism. They all contributed to and carried on a tradition of scholarship, rooted in a thorough knowledge of the ancient classical languages and the ancient semitic languages, and they all knew that hard scholarly work on texts could be the most exciting pursuit known to humanity. They helped to establish as a fact that no one could advance the study of scripture or of philosophy without becoming immersed in the German books on the subject.

I deeply admire this tradition but I believe this tradition is flawed. The flaw consists in some oversimplifications, the oversimplification that thinks supernaturalism too untidy to be viable, and the oversimplification that thinks the slow-moving succession in history of one age giving way to another shows that history is an entity controlled by an inherent rational spirit. The double flaw has led to a curious result: biblical criticism based on a rejection of supernaturalism has led to the elevation of the authority of the Bible, not as a witness to God, but as the key to something called History, the Book that gives us the clue to the working of Spirit. This myth has become the most powerful myth in our world. I scarcely think the myth will lose its hold over us until its origins, in the study of Biblical criticism and Biblical authority, are patiently explored and understood.

I am conscious the portrait gallery should have included a portrait of Schleiermacher, as I wish I had been able to include deWette, Ritschl, H. J. Holtzmann, William Wrede, Johannes Weiss and Troeltsch as well. Schleiermacher was omitted in the early days of this project, when I was lecturing on Biblical Criticism and Authority, because he was a major figure in a parallel course on modern theology. I confess I was also put off him by Hegel's dismissal in the preface to Hinrichs's book on religion (1822): 'If a man's religion were founded merely on a feeling, this would indeed have no further determination beyond being a *feeling of his dependence,* and then the dog would be the best Christian, for he has this feeling most intensely and lives most in it'.[2] Then I discovered how difficult Schleiermacher was; not for nothing did Nietzsche draw attention to the aptness of the name Schleiermacher, Maker of Veils. 'Germans are represented in the history of knowledge with decidedly ambiguous names, having ever produced only 'unwitting' forgers (– Fichte, Schelling, Schopenhauer, Hegel, Schleiermacher deserve the reputation of forger quite as much as Kant and Leibniz; they are all simply Schleiermacher).'[3] He certainly is important. Bultmann once protested to Barth against the hard things he used to say about Schleiermacher to his students ('Whereas I for my part rank him in the roll of honour, Jeremiah – Kierkegaard; yes, really'), and Barth ever after spoke of him with respect.[4] Perhaps, then, I

---

[2] *Berliner Schriften, 1818–1831* ed. J. Hoffmeister (1956), p. 74, translated by Walter Kaufmann, *Hegel: Reinterpretation, Texts, and Commentary* (1965, London, 1966), p. 239 note 18.

[3] *Ecce Homo*, xiii. 3.

[4] Letter to Barth, 31 December, 1922, *Karl Barth – Rudolf Bultmann Briefwechsel*

am trying to present Hamlet without the prince – except that the voice of the prince is heard throughout the book.

The reader must be warned that this is a very shocking book to many contemporary academic theologians. I have worked on the assumption that God's existence can either be seen by reflecting on the nature of the universe – in which time is real, that contains thinking beings like us, where events occur that reveal God –, or else his existence must be denied. That is, I reject the idea that we can consistently deny that God's existence is accessible to thought and still affirm God's living religious importance for ourselves – and not just in providing material for anthropology. I reject the defence of the existence of theological faculties in our universities which relies on theological thinking's being different in kind from other thinking as carried out in the rest of the university. If the history or philosophy as carried out elsewhere is precluded by the nature of the disciplines from discerning God, then the history or philosophy pursed in the divinity faculty is likewise precluded; if the historians and philosophers in Arts are not allowed to entertain the existence and the action of God, then neither are the historians and philosophers in Divinity. Nor can theologians choose arbitrarily and without evidence a theory that allows room for the church, for the church can be justified by no other arguments than the arguments of philosophy and history as carried on wherever people think.

In saying this, I realize I am contradicting the cherished beliefs of many good church people who gain their living by teaching theology in the universities. They do not believe God is a being who can give actual benefits to all people as well as to particular individuals, some of which benefits were asked for from him and received at his direct command. That would be a God who could be discerned in history, and their methodology precludes this possibility. They accept Lessings's case for there being a ditch no one can jump between accidental truths of history and necessary truths of reason (among which Lessing put the truths of religion), not being aware, it seems, of the untenability of Lessing's disjunction. Lessing's move is one of the 'dogmas of empiricism' so devastatingly challenged by Quine.[5] If they find my estimate of some of the people portrayed in this book shocking, let them reflect on the careers of Wellhausen and Overbeck, who read the lives of their contemporaries much as I do, and take what comfort they can find. My position may seem harsh, but, if I am right, something has to give. I do not think what has to give is the Christianity of the ancient creeds. Note, however, that I am not supporting theologians of today who regard Kähler and Barth as defenders of the faith; I fear that Kähler and Barth, too, are not as orthodox as they sound.

There are bound to be many mistakes in this book, and I should like to have them pointed out to me. If, however, the reader is tempted to think I have simply misjudged or caricatured the views of any of the thinkers I portray, I should be glad to be referred to actual passages in which the subject directly contradicts the view I attribute to him; it is not sufficient to say, This thinker could not possibly have thought as O'Neill says he thought. With all us human beings, I am afraid, the impression we wish to convey is not always the same as what we in our hearts believe, which both out deliberate and our unguarded words and deeds betray. That is one reason why the study of history is such an uncomfortable business.

---

[5] W. van O. Quine, 'Two Dogmas of Empiricism', *From a Logical Point of View* (Cambridge, Mass., 1953), pp. 20–46.

I

Lessing

Gotthold Ephraim Lessing was the oldest surviving son of an orthodox Lutheran pastor in Saxony. His paternal grandfather was town-councillor and mayor of Kamenz, and had written his doctoral thesis on the toleration of religious societies: toleration was Lessing's heritage.[1] His father married the daughter of the Pastor primarius of the town, and moved into his father-in-law's position and his parsonage when Lessing was four. Lessing was of a family of twelve; an older sister and four brothers grew to be adults. In 1741 the twelve-year-old Lessing had to pass an entrance examination to the famous St Afra Prince's School at Meissen, founded in the sixteenth century on old monastic lines to give a good religious and classical education to future civil servants (which of course also included the clergy).

At school Lessing soaked himself in the ancient Greek and Latin comedians: Theophrastus, Aristotle's pupil and friend, who wrote witty character sketches to illustrate human failings, and the Roman playwrights, Plautus and Terence.[2] He was also well-grounded in mathematics, English and French. One of his later great critical achievements was to make the English theatre a model for German drama in place of the French. His father was one of the first translators into

---

[1] See Alexander Altmann, *Moses Mendelssohn: A Biographical Study* (Alabama & London, 1973), p. 37.

[2] Preface to the 3rd part of his early Works, 1754, aged 25. *Gotthold Ephraim Lessings sämtliche Schriften*, edited by Karl Lachmann, 3rd revised and enlarged edition by Franz Muncker (vols. i–xi, Stuttgart; xii–xxi, Leipzig; xxii–xxiii, Berlin & Leipzig, 1886–1924), v. 268.

German of the superb English stylist, the tolerant Archbishop of Canterbury, John Tillotson (1630–1694).[3]

Lessing was allowed to leave school early, soon after he turned seventeen. He had already written poems and tried his hand at a play. His headmaster told his father, 'He's a horse needing double fodder. Passages that are too hard for the others are child's play to him. We are scarcely able to keep him occupied.'[4]

He went to Leipzig to study theology in September 1746. Christlob Mylius, his cousin, was already there studying medicine, but more interested in literature and the theatre. Mylius introduced him to the dangerous ideas of Benedict Spinoza, whose *Ethics* had been translated into German years before by Johann Lorenz Schmidt (1702–1749); Schmidt had had to preface it with an introductory refutation by Christian Wolff to get it past the censor. Lessing used to discuss Spinoza intensively with his best friend Moses Mendelssohn (1729–1786) whom he met in Berlin when he was twenty-five; he praised Mendelssohn as 'a second Spinoza' – save the errors (but Lessing is careful not to commit himself on whether the conventionally regarded 'errors' of Spinoza really were such). Spinoza denied the orthodox view of God as the Being who created a universe containing free creatures; rather 'whatever exists expresses in [an absolutely] certain and determined manner either the nature or essence of God, that is, whatever exists expresses in a certain and determined way the power of God, which is the cause of all things . . .' (Ethics, Part I, Proposition xxxvi, Proof). Lessing was long suspected of agreeing with Spinoza, and rather ambiguously conceded he was a Spinozist in conversation with Friedrich Heinrich Jacobi in the summer of 1780, the year before he died – but his friends and admirers could scarcely believe it, such was the power of conventional orthodoxy; and the controversy has continued to this day.[5]

---

[3] Letter to J. D. Michaelis, 16 October 1754, Lachmann-Muncker xvii. 39–41.

[4] Karl Gotthelf Lessing (1740–1812, Lessing's youngest brother), Gotthold Ephraim Lessings Leben, nebst seinem noch übrigen litterarischen Nachlässe (Berlin, 1793), p. 40; cited in Gerd Hillen, Lessing Chronick; Daten zu Leben und Werk (Munich, 1979), Spring 1746.

[5] Conversation with Jacobi, Rilla 8.261, H. Scholz. An attempt to argue that

Lessing's first poems and tales were published when he was nineteen. At twenty he was summoned home for three months because of his interest in the theatre and his friendship with Mylius; in August that year he started a medical course at Wittenberg, but soon gave up further study to follow Mylius to Berlin to work on the new free paper Mylius had begun to edit. Lessing's life as a critic of critics, a reviewer, had begun. He did go back to Wittenberg in the winter 1751–52 to get his master's degree, but otherwise he spent the rest of his life as a writer; indeed, supported himself by his pen for the rest of his life. He was General von Tauentzien's secretary in Breslau from 1760 to 1765, adviser and publisher for a new theatrical venture in Hamburg from 1767–70, and librarian of the Duke of Brunswick in Wolfenbüttel from 1770 until his death at the age of just 52, in February 1781. He was poor all his life – yet very generous to his family and friends. His health was never good. The one period of great happiness, his marriage to Eva König, a widow of an old Hamburg friend, the silk merchant Engelbert König, who died in 1769 was postponed for ages because the Duke took more than three years to carry out the promise he had made to give Lessing another additional post with an additional stipend. When they did marry, in October 1776, Eva was 40 and Lessing 47. Their son Traugott was born on Christmas Day 1777, but died twenty-four hours later. Eva herself died on the 10th January 1778. Lessing allowed little of his suffering to appear; he rarely spoke of himself.

In 1774 and 1777 Lessing slipped into his series of contributions to history and literature from the ducal library at Wolfenbüttel some fragments from an unknown author in criticism of the history of the Bible. Lessing knew these fragments did not actually come from the manuscripts held in the library. They were in fact part of a large book written by Hermann Samuel Reimarus, teacher of Hebrew and Oriental literature in a Gymnasium (grammar school) in

Lessing went beyond Spinoza is made by Reinhard Schwarz, 'Lessings "Spinozismus"', *Zeitschrift für Theologie und Kirche* 65 (1968), 271–290; answered by Friedmann Regner, *Z. Th. K.* 68 (1971), 351–375.

Hamburg, and entrusted to Lessing by Reimarus's daughter, Elise, after her father's death, on the strict understanding that any publication should be anonymous. In 1778 Lessing published a third section, but then had to desist because of the uproar the publication caused; his employer withdrew the right to publish without censorship.

Reimarus argued that Jesus' aim was different from the aim later attributed to him by the disciples. Jesus preached repentance to prepare for the coming of the Kingdom of God on earth, and saw himself as the Christ or Messiah. This hope was shattered when he was crucified. Out of the disappointment the disciples manufactured a new spiritual religion; they stole the body of Jesus from the tomb in Joseph's garden, and put around the story that Jesus had risen and been taken up into heaven, from whence he would come in glory. They then turned Jesus' simple call for trust in him into a system which demanded belief in the trinity of persons in God, and belief in redemption wrought through Jesus the Son of God, the God-Man, doctrines which fully misunderstand what Jesus believed and taught, although doctrines which grew out of such simple antecedents as Jesus' consciousness of sonship, and his baptism by the spirit of God.[6]

Lessing sympathised with Reimarus's historical conclusions, and challenged all the pamphleteers who argued, for example, against the ten contradictions Reimarus found between the Gospel accounts of the resurrection, that they had to answer all ten if they were to succeed. But Lessing himself wanted to lift the whole discussion on to a new plane. Reimarus argued that the orthodox trinitarian creed which confessed Jesus the Son of God as the redeemer was a distortion of Jesus' own message, and that Jesus' own message, shorn of its particular Jewish trappings about a coming kingdom of God on earth, was an admirable version of the natural religion of moral virtue. Reimarus provoked defenders of orthodox

---

[6] See *Reimarus: Fragments* ed. C. H. Talbert, trans. R. S. Fraser (Philadelphia, 1970; London, 1971). The whole of Reimarus's book, Apologie oder Schutzschrift für die Vernünftigen Verehrer Gottes, ed. G. Alexander, 2 vols. (Frankfurt am Main, 1972).

Christianity to try to prove his historical reconstruction of the origin of Christianity mistaken; they tried to show that Jesus really did rise bodily from the dead, and they thought they had proved the truth of their creed.

Lessing argued that both Reimarus and his opponents were on the wrong track. Even if Reimarus proved his case against the fulfilled prophecies and miracles of the Bible, even if the opponents of Reimarus could show that the prophecies were fulfilled and that Jesus both raised the dead and was himself raised from the dead, neither would either shake or confirm the truths preserved in the Christian faith. In this extract Lessing is dealing with Reimarus's opponents and for the sake of argument concedes their case; but he could just as well have been dealing with Reimarus and conceding his case.

Fulfilled prophecies, which I myself experience, are one thing; fulfilled prophecies, of which I know only from history that others say they have experienced them, are another.

Miracles, which I see with my own eyes, and which I have the opportunity to verify for myself, are one thing; miracles, of which I know only from history that others say they have seen them and verified them, are another . . .

. . . I am no longer in Origen's position; I live in the 18th century, in which miracles no longer happen. If I even now hesitate to believe anything on the proof of the spirit and of power, which I can believe on other arguments more appropriate to my age: what is the problem?

The problem is that this proof of the spirit and of power no longer has any spirit or power, but has sunk to the level of human testimonies of spirit and power.

. . . the reports of fulfilled prophecies and miracles, have to work through a medium which takes away all their force.

. . . What is asserted is only that the reports which we have of these prophecies and miracles are as reliable as historical truths ever can be. And then it is added that historical truths cannot be demonstrated: nevertheless we must believe them as firmly as truths that have been demonstrated.

To this I answer: *First,* who will deny (not I) that the reports of these miracles and prophecies are as reliable as historical truths ever can be? But if they are only as reliable as this, why are they treated as if they were infinitely more reliable? . . .

If no historical truth can be demonstrated, then nothing can be demonstrated by means of historical truths.

That is: *accidental truths of history can never become the proof of necessary truths of reason.*

. . . If on historical grounds I have no objection to the statement that this Christ himself rose from the dead, must I therefore accept it as true that this risen Christ was the Son of God?

. . . But to jump with that historical truth to a quite different class of truths, and to demand of me that I should form all my metaphysical and moral ideas accordingly; to expect me to alter all my fundamental ideas of the nature of the Godhead because I cannot set any credible testimony against the resurrection of Christ: if that is not a μετάβασις εἰς ἄλλο γένος [a shift into another class of things], then I do not know what Aristotle meant by this phrase.

. . . If you press me still further and say: 'Oh yes! this is more than historically certain. For it is asserted by inspired historians who cannot make a mistake'.

But, unfortunately, that also is only historically certain, that these historians were inspired and could not err.

That, then, is the ugly, broad ditch which I cannot get across, however often and however earnestly I have tried to make the leap. If anyone can help me over it, let him do it, I beg him, I adjure him. He will deserve a divine blessing from me.[7]

---

[7] 'On the Proof of the Spirit and of Power' (1777), xiii. 1–8; translated by Henry

Lessing silently jettisons the weakest part of Reimarus's case, the thesis that the disciples deliberately played a trick on a credulous public. He concedes that the original disciples thought they experienced miracles, thought that they saw prophecies fulfilled, and thought Jesus had risen bodily from the grave. As far as they were concerned, the miracles had happened.

Then Lessing made his key move, a move that marks a turning point in the history of European thought. The contemporaries of the apostles had the witness of the apostles to miracles and to prophecies that were fulfilled. These contemporaries might deny the truth of the events, but in principle miracles were possible and, if they happened, these miracles could prove that Jesus was what the apostles claimed he was. The contemporaries of the apostles often had to rely on reports of miracles rather than immediate experience, but they could and did rely on those reports so long as they belonged to an age when miracles happened. The contemporaries of the apostles were not forced to argue from a miracle or a fulfilled prophecy to a particular metaphysical conclusion – the miracle could be a trick of the devil to deflect men from true religion – but they thought miracles, if truly done in the power of God, did indicate truths which God wanted them to believe, and if falsely done, showed the power of the great deceiver.

Lessing argued that the age in which people could move confidently from observed events across to metaphysical beliefs lasted at least until the time of Origen in the third century, but existed no longer. Reimarus tried to show that the miracles did not happen. Lessing agreed with him, but was content to leave that question on one side. Even if they did happen, even if Christ rose bodily from the grave, that would prove nothing to someone living in the eighteenth century. 'I live in the eighteenth century, in which miracles no longer happen.' Lessing does not mean that surprising events like the events labelled miracles by Origen do not

Chadwick, *Lessing's Theological Writings* with an Introductory Essay (London, 1956), pp. 51–6 (with one slight alteration).

actually occur as they used to occur. He means that these events occur as always (sudden cures of seemingly incurable diseases; instances of events foretold long before). What has changed is that these events, even if they happened, no longer had the power to change the metaphysical and moral beliefs of anyone in the eighteenth century. What had changed was not the result of a temporal gap between the first century and the eighteenth century; there was a temporal gap between the first century and the third century in which Origen lived, but the miracles that occurred in Origen's own day confirmed the miracles that occurred at the time of the apostles and Jesus. What had changed was the assumption that observed events in history had the power to alter metaphysical and moral beliefs, the assumption that if Jesus rose from the dead he could well be the Son of God.

Lessing formulated his position in the memorable words, 'accidental truths of history can never become the proof of necessary truths of reason'. On the one side of an ugly broad ditch, accidental truths of history; on the other side, necessary truths of reason. No way to jump across the ditch from one side to the other. Lessing ironically promising to say 'God bless you' to anyone who could help him across; ironically, because if anyone could show Lessing how to make the leap, they would have transported Lessing back into a never-to-be-recovered age of faith, where blessings from God could be meaningfully given and received.

One of Lessing's necessary truths of reason consisted of the absolute presupposition that there were no accidental truths of history. He knew, of course, that historical facts were hard to discover and always the subject of debate, but his substantial point was that no historical fact, however well established, could alter the necessary truths of reason we now hold without question. Jesus did teach something necessarily true, which his contemporaries believed because they thought miracles required them to believe it; we know both that miracles cannot require belief and that the belief is true. Lessing hinted at the sort of belief that was necessarily true by his enigmatic conclusion to the pamphlet we have been quoting. 'I break off with the wish: may all whom the Gospel of John divides, the Testament of John reunite! Granted this Testament is apocryphal, but not for that reason any the less divine.'

The Testament of John was the apocryphal story that the Apostle John, as he lay dying, said 'Little children, love one another.' The Gospel of John was the source of many of the ideas about the Son of God which divided orthodox Christians from unorthodox. Lessing implies that the injunction to love one another and to be tolerant of one another is grounded in a necessary truth of reason.

Lessing is no builder of systems, but it is clear to me that he held a system which can be discovered by patient attention to what he said. 'Lessing had his own thought-through speculative system.'[8] The Testament of John bore witness to the necessity of toleration, not just as one piece of moral advice among others, but as a clue to the constitution of things. The necessity of toleration and the impossibility of jumping the ugly broad ditch from accidental truths of history to necessary truths of reason belonged both to the fundamental part of Lessing's system.

In Lessing's system, no eighteenth-century man could argue from events in history to metaphysical beliefs because he no longer held that events in history could be affected from outside, as it were, by a God who willed thereby to show people truths about himself and the world and themselves. No event could be the sign that God was responsible for it in a way analogous to our observing the arrival of a gift on our doorstep as pointing to a giver. In Origen's day this was still believed, but humanity has advanced since then and eighteenth-century man (says Lessing) can no longer believe in a God who shows things by miracles.

Lessing, however, is not arguing that the beliefs of the past are entirely irrelevant. On the contrary, he holds that all that happens happens of necessity, and that the whole process is a necessary advance. He expounds his beliefs in fifty-three theses on the Education of the Human Race he attached to his

---

[8] Guhrauer, 1841, cited by George Voss, *In welchem Sinne ist Lessing Determinist?* (Nürnberg, 1911), p. 25, note 1.

editorial remarks on the Fragments of Reimarus in 1777. In 1780 he published the tract as a separate pamphlet, filled out now to a full one hundred theses and given an illuminating new preface.

Here is Lessing's system, and from this we can understand how the principle of toleration enshrined in 'Little children, love one another' and the impossibility of leaping the ugly broad ditch go together.

The 1780 preface gives a sketch of the main thesis, which the hundred paragraphs expound. Lessing pictures himself as set a little apart on a hill from which he can observe the whole of human history. What particularly engrosses his attention are the 'positive' religions, the religions that claim to rest on revelation. These religions are a source of amusement or scorn to his enlightened contemporaries, but Lessing begs leave to doubt whether amusement or scorn are deserved of anything in the best of worlds; is it right that only the religions deserve them? Granted the positive religions are mistaken, has God part only in what is not mistaken?

In the theses Lessing argues that the truth of reason that God is one – which is now made certain by the necessary truth concerning the infinity of the universe (§ 14) – was first taught to humanity in the experience of a slave folk, allowed no god by their captives, who yet escaped captivity in the Exodus, and so ascribed their release to the most powerful one God. Similarly, the necessary truth of the immortality of the soul was first reliably and practically taught by Christ. Just as men no longer need the Old Testament to hold the unity of God, so they will no longer need the New Testament to hold the immortality of the soul. Even the despised doctrines of the church (the Trinity, Original Sin, the satisfaction offered God through the Son) may enshrine necessary truths. And mankind is moving on inevitably to the third age, the age of the new eternal gospel, which fanatics in the thirteenth and fourteenth century saw before time. In the third age the New Covenant would be outmoded as the Old Covenant had been outmoded. Then men would do the good because it was good, not because arbitrary punishments were attached to it (§ 85).

There is a paradox here. The whole tendency of the argument is to show mankind gradually freeing itself from the idea of a teacher: the picture is of the teacher giving his pupils elementary textbooks (first the Old Testament, then the New Testament) in order to train up the pupil to live without the textbooks by reason alone and so to live without an external teacher any more. But paradoxically, that process of education does not lead Lessing to posit the complete autonomy and freedom of man. Past history is not seen as a series of hit and miss attempts to find ʰhe truth, but as a process of education as if from outside; nᵤ her is present nor future history a story of mankind making its own history in full awareness of its freedom. Present and future history is just as much subject to necessary progress as was past history. 'Take thy indiscernible step, eternal providence! Only let me not doubt you because of this indiscernability! – Let me not doubt you, even when your step should seem to me to go backwards! It is not true that the shortest line is always the direct line. You have so much to take with you on your eternal way, so many sidesteps to make' (§§ 91, 92a). The argument about the progressive education of the human race appears to a superficial glance to be an argument about how mankind realises its own autonomy, but under Lessing's hands it isn't. His tract comes to its climax in a mechanical picture of progress, the progress of a wheel driven forward by smaller wheels which seem to run backwards. The seeming regressions in history are not really so. Why, it is as good as obvious that the large slow wheel that bears the human race nearer and nearer to perfection would only be set in motion by small faster wheels, each of which contributes its own individual unit to the progress (§ 92). Here is one of Lessing's favourite images, the image of wheels in a machine (see *Ernst und Falk*, 1778, first dialogue). The small wheels seem to be going backwards, but they are really part of the machine as a whole that is inevitably moving forwards.

If we now return to Lessing's original puzzle, the seemingly impossible problem of how to leap from accidental truths of history to necessary truths of reason across the ugly broad ditch, we now see that Lessing was really teasing us. It is only an illusion that there are accidental truths of history. In so far as they are seen as accidental, they cannot of course prove necessary truths. When the truths of history were seen as proving truths of reason, that was a sign that the age was yet in its infancy, believing that the miracle of the exodus from Egypt showed there was one God, or believing that the miracles of Christ guaranteed his teaching about the soul's immortality. Lessing's age did not need such spurious proofs. Lessing's age, however, did not in consequence reject the history of the past age as simply mistaken. The mistakes were themselves inevitable if the process should advance towards its inevitable goal. The seemingly accidental and dispensable historical events by which the human race advanced were themselves necessary. Whatever the historian discovered would be a necessary movement of a little wheel within the larger slower wheel of progress to perfection. The ditch of the original picture is itself an illusion; the attempt to jump from accidental truths of history to necessary truths of reason is simply a sign that the old age, the age in which men naturally moved from signs of God's special activity to truths about God, the world, and themselves, is passing away. Both Reimarus and his opponents were still half living in the old age, for Reimarus thought he discredited Christianity by showing the miracles didn't happen and his opponents thought they were proving Christianity true because the miracles did happen. Lessing himself had come to see the new age was dawning in which the Christianity which could be attacked or defended on grounds drawn from what happened in history was itself being superseded. The human race was entering the third age in which the necessary truth that everything that happened in history was necessary would be acknowledged. In this age toleration was the necessary balm to ease the pain of the transition. Those who were mistaken were as necessary to the process as those who were not mistaken. The Testament of John should unite those whom the Gospel of John divided.

Lessing's whole argument is brilliantly presented and appeals to the noblest of human instincts, toleration springing not from indifference but from love and from human understanding. Although Reimarus and his opponents were both in the wrong, the one in seeking to overthrow what could not be overthrown and the others in defending what could not be defended, both sides had their part to play in the progress of humanity.

The difficulty is that Lessing's argument cannot escape his own strictures. The nub of his case is that by observing what happens among us and by thinking about those happenings we cannot leap over to necessary truths of reason. Accidental happenings and the reasoning about those happenings that unenlightened man in the past engaged in cannot deliver necessary truths of reason, because the key necessary truth of reason is that whatever happens contributes to the inevitable progress of the human race. The difficulty is that Lessing patently does present us with a large tableau of accidental happenings and a reasoned explanation of those happenings. It is true that he does not argue from events as miracles to a God who brought about those miracles, but he does reason from events as movements of a sprocketed wheel to a large process involving many small wheels and each within a large wheel leading to a goal. He is leaping a ditch he said could not be leaped.

If I have described his argument correctly as yet another attempt to argue from accidental truths of history to necessary truths of reason, he may be right or he may be wrong. The trouble is that he expressly denies that his argument is of this character. He alone has seen through the illusion that one could argue from accidental truths of history to necessary truths of reason; he alone sees that strictly there are no accidental truths of history, that what seems to us accidental is really a necessary part of the progress of the human race.

Here is the final difficulty in Lessing's position. If he is right, his argument itself as well as my attempts to assess its truth or falsehood are necessary elements in the working of the machine. He claims to be right and I wonder if he is right or wrong or right in part, but his activity and mine are both (according to his theory) part of a larger process, a process that simply (according to his theory) has to be recognised as taking place. No value of truth or falsehood can (according to his theory) be attached to his cerebral processes and his activities of writing and publishing or to mine. But neither he nor I can surrender the possibility of being convinced, even if only for a day, that we are wrong; the possibility of being right, even if either of us never knows for sure we were so.

The very process of thinking which was so dear to Lessing, the very process of arguing a case and defending a position, depends on the universe not being the machine Lessing thought it was. He thought he had shown the Old Testament and the New Testament to be superseded primers that had done yeomen service and should by no means be despised. He thought his theses, like the 95 theses of Luther before him, were ushering in a new age, long foretold but slow in coming by the inevitable slowness of providence. But in order to eliminate the to him false idea of a God who could bring about contingent events he had to eliminate contingency altogether; and contingency eliminated spells also the elimination of the force of his own argument.

However, Lessing had one trick to play which might sustain his case. He could happily see the possibility of argument from evidence go, if in its place he could put a new religion which did not, any more than the old, depend on argument. Perhaps that was what he was really doing. Perhaps Lessing knowns that he must not argue on evidence. Perhaps he is simply preaching without seeking for any external support to prop up his message. Sometimes he sounds like that. We recall his admiration for the old orthodoxy which was tolerant because it did not try to reason with its opponents: as he wrote to his brother Karl, 'and I only prefer the old orthodox theology (at bottom tolerant) to the newer (at bottom intolerant) because the old obviously clashes with sound commonsense, and the newer would prefer to corrupt it. I make my peace with my obvious enemies in order to be able to be better on my guard against my secret ones.' (20 March 1777). Perhaps 'sound common sense' is something he thought too obvious to need argument. In that case we should have to surrender to him, for only the religion that knows without a shadow of regret for past arguments that all argument is beside the point can claim our complete and utter unreserved allegiance. Only this religion renounces completely all the seeming arguments.

Lessing's noble calm in the midst of his hard life perhaps springs from such a religion. His argument to end argument was immensely influential and remains influential. He raised the issues and sketched in a seemingly impregnable way to handle them which has fascinated everyone who has thought about the history of the world ever since. He dethroned the Bible and set another authority in its place without eliminating the Bible from our discourse. The problem of Biblical authority did not disappear; his consciousness of having deprived the Bible of its authority paradoxically helped to keep alive the problem of the Bible's authority even among thinkers who believed they had outgrown its power.

2

Michaelis

Lessing's argument in *The Proof of the Spirit & of Power* (1777) was that, even if we concede the historical accuracy of the Biblical miracles, this does not begin to prove the truth of the Christian religion. His key move was the assertion that, in the eighteenth century, miracles no longer happened. The 'historical proof' only reaches to showing that people in the first century were sure that they had experienced a miracle and that they were not tricksters; Lessing will concede that. What he denies is that this high degree of certainty can do anything for someone in the eighteenth century who worked on other presuppositions. Lessing accepts as beyond argument the presupposition that all events were determined and that no event could be evidence of the intervention of God from outside (as it were); this is part of his definition of someone living in the eighteenth century.

In this chapter I want to present an eighteenth-century man who scorned all systems of thought that tried to reduce the diversity and variety of the world of events in human history to any sort of unity.

This eighteenth-century man, Michaelis, was the greatest obstacle to Lessing's grand scheme, and I think Lessing knew he was. Johann David Michaelis was born twelve years before Lessing (in 1717; Lessing, 1729). He came from an academic family in Halle where his father and his father's uncle before him had been professors of oriental languages and theology. Our Michaelis early broke free from the pietistic orthodoxy of his family. As a school boy he had had to be confirmed in private because he confessed to the pastor who prepared him that he was a semi-pelagian, believing that free will played a part in a man's salvation. As a young university teacher in his mid-twenties he visited England, where the court was of course German-speaking and the Lutheran court chaplains ready to introduce young theologians to English intellectual life. There, to his relief, he found a high regard for a moral Christianity and a low regard for Lutheran or any other sort of orthodoxy. Scriptures was read in England not as a source book for dogmatic theology bu: as the record of natural human response to God. The Bible was regarded as literature. In an extremely happy month in Oxford Michaelis met the great Hebrew scholar Robert Lowth, who became a fast friend. Lowth had just been appointed Professor of Poetry (an occasional lectureship that still exists in Oxford) and gave in Michaelis's presence his second series of lectures, De sacra poesi Hebraeorum, *On the sacred poetry of the Hebrews*, in which he displayed the characteristic mark of Hebrew poetry, which depended not on rhythm nor on rhyme but on the parallelism of ideas (synonymous, antithetic and synthetic). Michaelis later wrote notes to the published lectures, and these Michaelis notes of 1750 and 1762 were incorporated into the Clarendon Press edition of 1763. (Lowth was in no position to develop and consolidate his own seminal work. He had to abandon a scholarly career at the age of forty, when preferment in the church and marriage removed him irrevocably from university life.)

Michaelis's time in England was crowned by his discovery of a new literary form, the paraphrase of scripture. Paraphrase was the attempt to render into a language that would speak to a modern audience the thoughts and ideas of the Biblical writers, on the assumption that they too were rational and respectable thinkers who communicated with ease and felicity to their contemporaries.

Paraphrases of books of the Bible were the rage in reaction to the alleged scholasticism of the theologians who found doctrines in St Paul, for instance, which led to bloody and inconclusive wars of religion and on which no one could agree. It was suspected that these disagreements arose from neglect of 'Understanding of St Paul's Epistles, by Consulting

St Paul Himself', as John Locke put it in his popular paraphrase and notes on Galatians, I and II Corinthians, Romans, and Ephesians.

In short, the Bible was discovered to be a realistic book, written out of human experience and speaking to human experience, written by men whose inspired words could be trusted to speak to every reader who applied himself to understand them. It is no accident that the age of the paraphrase was the age of the rise of the novel. The new novelists hoped, by telling a realistic story, to move readers in a way they all, novelists and readers, were accustomed to be moved morally by the plain words of scripture. The age of the paraphrase is the age of *Clarissa*.

It is no accident that the two ages coincided in England, but the important point for our understanding of Michaelis the Biblical scholar is that he was soon to belong to a scholarly community where the rise of the novel was specifically noticed as an important change in European consciousness. When he returned to his lectureship at Halle he found pietist orthodoxy even more constricting than before. Fortunately he was rescued from Halle and appointed first a lecturer (1745) and then very quickly a professor (ausserordentlicher, 1746; full, 1750) at the new Hanoverian university of Göttingen, where freedom of enquiry and publication was guaranteed. One of his first tasks in Göttingen was, at the behest of Haller, the Vice-Chancellor, to translate the first four parts of Richardson's *Clarissa* into German; this was even before the final parts had yet appeared in England. Haller also directed that the scholarly periodical of the University, the *Göttinger Gelehrte Anzeigen* should draw attention to the importance of the novel. Why? Because the novel tended to promote the love of virtue and because of its exact realism: 'For Nature is here depicted in all its detail, and Nature alone can convince us and move our heart.'[1] If

[1] Haller, 'Beurtheilung der beruhmten Geschichte der Clarissa', *Sammlung kleiner Hallerscher Schriften* (Bern, 1756), p. 356. See Theodor Wolpers, 'Haller, das gelehrte Göttingen und Richardsons *Clarissa*: Eine literarische Rezeption und ihre Rückwirkung auf den Autor', Catalogue of the Haller Exhibition, Georg August University Library, Göttingen, 1977; also 'Richardson, *Clarissa*', in F. K. Stanzel

the Bible was, and remained, for Michaelis literature, we must never forget that literature was for Michaelis and Michaelis's Göttingen the novel.

I do not mean that Michaelis though the Bible was fiction; far from it. I mean, rather, that Michaelis looked in the Bible for personal testimony to events that changed lives. He assumed that what worked then still worked in the eighteenth century.

Lessing assumed that the Bible regarded as the history of past events and read by people in the eighteenth century no longer had the power to affect them. Even if anyone should argue that the accounts of miracles done by Jesus and the apostles were accounts of people who could be trusted, that could no longer convince people in the eighteenth century – because miracles no longer happened in the eighteenth century. This argument of Lessing's was a direct answer to an argument of Michaelis's, published earlier in the same year, 1777.

In 1750, when Lessing's youthful poems and plays were beginning to make a mark, Michaelis published an Introduction to the New Testament, a scholarly handbook on the date, authorship and text of each of the books in the canon. This first edition of the Introduction caused little stir. Not so the second edition of 1765–8. Michaelis was by this time famous as the man who had inspired and directed the Danish expedition to Arabia to collect information about geology, botany, customs and language. But he was also infamous to the orthodox because of his liberal theological dogmatics; for example, his Latin Dogmatics was banned in the Lutheran kingdom of Sweden. He was constantly attacked for his independent line, yet he gave no comfort to the deists and rationalists. They denied that the Old Testament contained genuine prophecies of the coming of a Messiah (or

(ed.), *Der englische Roman*, vol. i (Dusseldorf, 1969), pp. 144–197. Michaelis in his anonymous foreword to the first two parts, dated 20 September 1748, states that he would not have undertaken the task of translation had he not believed that he did the world a genuine service (p. 4). His attempt was to transmute the different styles that distinguish the letters of the different people, not translating word for word but using freedom to put the meaning into German. He broke up the overlong English sentences and occasionally changed an English joke into an equivalent in German. I am indebted to Dr N. Boyle for these references.

Christ); he said it did. One of the key rationalist arguments against the alleged Old Testament prophecies was that the wording of Isaiah 7.14, *A virgin shall conceive*, rested on a mistaken translation of the Hebrew word '*almah*, which means 'young woman' not 'virgin'. (Most modern English translations of Isaiah 7.14 now accept this old rationalist point.) Michaelis, on the contrary, argued that '*almah* did mean 'virgin' – and I must say I think he is right. Nevertheless Michaelis did not then go to the aid of the orthodox who believed that Isaiah prophesied a miraculous virginal conception; he argued instead that Isaiah intended the sign to be not a miracle but simply a marker of the time at the end of which the prophecy would be fulfilled: some woman now a virgin would bear a son in nine months.[1a] This strikes me as rather too unexciting a sign, but my point is that Michaelis was no party man. He was above all an historian who loved working on the evidence to discover what was true. He was endlessly curious and inventive. He believed that Christianity could be shown by historical investigation to be true, but he was not the least dismayed to find some traditional Christian arguments and dogmatic positions untenable.

In 1777 Michaelis brought out a third edition of his Introduction (preface dated the 12th April), and the whole of the first section was completely rewritten. The decisive question was, Were the books of the New Testament made up or not?

> In deciding the divine nature of the Christian religion the genuineness or spuriousness of these books is far more decisive than anyone would think at first sight. I almost wonder why not every opponent or doubter of the Christian religion does not start by declaring the entire corpus of the New Testament to be spurious. For if these writings are old, and if they belong to the authors whose names they bear, then is proven not, I admit, absolutely directly, the divine transmission of these writings themselves, but still the truth and divine nature of the Christian religion. The epistles of the

---

[1a] *Deutsche Uebersetzungn des ATs, mit Anmerkungen für Ungelehrte*, 8. Theil, Göttingen, 1779, pp. 35–40.

apostles rest on definite miraculous gifts by which God, through the laying on of the apostles' hands, empowered their oral and written teaching. If the epistles are old and genuine and written by Paul himself to the churches to whom the title dedicates them: then it is not really possible to deny these miracles.

The matter then seems to be quite otherwise from the case of an historian who recounts miracles: for an historian if he is credulous or a liar can retail falsehoods to his readers about something that happened in another country or at another time – at least not before their eyes. An opponent of religion can deploy just this argument against the Gospels.

But to write to people among whom I had been that I had in your presence done miracles, indeed that you yourselves had through me received the ability to do miracles and to speak foreign languages, if nothing of the sort had happened, would have been far too incredible audacity; the man who had such audacity would be immediately discredited by those to whom he was writing and very soon by the whole world, especially if it should be the case that those to whom he was writing entertained doubts about his teaching or were inclined to oppose him.[2]

Michaelis went on to vindicate the Gospel historians by the argument that they had written before the destruction of Jerusalem in AD70 and yet their books contained accurate predictions of that event.

The important thing to notice, however, is that Lessing's argument in his 1777 pamphlet on the Proof of the Spirit & of Power is precisely designed to answer Michaelis. Lessing has to agree that Michaelis's argument sticks: that the people who knew Paul and received his letters did experience miracles at the hands of Paul; no historian who was reporting miracles from another place and another time stood between them and the miracles. The miracles they experienced

---

[2] *Einleitung in die göttlichen Schriften des Neuen Bundes.* Erster Theil. Dritte und vermehrte Ausgabe. Göttingen, im Verlag der Wittwe Vandenhoeck, 1777, pp. 13 f.

themselves would have proved to them the divine authority of Paul's message. Lessing found the argument convincing. However much he also wanted to exploit Michaelis's concession, that historians reporting miracles that happened in another place at another time could be lying, he cannot avoid Michaelis's positive case.

So Lessing turned to a large-scale metaphysical assertion: miracles do not happen in the eighteenth century and therefore the past miracles no longer convey the proof of the spirit and of power. This assertion is no longer a strict historical assertion because Lessing has ruled out in advance the testimony of any people living in the eighteenth century who claim to have experienced miracles.

Michaelis did not answer Lessing's argument. He was content to be an historian busy at work on the historical arguments against the Christian faith. Some years before Lessing published the Wolfenbüttel fragments Michaelis offered a series of lectures on the historical objections to the historicity of the bodily resurrection of Jesus. When the fragment on the resurrection was published in 1777 he repeated his course of lectures, and then again in 1782 at the request of some lawyers. He published the lectures in 1782, a year after Lessing's death.

Reimarus, the author of the anonymous fragments, had adduced ten contradictions in the Gospel accounts of the resurrection. Lessing, in his comment on the fragment, challenges the defenders of the historicity of the resurrection with the necessity of answering each and every one of the contradictions.

> Let us accept there might remain contradictions between the evangelists, (yet scarcely as many as the ten the author of the Fragments counts, since some of them fall away at first sight — in fact he has simply made them up, attributing something to one of the evangelists of which not one word appears in him; nevertheless there are some contradictions). From that it does not at all follow, as the late G. E. Lessing very well reminds us, that the resurrection of Christ would be historically

false, the invention of his disciples, or lies, but merely this: the evangelists are no God-inspired, no infallible writers. When Lessing asserted this he certainly did not prove himself an enemy of the Christian religion, but a friend and defender, or at least a valuable and perceptive observer.

Given that four men, men not rendered infallible by a divine miracle, men like ourselves, are painstakingly describing something, partly as eyewitnesses, partly as they have heard it from others; and granted they are decidedly not together correcting their account according to one already existing book on the subject, it is scarcely possible that they should not fall into some contradictions, simply because of the fallibility of the human memory, and because of other tendencies to err . . .

But we do not believe even the resurrection of Jesus merely on the testimony of the four evangelists whose works are still to hand, and from which we gather the more particular reports of it; but, as Lessing has very well remarked, before these evangelists had written, the resurrection was just as completely certain and credible as it is now, after 1700 years – indeed, because of the proximity to the event, still more certain. The case for the Christian religion was won before ever the evangelists and apostles had written. We believe the resurrection on the testimony of the apostles who attest that they were eyewitnesses of this fact and had seen the risen Jesus, and who dared to say this in face of the whole Sanhedrin though they knew that persecution, scourging and death could follow it . . .

So then, what would we lose if we so regarded the evangelists in historical matters as we do other writers, not as inspired but as honest human writers writing in the very period in which the events had taken place? . . .

From this, one can see that I hold that what Lessing has written [in his 'Objections of the Editor' appended to the Fragments of an Unknown Author] is very important and weighty, worthy not of being branded as heretical or of being damned, but worthy of a running commentary. I would wish Lessing's remarks to be read as a whole. Only right at the end does one requirement of Lessing's strike me as too hard, and at this point I part company from him. If he were still alive he could say whether he might not relax this requirement.

It is this: 'It follows that the man who asserts the inerracy of the evangelists finds here still untilled ground enough. Let him attempt it, and let him answer the ten alleged contradictions listed in our Fragment. *But let him answer every one of them.* For to set only something probable against this and that contradiction, and to pass over the rest with triumphant disdain means to answer none of them'.

Against this I have to remind him,

(1) that to answer them all is certainly not necessary for the prescribed purpose, for if contradictions between the last twelve verses of Mark [Mark 16.9–20] and the other evangelists should remain unanswered (just here is the richest field of contradictions), and if only all the contradictions in the remaining evangelists were answered, no one would have for that reason to give up the doctrine of the inerrancy of the evangelists . . .

(2) This requirement appears to me too hard, also, because I ought to think here exactly as I do in the case of other historical enquiries. One man is not in the position to do everything; he might resolve one, he might resolve quite a few of the difficulties, but one such can indeed well remain over for some future investigation; when I see that one after the other is removed, so I may hope that those still remaining will also be removed. That is how we proceed elsewhere in the realm of probability; we believe something on the basis of overwhelming reasons, even though there remains one unresolved difficulty.

It could be that a few readers would here require of

me yet more; I should speak not hypothetically, not doubtingly (true I cannot keep myself ever free from all doubt, cannot so definitely affirm and deny everything the way a perfect non-Cartesian can). They require me to say whether I hold the evangelists to be inspired in historical matters, or not.

To answer frankly, but without pressing my ideas on anyone else, I pretty much agree here too with the late G. E. Lessing, although I confess I thought otherwise twenty years ago. I see no proof of the inspiration of the evangelists in the historical matters they had either already known as eyewitnesses or which they had, like Luke, read in other older fabulous Gospels and enquired from eyewitnesses as to which of the facts were true or false (Luke 1. 1–4). Jesus' pledge in John 14.26 applies only to his words, the last and highest ground of our faith, words which the Holy Spirit was to bring again to the remembrance of the apostles (not of Mark and Luke); it does not apply to the history and its smallest details'.[3]

Notice Michaelis does two things in this passage. First, he gently chides Lessing for asking more from historians than probable conclusions. This is surely right, but it leaves unanswered the question of the seeming disparity between probable historical results and the certainty usually associated with faith. Lessing exploited this disparity to suggest that there was no connection between the two sorts of conclusions, only an ugly broad ditch. Michaelis simply marvelled at the sort of certainty Lessing and his opponents seemed to think they needed.

[3] Erklärung der Begräbnis und Auferstehungsgeschichte Christi nach den vier Evangelisten: Mit Rücksicht auf die in den Fragmenten gemachten Einwürfe und deren Beantwortung. Halle, 1783. An Explanation of the history of the Burial and Resurrection of Christ according to the Four Evangelists: With Regard to the Objections Made in the [Wolfenbüttel] Fragments and their Refutation. Compare the English translation (shortened and not always accurate), London, 1827. pp. xviii, xx, xxxv, xxxvi, xxxxvi, liiii, lv, lvi, lvii, lviii; cf. English pp. 5, 11, 16, 21, 22.

Second, Michaelis withdraws a little from his earlier conclusion that Matthew was inspired because he was an apostle. (Mark and Luke, he held, were not inspired because they were not apostles). He had modified that position somewhat already by suggesting that our translation of the original Hebrew Matthew could also be defective, but there he tentatively proposes that inspiration attaches only to the *words* of Jesus not to the historical reports about him. This strikes me as a rather sensible distinction; it is much more likely that words of the Lord would have been transmitted accurately than historical reports about him (although words, too, can be contaminated in the transmission). I would hold that all our Gospels are much younger than Michaelis thought, and therefore much more prone to the corruption he noticed, but the important thing for our present purpose is to see how open Michaelis was to the evidence. His freedom from large-scale theories about plots of Jewish Apostles to distort their Master's teaching and about laws of historical development is notable. New Testament scholarship has scarcely ever been free from such theories since his day.

Michaelis broke clearly and thoroughly from dogmatic attempts to read all the evidence according to a set theory. In doing, so he founded and established modern critical and historical study of the Bible. His sort of work has never ceased, if it has rarely been pursued with quite the same learning and zest; but soon, too soon, the method itself was raised into a new dogma.

3

Semler

Michaelis escaped from the narrow pietism of Halle to the freedom of the new university of Göttingen. Johann Salomo Semler, only eight years his junior (born 1725), spent almost all his life in Halle and never found its atmosphere cramping. Yet he, too, needed to escape the confines of Lutheran orthodoxy; but he found an entirely different means: the freedom and spaciousness of an inner and moral religion.

Both Michaelis and Semler were students of the one teacher, Sigmund Jacob Baumgarten. Michaelis perhaps heard him at a bad time, before Frederick the Great came to the Prussian throne and relaxed the censorship and allowed the philosopher Wolff to return to Halle from his exile in Marburg; whatever the reason, Michaelis never liked Baumgarten. Semler, on the contrary, completely fell under Baumgarten's spell. As a student he started taking his evening meals at Baumgarten's table where he met notable visitors like Voltaire and Wolff; he made himself useful to his revered teacher by getting him pre-1500 books through his father, a pastor in Saalfeld, who was also a great book collector. Baumgarten at table in his own house revealed to his pupil something not easily discoverable from his public lectures: the complete distinction he made between public state religion and technical theology on the one hand, and private religion, the divine teaching leading to salvation, on the other hand. He also initiated Semler into English theology of the latitudinarian kind, with leanings toward socinianism (unitarianism, the denial that Jesus Christ was the eternal Son of God). Baumgarten directed a number of schemes to translate large collections of English historical and theological writings into German, including a Dutch composite commentary on the whole Bible drawn from English seventeenth and eighteenth century commentators. Semler was to complete his master's work and to carry on in the same tradition: he himself supervised the translation and publication of Daniel Neal's *History of the Puritans*, Samuel Clarke's *Scripture-Doctrine of the Trinity*, Arthur Ashley Sykes's work on sacrifice and his paraphrases of Hebrews, Hugh Farmer's *Letters to the Rev. Dr. Worthington, in Answer to his late Publication, Intitled, An Impartial Enquiry into the Case of the Gospel Demoniacks*, and Thomas Townson's *Discourses on the Four Gospels*.

Semler had no thought of an academic life as a theologian, although he had qualified with a dissertation that proved the authenticity of the 'Johannine Comma' which stated the doctrine of the Trinity (1 John 5.7 f.), a theory Semler later gave up; the passage today is universally agreed to be spurious. After a year as editor of a local newspaper and unpaid schoolteacher, he was called to the Chair of History and Latin Poetry at the beautiful well-endowed ancient university of Altdorf near Nürenberg. Within a year Baumgarten arranged for him to receive a call back to Halle, a call Semler was very reluctant indeed to accept; he had no relish for the battles between pietists and the exponents of 'scientific theology' which he saw lying ahead. He was only twenty-seven years old. In the event, he was extremely happy in Halle, avoiding criticism at first by carefully adhering to Baumgarten's public teaching and using Baumgarten's books as the text books of his lectures. He even found his handwriting became like Baumgarten's.

But Baumgarten did not cramp Semler's development; rather, he provided the secure fatherly protection necessary for the growth of a powerful independent teacher whose own influence was to be far deeper and more widespread than Baumgarten's. There is hardly a theory or a hypothesis in New Testament studies from his day to ours that does not depend on Semler's teaching. More than that, Semler's picture of the development of catholic Christianity from an alleged clash between a particularist Jewish Christianity and a universalist gentile Christianity lies behind Hegel's dialectical scheme of historical development and Marx's derivative version, as well as behind the distinctive philosophy of Friedrich Nietzsche. Already we have been in touch with Semler's influence in discussing Lessing. Lessing learnt from Semler the theory that inward genuine religion was safe even if the outward historical props like miracles were knocked away. Even the detailed theories Lessing expounded, like the theory that the first three Gospelss were independent translations from Hebrew or Aramaic originals, his theory that John's Gospel was a late attempt to recover the true spiritual message, or his theory that the canon of Scripture was a late device simply to save the outward unity of the church, came straight out of Semler. Some of the best New Testament scholars of the age were his pupils, men like Johann Jakob Griesbach and Johann Gottfried Eichhorn (whom I shall discuss in a later chapter), and they got all their best ideas from Semler, but Semler's name has scarcely ever appeared in the New Testament textbooks, let alone in the histories of European thought, from that day to this.

Why was Semler forgotten, while those who freely borrowed his ideas became famous? Part of the reason was that he threw out ideas at a great rate in obscure corners of his vast literary output and rarely stopped to develop them. But the chief reason was that from about 1779 onwards, his mid fifties onwards, he showed himself a strict upholder of the right of the Prussian state and the state's theological faculties to censor anti-Lutheran and unorthodox teaching. In 1780 a brilliant young lecturer called Carl Friedrich Bahrdt was denied a theological chair because he did not believe in the working of the Holy Spirit, the occurrence of miracles, the historicity of the resurrection, and the primitiveness of the doctrine of the Trinity, and because he argued that the doctrine of the inspiration of the Bible was a late invention. To his astonishment, Semler publicly supported the right of the state to exclude Bahrdt from university teaching, and Semler explicitly acknowledged the duty of university theologians to maintain and uphold the local beliefs of the state they happened to serve. Theologians could discuss the doctrines and suggest in technical theological books the sort of positions Bahrdt maintained, but their public duty was to back the state religion and to see that it was enforced. Semler said this, even though he in fact shared most of Bahrdt's positions (as Bahrdt tartly remarked).

Semler's position may seem fantastic to us, as it did to most of his liberal-minded contemporaries, but we should remember that most intellectuals in Communist countries used to operate on the same principles, and that even in tolerant countries like Britain theologians who hold Semler's critical views retain positions in established churches which involve them in conducting public worship and reciting creeds which they interpret in a sense far removed from the original. It is easy to pour scorn on Semler, particularly when we learn that his private religion consisted not only in a pious and entirely 'spiritual' faith but also in a belief in alchemy and in the virtues of Luftsalzwasser (aerial-salt water) as a cure-all: public medicine might like to think that Luftsalzwasser was nothing, but every man had a right to his private medicine as much as to his private religion, and private medicine no more than private religion should be despised and attacked by the authorities, provided, of course, it kept its place and did not try to disrupt public unity and order! It is easy to pour scorn on Semler, but we do better to try to understand what he was arguing for; as I have said, his arguments exerted an immense influence on European thought, and are still alive today.

Semler's first and most fundamental move was to show that the so-called sacred writings of the Bible were not above criticism. The reason was that no alleged revelation could have been conveyed without using ordinary language, and ordinary language brought with it the ordinary assumptions about what was reasonable and true and what was unreasonable and false. Far from scripture contradicting reason, scripture could not convey any new truths without assuming the basic axioms of reason. And reason was required if we were to discover what the scriptural writers were saying. If there were a dispute about the meaning of scripture, no one could avoid using reason to try to discover the true meaning of the words under discussion; it is impossible to stick to the words themselves because it is just these words that are in dispute.

All biblical writings, like all other books by rational authors, consist of written discourses which were originally set down for particular readers, in a particular country, at a particular time, and, despite any other general usefulness, for a particular occasion . . .

So, when long ago God wanted to teach men certain important matters specifically by written revelation and through the Bible, he certainly could not adopt, invent and use for the purpose some new, non-human language. Otherwise he would have had to introduce a new set of signs and associated concepts, and men would have had first to be instructed in a hitherto unknown language. Even supposing that Holy Scripture, as regards its contents, consisted simply of pure revelations, and contained matters and subjects which were from beginning to end unknown to men, which by their inner nature could not be conceived of, God would still need to have even these revelations conveyed and expressed in just the signs and words and in just the manner of expression customary among men . . .

Unless revelation should lack all true morality, it could only be conveyed to men for their further use when, alongside revelation, the other principles of all human understanding and the use of the senses necessary for general cognition were taken for granted and kept unchanged . . .

The genuine powers and abilities which man as man essentially possesses are not actually taken away from him and cancelled [by the Fall], but are displaced from their first and best connection. Man after the Fall has just the same natural universal principles of all knowledge as knowledge gradually expands through the use of the senses and the understanding as he had before this disaster: that nothing can both exist and not exist, that a part is less than the whole, and the like. He would otherwise be deprived of all helps in understanding anything and in extending the bounds of understanding inwardly and outwardly and in dealing with questions from a moral point of view. He is otherwise not in a position to discover with all his natural understanding the very truths and to assent to those things which he must completely accept and obey if he wants to be united with God in the best way possible . . .

God could not, through the old special revelation, have contradicted natural general revelation or the knowledge which men by the use of their natural powers of understanding and reason can obtain as men. For God was as much the author of the one as the other; special revelation could never have taken place if he had not intended men to be as much rational creatures as living creatures. So all the mediators he has employed for special revelation must also surely have proved themselves to be rational teachers who have to do with rational creatures . . . So the presentation adopted by the mediators of the written revelation, their clothing and arranging of the expressions that make up the content was, in fact, in every case their own, although, to be sure, not without God's permission.[1]

This move of Semler's, as far as it goes, is perfectly correct: if the meaning of a text is in dispute, we can only discuss what is the true meaning by assuming certain axioms of reason and by using a language which has been shaped in centuries of rational discourse.

However, Semler is not discussing the meaning of any old text; his problem is the meaning of books held to be part of the sacred scripture of the church. Scripture contained special revelation from God. Presumably, if an investigator discovered the meaning of a passage in scripture, he was

---

[1] Historische Einleitung in die Dogmatische Gottesgelehrsamkeit von ihrem Ursprung and ihrer Beschaffenheit bis auf unsere Zeiten, which is Semler's 105-page introduction to his edition of S. J. Baumgarten's *Evangelische Glaubenslehre*, vol. i (1759), beginning on p. 34. These extracts are from pp. 35, 36, 37 f. and 40.

discovering a meaning God had revealed. Of course that meaning would have had to be couched in words and sentences of a particular language at a particular time. This move is again perfectly true, but it gave Semler the opportunity to introduce another idea which is far more problematical.

There was a long tradition in Christian theology, going back to the writings of Jewish theologians like Philo of Alexandria that the external literal sense of scripture could be false or misleading or unimportant compared to the internal spiritual message God really wanted to convey. Semler took up this theme and used it for a thoroughgoing theory that God had accommodated himself to the false notions or prejudices of those to whom he made revelations in order to lead them onward to the true inward spiritual religion.

Semler found evidence in the teaching of Jesus itself for his distinction between outward accommodating discourse and inward true teaching.

> We only have to observe more closely the history of the teaching office exercised by Jesus and Paul to recognize that there was a sort of *condescension* [accommodation] by which many mistakes in the thinking of the hearers and readers were for long deliberately overlooked. Right at the beginning it is expressly noted in Mark 4.2 that Jesus taught the people only in parables, . . . whereas when he was again *alone* and with his disciples he said, To you it is given to know and understand the mystery of the Kingdom of God, which I concede has been very unclearly presented in the parables.[2]

Jesus accommodated himself to his Jewish hearers by talking about angels, demons, Abraham's bosom and such like so as not to put them off; otherwise they would not have been able to absorb his true inner religion which consisted of 'free moral truth'.

---

[2] *Versuch einer biblischen Dämonologie* (Halle, 1776), Anhang, pp. 342 f., cited in Gottfried Hornig, *Die Anfänge der historisch-kritischen Theologie: Johann Salomo Semlers Schriftverständnis und seine Stellung zu Luther* (Göttingen, 1961), p. 222, note 28.

The Gospels and the whole idea of a sacred canon of scripture was similarly a device to preserve the outward unity of the church, and this canon could be and was misused to impose restrictions on the consciences and inner freedom of Christians to hold to the truths taught by Jesus and Paul . .

[On a close reading of Eusebius, Irenaeus and Tertullian on the four Gospels etc] one finally discovers that the canonical books . . . as little contain the universal unalterable complete sum of the Christian religion as those other books not in the canon: the Epistle of Barnabas, the writings of Hermas and of Clement in Rome. They are very good treatises for the first teachers in the then-prevailing circumstances; but any further decision, whether of the church or of many private Christians, that such-and-such a divinity attaches to these *canonical* writings has no part in the *universal content* of the Christian religion. Rather, such a judgment is part of the local particular history of Christians who now use or misuse these books for their own cognition, for their own ends; and who now employ them against one another in order to present, once and for all, an exlusive summary of the Christian religion – namely, their own –; use them to put themselves over one another. This misuse of the New Testament is as visible, as patent to all morally alert men as the quite strange coupling of all the books of the Old Testament, in the form of a current very dubious Greek translation, with just this New Testament. The Catholic Church now teaches that a monotonously simple repetition of the historical content of the Gospels comprises the chief content of the religion of all Christians once and for all – completely against the teaching and the example of Jesus, completely against the perfectly clear axioms of Paul, and of all the Apostles so far as they, too, observed a certain 'economy' and stewardship and dealt tenderly with their weak contemporaries. But it is quite certain that these Gospel narratives were all written only with the purpose of bringing those (who up till then were Jews) to the point where they could let go their traditions and opinions about a Messiah and follow their own moral judgment concerning the God-pleasing destiny of his Son. All readers were left free, according to their ability, to attach themselves to every one of these narratives, but this dependence of individual readers could not then become part of the universal and external new religion, in so far as this new religion itself had only just begun to take small steps upwards. The fact that the Church or the official teachers have made this a part of the essence or main content of the Christian religion on which should hang even the everlasting blessedness of all Christians: that belongs on the contrary to the history of the Church. This can only be regarded by unskilled and unthinking Christians, quite erroneously, as something they have to believe about Christ as of highest importance and significance. Just as little do the Epistles or the other books of the New Testament automatically belong to the best and most perfect content of the Christian religion. They contain instructions for the first teachers of that time how they should deal with their contemporaries. Of course individual Christians are free to affirm in their own mind the whole content, every line and every paragraph, however little they understand them, and thereby to make this the additional content of their own religion. But no Church, no teacher can elevate this to the genuine main content of the whole Christian religion of all time. From the nature of the case it is impossible. At the very least, all Christians who see this must remain utterly and completely free to distinguish between their present Christian knowledge and practice and what was once the knowledge and practice of those Christians who lived in Galatica, in Rome etc.[3]

Semler's view of the true nature of Jesus' message – a set

[3] *Neue Versuche die Kirchenhistorie der ersten Jahrhunderte mehr aufzuklären* (Leipzig, 1788), pp. 107–9.

of inner free moral truths, clothed in Jewish terms and later transmitted by Jewish followers who took the outer clothing for the inner substance – led him to oppose most sharply the reconstruction of Jesus' teaching proposed by Hermann Samuel Reimarus and published by Lessing as fragments of an unknown writer.   Reimarus (largely indebted to the English Deist Thomas Chubb's The True Gospel of Jesus Christ published in 1738 in London) argued, you will remember from chapter one, that Jesus had taught no new doctrines, that he adhered to the Mosaic Law, and that he expected to be the Jewish national deliverer who would reign in the coming Kingdom of God. The spiritual gospel, which abandoned these Jewish ideas, was (according to Reimarus) a late invention of the Apostles, long after the Resurrection (which they themselves faked), when they saw that the Jewish ideas could not win them the success they needed.

Semler opposed this reading of the evidence with the utmost vehemence; his whole religious position as well as his whole elaborate history of the growth of Christianity was at stake.

Semler, no more than Reimarus, was original. His picture can be found in the writings of another English Deist, and was probably derived from there. This was Thomas Morgan (died 1743) who published in four parts an anonymous dialogue between a Christian Deist and Theophanes, a Christian Jew (meaning, of course, an orthodox Christian), the first volume in 1737. Here is the origin of Semler's ideas and the ideas that have largely dominated New Testament scholarship ever since.

> Theophanes [a Christian Jew]: But did Jesus himself own or take upon him this Character, as *Jewish* Messiah, or the Restorer of the Kingdom to Israel, in their national and well-known Sense?
>
> Philalethes [a Christian Deist]: No: He renounced it to the last, and died upon that Renunciation, by declaring before Pilate, that his Kingdom was not of this World, and that he had no such worldy, ambitious Views, as the Priests and Rulers charged him with, and put him to Death for, nor could they

prove any such Thing against him; and therefore Pilate, upon Examination would have acquitted him had it not been for the Violence and Outrage of the Populace, who could not be satisfied but by his crucifixion . . . It is plain, that the *Jewish* Populace or Mobility had generally a Notion of him, as their Messiah, national Deliverer, or Restorer of the Kingdom. Upon this Supposition only they had follow'd and adher'd to him for a Twelve-Month together, and were all ready, at this Time, to take up Arms for him, and make him King even by Force. They had Expectations and strong Hopes, that he would declare for them to the very last. But when they found that he disclaimed it before *Pilate*, and quitted their Interest upon his Trial, they were all turned in a Moment, and as one Man cry'd out, *Crucify, crucify him,* it is not fit that such a Fellow should live, away with him from the Earth . . .

Nay, his own Disciples had all along adhered to him upon this vain Hope, and even after his Resurrection, they never preached Jesus as the Messiah or Christ in any other Sense. No Christian *Jew* ever believ'd in Jesus as the common Saviour of the World, without Distinction between *Jew* and *Gentle*. This was St. *Paul's* Gospel, which he had received, as he declared by immediate Revelation from Christ himself; and had never advised or consulted with any of the *Jewish* Apostles about it, as well knowing that they would never come into it.

Theophanes: Christianity then, as you represent it, was nothing else but as political Faction among the Jews; some of them receiving Jesus as the Messiah or Restorer of the Kingdom, and others rejecting him under that Character.

Philalethes: I take this to be the plain Truth of the Matter; for they who received him as the Messiah, were as zealous for the Law, and as great Sticklers for it, as the rest who rejected him.

Theophanes: . . . What, I beseech you, did the Apostles

of Christ preach two different Gospels? Did *Peter,*
James and *John* preach one Gospel, and *Paul* another?[4]

Semler took hold of Morgan's theory of the double origin
of Christianity and made it more subtle by drawing on his
accommodation theory, that Jesus and Paul had accommodated their teaching to the weakness of their hearers
by adopting ideas like that of demon-possession or the
apocalyptic hope of a coming earthly Kingdom of God which
they did not themselves believe to be literally true. This
modification allowed Semler to argue that the misunderstanding of Jesus' teaching was not completely surprising.
But Semler also argued that Jesus explained the inward truth
in secret to his disciples, and that Paul also made a distinction
between what he said to fleshly hearers and what he kept for
the spiritual. So Semler could argue that all the Apostles
knew the true spiritual gospel at first; only later did they
contaminate it by Jewish ideas. When that happened, Paul
opposed them, and at this point there came about the great
split and division that is so important for understanding the
rise of the Catholic Church, which was a reconciling of the
two parties after the death of the Apostles.

Here is Semler's theory in more detail as it can be gathered
from scattered references in his writings.

Jesus was not a zealous Jew. He did not appeal to the
Mosaic Law, but rather to the better moral insight of his
hearers. To be sure, he did employ some of the current
pictures about the coming Kingdom of God in Jewish
external terms, but this was only to accommodate his
teachings to the capacity of his hearers. In any case, this was
only in his public teaching; in private he explained everything
in purely spiritual terms. The Jews expected the Messiah to
bring in a worldly kingdom in which the enemies of the
Jews would be overthrown and they would enjoy riches and
power. Jesus contradicted this view and taught that the
Kingdom was already present (according to Luke 17.21). He

---

[4] [Thomas Morgan], The Moral Philosopher. In a Dialogue between Philalethes a
Christian Deist, and Theophanes a Christian Jew (London, 1737), pp. 349–54.
Volume II, 1739; Volume III, 1740; Volume IV, 1741.

was crucified because he never taught tax-collectors and so-called sinners to adhere first to the Mosaic Law, and because he contradicted Jewish ideas of the Kingdom of the Messiah. 'Jesus himself was executed because he had put his teaching and his life openly against the previous Jewish interpretations of the Kingdom of the Messiah'.

Paul taught the same universal gospel as Jesus against Jewish particularism: the gospel was universal and for all men equally. Like Jesus, Paul also accommodated himself to his hearers, and distinguished between the fleshly hearers, who had to be given pictures about the imminent return of Christ, and the spiritual who could be told the spiritual religion.

Peter and the Apostles knew about the spiritual religion, but they quite arbitrarily soon began to revive the old Jewish ideas, and to teach them as necessary beliefs. They started to appeal to Old Testament prophecies and to miracles and exorcisms in support of the truth of the gospel, and so came to make the Old Testament a part of Christianity. Paul opposed them in the name of the new eternal universal inward gospel, the 'moral ' religion which depends not on historical narratives about Christ but on a practical daily moral advance in the universal faith in Christ. So Christianity divided into two parties, the Jewish-Christian party led by Peter, and the gnostic, free, spiritual party of Paul.

The heretic Marcion from Pontus on the Black Sea in the second century and other so-called heretics tried to preserve the religion of Jesus and Paul. Marcion had a gospel which separated out the merely local and ephemeral Jewish elements from Jesus' teaching and so preserved its true import. (The story that Marcion had constructed his Gospel by cutting bits out of Luke's Gospel was a lie; his Gospel was in fact as old or older than the others and formed the basis of the canonical Luke.) But even Paul's party succumbed to the Jewish notion that the church should be one organized body with one canon and one creed, and after the death of the Apostles the parties of Peter and Paul drew together and formed the one Catholic Church. This Church wrote church history in its own image, and it is hard for us now, but not impossible, to penetrate behind this history to the true story of Christianity.

We have one canon which each Church (Roman, Lutheran, Reformed or Socinian) tries to use in support of one orthodoxy. But this canon in fact contains different strands which dimly mirror the true history of Christianity. The first three Gospels were written to attract Jews to Christianity and so they emphasize Jewish external beliefs (miracles, exorcisms, teaching about the future Kingdom of God, the resurrection as a physical event). Mark's Gospel was not written by John Mark, Peter's secretary, nor was Luke's Gospel by Paul's friend and supporter, Luke the Physician. Paul's Epistles were treasured by the gnostic Christians and represent that party. The Catholic Epistles were part of the unifying process which led to the one Catholic Church.

Not all the history of the first centuries of the church was a denial of the inward Gospel. The church necessarily adopted formulas like the Trinity and the Homoousion clause in the creed (that the Son was of one substance with the Father) to protect the social cohesion of the church required by the state for the sake of civil peace and unity; and only under such conditions could the private inner religion of enlightened individual Christians flourish. Semler seems to see these formulas, which he privately does not subscribe to, as necessary external accompaniments in the progressive development of the inner religion (just as Hegel was later to say that the doctrine of the Trinity was the axle of world history).[5]

Semler tried to discredit the traditional doctrine of the inspiration of scripture and yet, in a curious way, he injected reverence for scripture deep into European consciousness – European secular consciousness – by arguing that scripture was the necessary outward clothing of the deepest inward truth. Semler's ideas were influential far beyond the confines of Biblical scholarship or theology proper, although here too Semler propounded a theory that has been elaborated and

[5] For the best summaries of Semler's theories see Johann Gottfried Eichhorn, 'Johann Salomo Semler, geb. am 18ten Dec. 1725, gest. am 14ten März 1791', *Allgemeine Bibliothek der biblischen Litteratur*, vol. 5 (Leipzig, 1793), 1–202, and Bruno Bauer, Einfluss des englischen Quäkerthums auf die deutsche Cultur ... (Berlin, 1878), pp. 127–58.

enlarged (without acknowledgement) by technical scholars and popular teachers. We shall see his influence at work in the thought of all the other thinkers to be discussed in this book, as we have already seen it in Lessing.

4

Kant

There is a simple reading of Kant that would class him as a moralist who left the revealed religion of the Bible and the established churches of his day to one side, and taught a practical morality based on reason alone. If that was all that was to be said about Kant, there would scarcely be room for a chapter on Kant in a book about the authority of the Bible; Kant was simply a rational philosopher for whom the Bible had no authority; if the Bible happened to suggest and promote some true moral beliefs, well and good, but the fact that these true moral beliefs could be found in the Bible did nothing for their authority – moral beliefs held true if and only if the reasons for them held true.

Nevertheless Kant requires a place in a book about the authority of the Bible in an age of criticism because his definition of what belonged to the circle of pure reason was extraordinarily wide, and included many ideas that his contemporaries thought (and we might well agree with them) belonged to the sphere of Bible and revelation, ideas corresponding to the Creation and the Fall of Man, to Redemption, and to the Destruction and the Restoration of All Things.

Kant's whole life was lived in and around Königsberg, the capital of East Prussia, in whose cathedral Frederick I had been crowned in 1701.[1] Frederick marked his coronation year by allowing a small school in Königsberg to be called the

[1] Königsberg is now called Kaliningrad and is part of the Soviet Union (54.42 N 20.32 E).

Royal School. It became later the *Kollegium Fridericianum*. The school had been founded on the model of the Halle orphanage school Michaelis had attended; like it, a school devoted to making its pupils Christians on the pietist model. In 1733, Frederick I appointed the outstanding army chaplain Schultz, already town councillor, Doctor of theology and pastor, to be the school's head, and he it was who persuaded Kant's parents of his outstanding gifts, being a constant visitor to their house. He was a practical Christian – but also a close disciple of Wolff's.[2]

Kant, born on Immanuel day in the old Prussian calendar, 22 April 1724, was the fifth child, but only the second to survive, of a saddler. He believed his grandfather had emigrated from Scotland and settled first in Tilsit and then in Memel, and certainly his name was sometimes recorded in the school records as Cant, Cante, Candt, as well as Kant and Kandt.[3] In his eight years at the *Fridericianum* he learnt mostly Latin, some Greek, Hebrew, and French, and a great deal of Religion, which decidedly put him off. During this time, when he was thirteen or fourteen, his mother died, whom he adored. She died of a fever caught while tending a friend whose fiancé had deserted her; no wonder Kant always taught the radical evil of man, and himself found it almost impossible to trust in friendship. He used to quote Aristotle, My dear friends, there are no friends.[4]

At sixteen he went to the local University, called Albertina after its founder, Albrecht of Prussia (1541). He lived in a student hostel, and quietly made his own way in philosophy. The greatest influence on him was the teaching of the young professor Martin Knutzen, professor of Logic and Metaphysics, who of course also lectured in mathematics and natural sciences, an early Newtonian. Kant published his first monograph of 240 pages, at the age of 22. In it he ventured

[2] E. A. Ch. Waisianski, *Immanuel Kant in seinen letzten Lebensjahren* (1840), reprinted by Felix Gross, *Immanuel Kant: Sein Leben in Darstellungen von Zeitgenossen* (Berlin, 1912), pp. 250 f; = *Wer war Kant?* (Pfullingen, 1974), p. 245. Karl Vorländer, *Immanuel Kant: Der Mann and das Werk*, 2 vols. (Leipzig, 1924), vol. i, pp. 23–5.

[3] Vorländer, i.15, 36. Vorländer rather doubts the Scottish descent.

[4] Wasianski: for his mother's death, pp. 252 f.; for friendship, pp. 245 f.

to say that Leibniz was wrong, and justified his boldness in leaving the beaten track by the argument that only thus could knowledge of the truth grow.[5]

In May 1746 he left the University and in 1747 settled as private tutor in the house of a Reformed pastor in the Latvian village of Judtschen on the eastern borders of East Prussia where protestants from Switzerland, northern France and the Netherlands had been settled after the plague had decimated the village in 1709–10. In 1750 he took a similar post in a military household in the far west of East Prussia. At the age of thirty he returned to Königsberg and wrote an important essay of 200 pages on the constitution and mechanical origin of the whole universe treated according to Newton's principles, *Allgemeine Naturgeschichte und Theorie des Himmels*, in which he defended himself against the charge that he advanced atheism; on the contrary, he said, 'there is a God just for this reason: that Nature even in chaos cannot proceed except regularly and orderly'.[6] Quotations from Pope's *Essay on Man* (1733) in translation stud the work. Kant gained his M. A. by thesis (our doctorate) and his *pro venia docendi* (right to teach), also by thesis, the *Nova dilucidatio*, a new elucidation of the first principles of metaphysical knowledge.

His course was set. He had swept aside Newton's hesitations about ascribing a mechanical explanation to the whole universe, and he had squarely posed to himself the difficulty of proving the principle that nothing is true without a determined (or sufficient) reason. Hume may have had to waken him out of his dogmatic slumbers, but his dogmatic solution to the central problem was not given without careful thought.

As a university teacher he began a strenuous course of lecturing and writing, rising every day at 5 and going to bed at 10. He taught logic, metaphysics, mathematics, physics, physical geography, anthropology, and ethics, as well as aesthetics with classes in rhetoric and German style; never less

---

[5] *Gedanken von der wahren Schätzung der Lebendigen Kräfte* (Königsberg, 1746), Vorrede §§ vi, vii.

[6] Axxviii f. There is an English translation of part of *The Universal Natural History* by W. Hastic (Glasgow, 1900, reprinted Michigan, 1969).

than sixteen hours a week, and as much as twenty-six or twenty-eight in the 1760s, besides private lessons for the money.[7]

You had to listen in his lectures, to pay attention to everything, however small. He did not force his students to understand by constant repetition. He never tired of saying to his students, 'You will not learn philosophy from me but – *to philosophise*; not thoughts simply for repeating, but *to think*'.[8]

By the end of the Seven Years' War (1763), before Kant was forty, he was famous as the author of *The Only Possible Proof to Demonstrate the Existence of God*, and he was to publish two more well-regarded books in 1764 and 1766 before falling silent, effectively for more than twelve years. Since about 1768 he had wrestled with a problem not new to him, but which Hume had brought to his attention with renewed force. In the middle of 1780 he wrote down the results of that twelve years' thinking in four to five months, on the wing.[9]

The *Critique of Pure Reason* was published in parts in April and May 1781 in time for the Leipzig Easter Book Fair. Kant turned fifty-seven when this *Critique* was in the press. He went on lecturing until 1797, when he turned seventy-three, and during those sixteen years of his life he published thirty-two separate writings, and there were more to come.

What discovery released this extraordinary philosophical energy? It was the discovery that the comical contrast between the amazing descriptive achievements of natural science and the blind dogmatism of metaphysics could only be resolved if metaphysics gave up its pretensions:

> Go, teach Eternal Wisdom how to rule –
> Then drop into thyself, and be a fool![10]

---

[7] Vorländer, vol. i, p. 84. The reference to lectures on aesthetics and classes in rhetoric is to be found in Ludwig Ernst Borowski, *Darstellung des Lebens und Charakters Immanuel Kants, von Kant selbst genau revidiert und berichtigt* reprinted in *Immanual Kant: Sein Leben in Darstellungen von Zeitgenossen* ed. Felix Gross (Berlin, 1912), p. 87; = *Wer war Kant? [Pfullingen, 1974]*, p. 102.

[8] See his lecture plan for the Winter Semester 1765–1766, A5.

[9] Vorländer, i. 261.

[10] Alexander Pope, Essay on Man II. 29 f. (1733) quoted by Kant, *Der einzig mögliche Beweisgrund* (1762) A149.

Reason had to recognise that there were irresolvable antinomies at the limits of thought: between the world as having a beginning and a spatial boundary and the world as infinite in time and space; between causality combined with freedom and the complete absence of freedom in a world bound by nature's laws; between an absolutely necessary being as part of the world or cause of the world and no absolutely necessary being at all.[11]

When reason recognised these limits and discovered that these were questions to which no answer was an answer, it could then operate in giving scientific descriptions with perfect confidence.[12] Similarly, dogmatic unbelief led the young men of Kant's day to think that there were no moral laws. But if one applied the same critique to dogmatic unbelief in ethics as one had applied to dogmatic unbelief in the study of nature, one arrived at the same conclusion: pure reason lived by faith and discerned that, apart from all empirical considerations of pleasure or reward, there existed duties that bound everyone unconditionally. My will is determined by this 'something' that lies beyond any determination to be found in the world of sense. But this 'something' has no being; it is an idea.[13]

In the philosophy of nature and in the philosophy of morals, Kant is the apostle of faith; reason itself discerns the limits of reason and attains to reasonable faith (ein vernünftiges Glauben).[14] But when one says 'faith' in Protestant Germany one has said the only word which gives access to God, religion, and the Bible. *Sola fide*, by faith alone, is the key to everything.

Kant quietly and coolly applied to the Bible the principle of 'by faith alone', as Luther had advocated, and produced a

[11] A426 f., B454 f.; A434 f., B462 f.; A444 f., B472 f.; A452 f., B480 f. Kant said he started his *Critique of Pure Reason* from the Antinomies: these it were that woke him from his dogmatic slumber. Letter to Garve, 21 September 1798; Vorländer, i.250 f.

[12] Note A479, B507.

[13] *Grundlegung zur Metaphysik der Sitten, Foundations of the Metaphysics of Morals* (1785), AB 120–128, especially 125 f.

[14] *Ibid.*, AB 126 f.

most reverent and thorough-going representation of everything in it; but as an idea, necessary and valuable only for its practical moral import.

Creation, Fall, Redemption, the Destruction and Restoration of all things: the great doctrines of orthodox Christianity all have their place – to the horror of many of his enlightened contemporaries who wondered how Book One of *Religion within the Limits of Reason Alone* could be entitled 'On the Radical Evil in Human Nature'.[15]

This is very strange. Reason has to submit to authority if it is to be rational. It has to live by faith alone. A man who rejects the religion of the Bible needs the 'fiction' of the religion of the Bible in order to underpin all rational reflection, and he raids the Bible for his key moral ideas.

Let us examine in detail a passage where Kant actually discusses the meaning of a text from the bible in the setting of an essay on how to interpret the bible in general. The extract is from a witty book published in 1798 when Kant was seventy-four years old, but written at the same time as his *Religion Within the Limits of Reason Alone* (1793). It is entitled *The Strife between the Faculties*, that is, the strife between the faculty of Philosophy and the faculties of Theology, Law, and Medicine.

He begins the book with an attack on the 'man in the street's' attitude to the faculties. The man in the street ignores philosophy: Philosophers prattle on about what I have always known by myself. He demands of theology: Though I have lived a profligate life, I want an entry ticket to the Kingdom of heaven just before the gates clang to. He demands of law: How can I win my case though I'm in the wrong? And of medicine: Thought I have done exactly what I wanted with my body and misused it, how can I stay healthy and live to a good age? The man in the street wants fortune-tellers and wizards, and Kant's purpose is to bring philosophy to bear on the other three faculties to rescue them from fortune-tellers

---

[15] The original title when the section was first published as an article in the *Berlinische Monatschrift*, April 1792.

and wizards and to make them reasonable and moral. In the strife between philosophy and the other faculties, philosophy must win.

In the conflict between philosophy and theology, Kant, true to his guiding principle, attacks the dogmatism of the theologians: reason overthrows all human pretentions.

He proposes four rules for the exegesis of the Bible. First, all theoretical doctrines proclaimed as holy and transcending reason can be judged by reason, and all those which contradict practical reason must be condemned by reason.

Second, everything in religion comes down to what one does. Therefore the articles of faith cannot be things that are simply required to be believed but what it is possible and fitting to believe from a practical and moral point of view. Ecclesiastical authority is necessary – but it must not rely on fear or hope. The authority of beliefs stems only from a judgement of whether or not they make better men.

Third, men are radically evil and come under the condemnation of the law, but grace can and should be more powerful in them. But grace should be taught, not as the infusion of something from on high, but as the development of moral impulses in men by their own effort.

Fourth, men by their own actions cannot attain righteousness in the sight of their own conscience. Reason must believe in a supernatural supplementing of defective righteousness; otherwise men will lack the courage to believe that they will attain blessedness and be well-pleasing to God.

Under his first rule for the exegesis of the Bible Kant includes a discussion of the resurrection of Christ.

> From a practical point of view we can be completely indifferent to the question of whether we survive only as a soul, or whether, the very same material out of which our body here consists being necessary to the identity of our person in the next world, the soul being consequently no distinct substance, our body itself must be resurrected. For to whom is his body really so dear, that he would gladly choose to drag it with him into eternity, when he could dispense with it?

Consequently the Apostle's logical argument, 'If Christ is not risen (come alive as a body), then we too shall not rise (definitely not live on after death)', is not binding. But the argument might indeed be unsound (since no one will hold that a particular inspiration is proof of an argument), yet the Apostle only wanted thereby to say that we had cause to believe that Christ still lived, and that our faith would be in vain if so perfect a man as this should not have lived after his (bodily) death. It was this faith, which reason instilled in him (as in all men), that stirred him to historical faith in a public event. He ingenuously held the event to be true, and he needed it as the basis of proof of a particular moral faith in the future life, without being conscious that he himself would scarcely have given credence to this legend without the latter, the faith. Thereby the moral intention was attained, even though the mode of presentation bore the stamp of the scholastic notions in which he had been educated.

By the way, there are important objections to the case. The institution of the Lord's Supper (of a sad occasion) in memory of him seems like a formal parting (not just merely till the next meeting soon). The sorrowful words on the cross express a disappointed intention (to bring the Jews simply by his life to true religion) rather than what the joy at an accomplished intention would have led us to expect. Finally, the disciples' expression in Luke's Gospel, 'We thought that he would redeem Israel' does not allow us to gather that they were prepared for an expected meeting again in three days, still less that anything about his resurrection had come to their ears.

But why should we allow ourselves to be entangled in such very learned investigations and disputations for the sake of an historical narrative that we should have always let be put where it belongs, among the *adiaphora* [things indifferent to faith] — when the real issue is religion, and for religion the faith that reason infuses into us is, for practical purposes, quite sufficient?[16]

---

[16] Der Streit der Facultäten in drey Abschnitten. Königsberg, 1798, pp. 52 f. The

Kant's argument is this. The doctrine of the Resurrection, like the doctrines of the Trinity, the Incarnation, and the Ascension, transcends reason but must be judged by reason. In the case of the Resurrection of Christ, reason discerns the true moral principle the doctrine is meant to convey, because reason sees that the particular expression of the doctrine in the form that Christ was raised from the dead bodily and that we shall be raised bodily was due to a prior reasonable belief in the immortality of the soul. If reason finds a doctrine which has a husk that does not conform to reason but contradicts reason, reason must – and does – condemn it.

Kant concluded his resolution of the dispute between philosophy and theology by arguing that he has saved the authority of the Bible. The Bible is a vehicle which leads men to religion – in so far as it furthers the public dissemination of the moral precepts of reason. But the Bible is a ladder which whoever climbs it can kick away. 'If the Gospel has not previously taught universal moral laws in their purity, pure reason would not have been able to comprehend them in such perfection; but since they are given, one can now convince anyone of their correctness and validity merely by reason'.[17]

In the case of the resurrection, Kant wanted to save the Biblical doctrine – so long as it is taken in a moral and practical sense. But he can hardly succeed. Paul must have been perfectly well aware of the doctrine of the immortality of the soul: the Sadducees, who denied the resurrection, affirmed the shadow existence of men after death in Sheol, for that doctrine (at least) could be gathered from the Law. As a Pharisee, Paul would have been accustomed to defending the doctrine of the resurrection of the body, long before he came to believe that Jesus had been bodily raised from the dead. Consequently, he would have judged his argument to

Strife between the Faculties, in three parts. First Part: Strife between the Faculty of Philosophy and the Faculty of Theology.

[17] Kant to Jacobi, 30 August 1789, translated by Lewis White Beck, *Early German Philosophy: Kant and His Predecessors* (Cambridge, Massachusetts, 1969), p. 495. I am much indebted to Beck's chapter on Kant.

have failed if Jesus were not raised bodily. Kant tries to save St Paul by discounting the husk of the argument and preserving the rational kernel. He sees that St Paul genuinely believed that Christ had been bodily raised, but he thinks that the truth of that is beyond recovery and, in any case, does not matter. Only the practical moral belief that good men live on after death matters.

But what is this practical moral belief? It is, as Kant explained at greater length in *Religion within the Limits of Reason Alone*, a regulative principle, not a constitutive principle. The belief in immortality is not giving historical information about whether or not life continues after death but, if it is a regulative principle, it expresses the moral satisfaction a good man feels: if another life awaits him after this, he may hope to draw nearer and nearer to the goal of perfection. Just as an observer of nature must posit a wise and almighty originator (but must also understand that no such being existed, only in idea), so moral man must posit continuing progress to perfection even after death. Immortality exists only as an idea.

If my exposition of Kant's position is right, the passage on the resurrection is not as candid as it looks. He seems to be arguing that reason accepts immortality while rejecting the bodily resurrection, but he is not really arguing about the content of the proposition to be believed (resurrection of the body or immortality of the soul), but about the *nature* of the belief. Historical belief is rejected and moral belief recommended. He could just as well have attacked the doctrine of the immortality of the soul as attacked Paul's doctrine of the resurrection of the body, for the immortality of the soul could be held historically too. He condescendingly excuses Paul for believing a legend and for loading on top of a truth of reason the scholastic accretions in which he had been educated. But Kant comes close to putting himself beyond his own excuses. Kant knows that the point at issue is how beliefs are held, yet he presents the case as though it were a choice between beliefs. The doctrine of the immortality of the soul is no more literally important than the doctrine of the resurrection of the body. The doctrine of immortality is a golden lie: a powerful and beneficent idea of a state that does not exist. Now a golden lie is still a lie, and Kant rightly condemned those who thought they had a right to lie. Furthermore, a golden lie is a moral truth told not because it is true but because it serves to promote morality, and Kant rightly condemned the teaching that we should judge the morality of an action by its effects on others.

Kant could well reply to these charges by saying that he deceived no one who paid attention to his teaching. The sense in which he taught God, freedom, and immortality was perfectly clear; he taught each as 'fictions', a sceptical method designed to confound sceptics (like Hume) as well as to confound dogmatists.[18]

That is his final defence: his critical method. By his critical method, he hoped to show reason its limits, to make room for faith, and then to vindicate this faith as reasonable. Only reason humbled, weak, and powerless was reason triumphant, strong and powerful. The system is beautifully put together, and appears completely consistent in all its parts, yet wherever we push it, the critical method turns into either dogmatism or scepticism. Kant is dogmatic about free-will in morality, but sceptical in natural science; he is dogmatic about the teleological principle of the natural order, but sceptical about teleology in morality. We must posit an almighty originator of the world, but we are to be completely sceptical about his existence.

For all this, the Bible is the paradigm. As Lessing and Semler and countless others had come to believe, the Bible taught, under the false appearance of historical truths, the truths of reason. The principle of 'by faith alone', which they had taken in with their mothers' milk, was beautifully suited to express their view of the world: a world in which God, freedom, and immortality were necessary truths, but truths which had no existence other than in the mind.

Kant's gravestone bears some of his own words. 'Two things fill the mind with ever new and increasing admiration

---

[18] *Critique of Pure Reason*, A424, B451. Dr Gerd Buchdahl gave me the phrase 'as a fiction', which of course Kant would not have used.

and awe, the more often and the more steadily we contemplate them: the starry heavens above me, and the moral law within'. He was one of the greatest contemplatives, and one of the greatest advocates of the reasoning mind, but his contemplation was not as steady as it appeared. It was not reasonable to be so unreasonable: we have to go either onwards to worship, or back to scepticism. Kant, however, was so powerful an influence that few men in the next hundred years dared to leave the protection he offered; few dared to go either on or back. That meant that in interpreting the Bible, too, they remained with Kant. The critical method of studying the Bible came to mean not so much an open and fearless historical investigation as an acceptance of the dogma that the Bible pointed to beliefs that were necessary, about a being that did not exist except in the mind.

5

Herder

Herder believed passionately in the authority of the Bible and preached the Bible's authority all his life, and that preaching deeply influenced European thought. He was born on the 25 August, 1744, in the little town of Mohrungen in East Prussia. His father had been a weaver but poverty spurred him to become a primary school teacher, bell-ringer and cantor: a quiet, earnest man. His mother, Herder said, taught him 'to pray, to feel, and to think'.[1] Every day closed with a family hymn and Bible reading, and Hamann was to envy Herder's intimate knowledge of all the hymns and their tunes.[2] His teacher Grim taught him Latin, Greek, a little Hebrew, Logic, and a thorough dogmatic theology. Herder didn't waste time playing with friends; he preferred to read. No book in the village was safe from him; no sooner he saw a book he hadn't read on a window-sill, than he went into the house and asked to read it.[3] He was a strong and healthy boy, yet a fistula which developed in his right eye when he was five seemed to put an end to all his youthful plans to study to be a theologian – a physical defect that was to dog him all his life, but which led him to Strasburg for an operation when he was twenty-six, and threw the young Goethe in his path, on whom he exercised a crucial and lasting influence.

When Herder was sixteen, he was taken into the house of Trescho, pastor of the town church, to act as amanuensis to

---

[1] R. Haym, *Herder nach seinem Leben und seinen Werken dargestellt* (Berlin, i.1, 1877; i.2, 1880; ii, 1885), i.5.

[2] Haym, i.6.

[3] Haym, i.8.

this self-important writer who needed just such an excellent penman to transcribe his books for publication. Trescho was a hard task-master, but at least he gave Herder access to a large, well-stocked library. He was not amused when Herder slipped a poem of his own, *A Song to Cyrus*, into the bundle of manuscripts sent to Kanter, the Königsberg publisher. Fortunately for Herder, a Russian medical officer named Schwarzerloch, quartered in Mohrungen in the winter of 1761–62, took him up and carried him off to Königsberg to become a medical student at his expense, in return for translating a book of his into Latin.

Herder lasted as a medical student for three weeks and then impulsively, with the prospect of little or no financial support from home, he changed to theology, and within a fortnight was sitting listening to Kant's lectures on Metaphysics (21 August, 1762). For that day on, he never missed a lecture of Kant's, whatever the subject. Once he was so excited by Kant's lecture that he went home and composed a poem embodying its content, which he recited to his fellow students the next day when they again assembled to hear Kant.[4] And Kant used to let Herder attend his lectures free, since Herder was quite penniless and, apart from some help from his home town, supported himself at university by teaching in the Collegium Fridericianum (Kant's old school). Herder never lost his admiration for Kant, yet Kant came to embody for him the fatal defect of the age, the pretension of philosophy, which by dividing and separating killed understanding of the living process of history. 'We have had enough of philosophical proofs.'[5]

Herder left Königsberg at the age of twenty and became a teacher and then a preacher in Riga. He became a freemason and advanced to become secretary of the lodge. He began to publish reflections on the new and reviving German literature of which Lessing was the brightest star.

In June 1769 he embarked on a grand tour: Paris (where he became tutor and travelling companion to a young prince),

[4] Haym, i.32 f.
[5] Provincial Letters, Herders Sämmtliche Werke, edited by Bernhard Suphan (Berlin, 1877–1913), vii.303 f.

Brussels, and Amsterdam. But his eye began to play up, and the contract with the prince was dissolved and he went to Strasburg for treatment. In Darmstadt he had already met Caroline Flachsland, a prominent member of the Damstadt circle of men and women passionately devoted to the inward-looking writings of Klopstock, Richardson, and Rousseau, and she was to become his wife. In Strasburg he brought Goethe under his spell – he was twenty-six and Goethe twenty-one.[6] He opened Goethe's eyes to the simplicity and naturalness of folk-songs (some of which, in particular the folk songs of 'Ossian', were not as 'natural' as they gave out to be). Together they planned to publish *Von deutscher Art und Kunst* which became the manifesto of Sturm und Drang (1773). Herder's essay on Shakespeare proclaimed him as 'happy child of the gods in his undertaking! The primal power of his inner calling displays what is indeed new, original, completely different'.[7]

After some delay because of his eye operation Herder went to Bückeburg as chief pastor. In 1772 he began the *Frankfurter Gelehrte Anzeigen* with Merck and Goethe, to be the organ of the movement, and his Berlin prize-winning essay *On the Origin of Language* was published. He mocked the assumption behind the question set by the Berlin Academy, that men *invented* language; rather, language defines man, and the origin of language was divine – insofar as its origin was human.[8]

On the 2nd May 1773 he married Caroline Flachsland. He was twenty-eight. That was the year Lessing published the first of the Wolfenbüttel Fragments, but Herder simply rose above the Fragments and the controversy;[9] not because he was uninterested in the interpretation of the Bible – far from it – but partly because he was securely grounded in Semler and could afford to ignore the questions raised by Reimarus,

---

[6] See Herder's letter to Karoline Flachsland, 21 March, 1772.

[7] Shakespear [sic], Suphan, v.218.

[8] Suphan, v.143–6: 'So the origin of language was only properly divine insofar as it was human', v. 146.

[9] For a rare reference, see *Briefe, das Studium der Theologie betreffend*, Suphan, x.162 f.

but above all because he was embarked on a campaign to preach a new gospel which had a new approach to the Bible at its centre.

Herder remained a pastor all his life. Goethe was instrumental in having him appointed General Superintendent of the church in Weimar. In the Weimar years Herder produced his great work *Ideen zur Philosophie der Geschichte der Menschheit* (1748–91) [Ideas on the Philosophy of the History of Humanity] which enjoyed a brief popularity but then was forgotten by the leaders of thought. Yet the book made a profound impact on the reading public and proved of more lasting importance than the great books that overshadowed it in its own generation.

What gave the long-winded but vivid and rhetorical writings of Herder their influence that the more polished works of his contemporaries failed to achieve? Above all, it was Herder's insistence that humanity could only be understood by reading humanity's history, in its own terms, according to the circumstances in which it was written; that all reflection on that history was secondary, and the more abstract and critical that reflection became, the further it was removed from the truth. Herder planted a deep distrust of abstract thought in Western consciousness and challenged all attempted to establish timeless and eternal truths by his relentless passionate appeals to history.

Reason was itself a product of history, developing with the progressive development of the human race. The very phrase 'the education of the human race', which Lessing had used as the title of a set of theses first published in 1779, had been used first as the leitmotiv of a remarkable series of books Herder published in 1774 and 1775.[10] Herder, however, did not set himself apart from the education he observed; there was no independent standpoint of

---

[10] The important published works of these two years are *Aelteste Urkunde des Menschengeschlechts*; *Auch eine Philosophie der Geschichte zur Bildung der Menschheit: Beitrag zu vielen Beiträgen des Jahrhunderts*; *An Prediger: Funfzehn Provincial-blätter*; and *Erläuterungen zum Neuen Testament aus einer neueröfneten Morgenländischen Quelle*. The words of Lessing's title are to be found in the *Provincial Letters*, Suphan vii.294; cf. *Elucidations of the New Testament*, Suphan vii.368 f. quoted below.

enlightened reason to which the observer could retire.

Even this reason, it is formed only through the process of time: so one sees that everything that has educated the human race, taught it, advanced it, was also forming reason. A child develops his reason only through education; so with all which has educated the human race: to that, reason is indebted for what it has become. It would be mere play to separate one from the other and try to make reason into an independent abstraction, when it is nothing of the sort. Similarly, it is mere play to set reason against revelation, and treat reason as something independent which is in opposition to revelation. As little as the human race could have come into being without creation, so little could it have endured without divine help, and have known what it knows without divine education . . .

Look, a spider depends on its house even though the house is not fixed, and supports itself on it even though the house itself has no support. If philosophy were what it ought to be, it would acknowledge its origins, its strength, and its limits and lose itself in revelation, that is, in the unfolding of the formation of the human race which also formed philosophy itself. Philosophy is only the thin cloud of abstraction which gently rises over the obscure growth of the rich garden of God, and which without this garden is nothing.[11]

This was a challenge to Herder's old revered teacher Immanuel Kant, and it is arguable that Kant's *Critique of Pure Reason* was an answer to Herder's position.

Herder's challenge to the Enlightenment was naturally not an abstract challenge based on abstract history, nor was the history to which he appealed some scholarly history reconstructed by study out of the available evidence. The history Herder put before his readers was a specific history contained in specific books open to all. The history Herder

---

[11] *Erläuterungen zum neuen Testament* (1775) Book I, chapter III, notes 5, 7; Suphan vii.369, 371 f.

urged his readers to attend was 'the oldest history of the human spirit, history recorded in the poetry and folk-sagas of the Old Testament'. He scorned all paraphrases of the scripture and continually urged his readers to turn away from learned discussions and theories about the writings to the writings themselves. The writings were to be read according to the circumstances of their own time under the restrictions of the audience for whom they were first written. Only then would they be seen as steps in the education of the human race, leading up to the spiritual fulfilment of their promises in Jesus Christ. Similarly, the Gospels must also be read in their own terms as simple artless brief accounts of the facts of the gospel. Furthermore, the facts of the gospel would be maintained not by learned discussion of doctrines or of historical probabilities but only in the facts of lives lived today as Christ lived his life long ago. 'Facts can only be attested and maintained by facts'.[12]

In this way Herder swept aside all the doubts and difficulties raised by Lessing's publication of the Wolfenbüttel fragments. Whoever gives way to these doubts has not surrendered himself to the history as history.

The Bible had to be read as a human book, for that is its purpose, to educate the human race in humanity.

> One must read the Bible in a human way, for the Bible is a book written by men for men: the language is human, and human the external means by which it was written and preserved; indeed, when all is said and done, the mind by which the Bible can be understood is human, as is every means of explaining it, as it is the whole purpose and use to which the Bible is applied. So you can certainly believe that the more humanly (in the best sense of the word human) you read the Bible, the nearer you come to the purpose of its Originator, who created men in his own image; and in all works and good deeds where he shows himself to us as God, he acts for us in a human way.[13]

---

[12] *Briefe, das Studium der Theologie betreffend* 2nd ed. 1785, 15th Letter, opening words.

The sense of the Bible must not be twisted for dogmatic ends. For example, the alleged Old Testament prophecies of the coming of a future messiah must first of all be read in their original sense, as prophecies given at a particular time to a particular person in particular circumstances. Psalm 110 is nullified if it is simply read as a prophecy of Christ, the subject of dispute between Jesus and the Pharisees. Its splendour is lost unless it is first read as a psalm about David's victory over his enemies, about how the people gather in festive garments to greet the King whom God has enthroned and to whom he has promised an eternal kingdom.

Nevertheless there is a development, there are fingerposts pointing to Christ's eventual appearing: events happen, poets and prophets colour in the picture of these events and build on them. The blessing of Abraham is general, the blessing of Isaac and Jacob and Judah more specific; Judah is given victory, a kingdom, and becomes a peace-maker; Judah is the ancestor of David. David becomes a King of Peace as a result of war; his kingdom fails, but Isaiah foresess a tiny despised shoot springing out of the stump of David; Micah sees insignificant Bethlehem as the birthplace of David's son; all the prophets begin to pair humility and majesty, and to show that the true grandeur of the eternal spiritual kingdom must spring from contempt and poverty.

> Abrahams Segen:
> Juda's Herrschaft und Ruhe:
> Davids Ewiges Reich des Friedens:
> Geistiger Art und Dauer:
> Aus Niedrigkeit, durch Verachtung und Leiden:
> Durch Wunder, Lehre, geistliche Gaben.
> [Abraham's blessing:
> Judah's reign and peace:
> David's eternal kingdom of peace:
> Of a spiritual nature and duration:
> Out of humility, through contempt and suffering:
> Through miracle, teaching, spiritual gifts.][14]

---

[13] *Briefe, das Studium der Theologie betreffend*, 1st Letter, second paragraph.
[14] 18th Letter, fourth point.

Daniel makes more specific promises of a time when the Temple will be restored and then again destroyed, and the Books of Maccabees say it will be soon. Then comes Jesus Christ, not asking men to busy themselves with his metaphysical nature. He simply announced, 'The kingdom is come'; he acted and taught and did miracles and allowed all these things to work.

This is great rhetoric and Herder is a literary critic who has the gift of making the texts speak to us in power and simplicity. He revealed the Bible to be literature of a particular kind, folk-literature which had to be read as folk-literature, as simple and child-like speech designed to celebrate public occasions, to be read aloud to people gathered in worship. He scorned the hyper-critics who would not let the literature be what it was.

Unfortunately it is true that writers who scorn metaphysics and philosophy and abstract thought cannot escape having their own hidden philosophy which can be just as abstract as the theories they so roundly condemn. Herder is no exception, and his appeal to history and his placing of history and revelation above abstraction and reason is not as artless and ingenuous as it seems.

He scorns the philosophers who make God such an exalted entity that they can say and think nothing about him, and he defends the simple who make an image or symbol of the God to whom they pray, in whom they trust, who has created them and sustained them. That is well said, but on closer examination Herder's God is not a God to whom people may pray in the expectation of receiving anything in answer to their prayers; his God is not the creator of the universe who is rightly adored and worshipped because he is not, like his worshippers, part of the universe he created. Herder's God is the universe as it evolves towards perfection out of its inherent laws by which order emerges from chaos, by which goodness and beauty emerge from the union of like with like, the separation of opposites, and the assimilation of the opposites that need each other for a final union.

His approach to the 'facts' about Jesus contains an explicit rejection of most of the orthodox estimate of Jesus. Christianity has made a religion about Jesus in place of Jesus' religion. Jesus foresaw this, and even this history cannot be despised, however much it misrepresented its origins: for out of seeming evil good comes.

> I bow in reverence before your noble form, Head and Founder of a Kingdom so great in its objects, so lasting in its extent, so simple and vital in its principles, so compelling in its motives, that the sphere of this earthly life seems too narrow for it. Nowhere else in history do I find a revolution like yours: so quietly and so quickly accomplished, planted in such an unexpected way by weak instruments, propagated everywhere on earth with results that can still surprise us, and cultivated to bring forth good fruit and bad. It has spread among the nations not under the name of *your religion* – your living plan for the welfare of mankind; but it has mostly spread as a *religion about you* – an unreflecting worship of your person and your cross. Your penetrating spirit foresaw just this, and it would be a desecration to dare to name your name in describing every muddy stream flowing from your pure source. As far as possible we shall avoid naming the name: let your quiet form stand apart, before the entire history that takes its rise from you.[15]

But what was Jesus' religion? Herder's answer, I think, is that those who follow Jesus' spiritual religion should see themselves not as worshippers of Jesus but as more or less complete embodiments of Jesus. Jesus stands for the humanity of the chosen souls, and chosen souls understand themselves as carrying forward the work of Jesus which they themselves as it were encapsulate. 'In Jesus the human race has been created and chosen'.[16]

---

[15] *Ideen zur Philosophie der Geschichte der Menschheit* (1784–91), Part Four, Book 17 (1791), Suphan, xiv, 291; edited by Heinz Stolpe (Berlin & Weimar, 1965), ii. 294; cf. *Outlines of a Philosophy of the History of Man; translated from the German of John Godfrey Herder* by Thomas Churchill (London, 1800), p. 429.

[16] *Erläuterungen zum neuen Testament*, Book 1, Chapter III.

Notice the word 'chosen'. Isn't it extraordinary that a pantheist pastor should choose the doctrine of election to explain the connection between Jesus and his readers? Yet it is really not surprising. Herder does not hold that there exists an extra-mundane God who could choose men out from their fellows as the elect. But nevertheless his whole system is based on the assumption that there do exist men who see farther than their fellow men and who are nobler. The human race has always had precious spirits whom only other like-spirits recognise: the invisible church.[17] These nobler souls are pantheists, who recognise God in nature and history and themselves. But these souls are a product of history, and the very fact that they can share in the power that pervades everything must mean that that power was once embodied at one point. If One is in All, All must also be in One. The arguments which led Leibniz to God as the primary unity or original simple substance led Herder, as a pantheist, to Christ. The perfection of Mankind is the constant unvarying plan of God – but, remember, God is not a person; God is the All. If Mankind's perfection is the goal, there must be One who will embody that plan and so be one with God. As other men participate in that One, so they fulfil the plan. Of course, when men do not participate in that One, they also fulfil the divine plan, for the plan embraces everything that happens; they are simply thereby less of men.

This explains the interesting and curious fact that Herder seizes on the one doctrine that most rouses the scorn of the deists and rationalists of the eighteenth century, the doctrine of predestination or election. World history is developing, not step by step but in revolutions. In the darkness of the slumber of the nations there are points of light for the enlightment and advance of the human race. This is the leaven of the nations. The people who are the lights or the leaven are those who are elect of God in Jesus.

Similarly, Herder chooses to defend the doctrine of the resurrection of the body and to reject the immortality of the

---

[17] *Briefe zu Beförderung der Humanität* (1793 ff.) ed. H. J. Kruse (Berlin & Weimar, 1971), p. 81 (= 2nd collection, letter 16), Suphan xvii.81.

soul. Like the doctrine of election, this doctrine, too, is the scorn of the enlightened.

> Christianity knows nothing of the immortality of the soul and I doubt whether anyone has much conception of it. Christianity teaches Resurrection of the Dead and moral transition and clear and decisive sentence after this transition: no one can image more spiritual laws of survival, of transition, of judgement more spiritual than this the simplest of religions unfolds . . .
>
> Nothing shall carry over into the other world except what has been accomplished *in Christ*, who became the model of the still, pure, universal love of God in human form. From all that the 'I' is, his religion seeks to free us in our conceptions, inclinations and actions; to seek not truths but the true, to love not good things but the good; to teach us to forget all that is picture, and to become one with him, one with all good, just as he is one with the Father and with us. His religion overcomes space and time, dispels fancy, sense and passions like mist; in the midst of earth his religion wanders in heaven, that is, among eternal things – or rather, in one eternal thing alone, God! whom this religion recognises in Jesus, in whom through the Spirit it participates. The more we are transformed into this heavenly nature, the more our soul drinks the sap of life, the more our soul is light, as he is light. And then, says the originator of our bliss, our soul 'already has eternal life in itself: it does not come to judgement but has passed from death to life' [cf. John 5.24]. We are not astonished when the stone falls and the flame leaps up: so shall we feel it to be a law of nature when the eternal goes to eternity, and darkness and earth sink into the great decay of the world.[18]

On close reading Herder's espousal of the doctrine of the resurrection of the body turns out to be nothing of the sort. Far from arguing that individual believers survive death and

---

[18] *Erläuterungen*, Book 3, chapters VI and VII, notes at end; Suphan vii.462 f.

are clothed in a spiritual body so that they may enjoy the peace of the kingdom of God and share for ever in the praise and worship of God, Herder uses the doctrine to teach the final absorption of individuals into the world process which can be called 'God' or 'Christ'.

Herder's ideas may strike us as bizarre and fantastic, and yet they exerted an almost magical power over European thought. People brought up on the Bible and familiar with its stories and poetry and images from their mother's knee were given the means of retaining their dreams without capitulating to the fierce enlightenment attack on all they held dear.

Herder succeeded for countless people of his generation and beyond because he quietly conceded the enlightened presupposition that there was no independent creator of the universe and that everything that happened was part of an eternal process governed by laws inherent in the universe. The people who drank in Herder also drank in a powerful sense that they themselves were the elect. What they saw was not some theory or dogma or abstract construct; what they saw was the whole process of the education of the human race not from outside but from within – they themselves were embodiments of the ideal towards which everything tended. This sense of election gave those who possessed it a sure self-confidence which had revolutionary consequences. It was just this sense of belonging to the elect that inspired the early communists to devote their lives to changing the world – or rather, to give their lives to the process that was, willy-nilly, changing the world; and it was just this sense of belonging to the elect nation that inspired national socialists to similar devotion to what they saw as the inevitable forward march of history. Herder's ideas helped produce strange results in the long run which he would not have welcomed.

The authority of the Bible was rescued by Herder but, in the rescue, transformed. European thought was made irrevocably historical. Historical philosophers like Hegel and Marx and Nietzsche owed much to the pioneering work of the preacher Herder.

6

Eichhorn

Eichhorn belongs to a new breed, the breed of the professional historian. He was made by the best school of history in Europe, the Göttingen school. In his systematic attempt to show that every book of the Bible not only talked about history but had a history (that each book was written in specific historical circumstances, drew on older myths and sagas and written sources, was perhaps edited and enlarged, and continued to exercise an influence different from the intention of the writer) he showed himself a Göttingen historian, and the pupil of Heyne.

The University of Göttingen had been founded in 1733 and inaugurated in 1737 by George II of England, the Elector of Hannover, at the behest of his wife, Queen Caroline, Leibniz's pupil. Michaelis was one of the early appointments and he was, as we have seen, one of the pioneers of the new historical approach to the scriptures. But the Göttingen school of history was primarily concerned with the historical approach to classical antiquity. The founder of the school was J. M. Gesner and his successor Eichhorn's teacher Christian Gottlob Heyne, the close friend of Herder.

What were the broad and well-known characteristics of the Göttingen historical approach? The first note was that of freedom of enquiry. Although the Göttingen professors had to satisfy the authorities of their religious orthodoxy (by Lutheran standards), they were then left free of censorship to publish whatever they discovered. Secondly, the Göttingen historical school was dedicated to an exact and wide investigation of the sources, free from all dogmatic presuppositions. Thirdly, the Göttingen historians were looking for a comprehensive view of the progress of human history: to show how one historical period followed naturally on another. These had been the clearly stated ideas of Johann Lorenz von Mosheim (1694–1755), who had played a leading part in founding the University in the first place, and who ten years later came to the University as Chancellor and Professor of Theology. There he exercised a great influence on Johann Rudolf Schlegel, who was later to edit his Church History, and who was the rector of Eichhorn's high school (Gymnasium) in Heilbronn. Schlegel taught Eichhorn his love of history, and no doubt ensured that Eichhorn should go to Göttingen to study.

Eichhorn was born on 16 October 1752 in Dorrenzimmern. His father was a Lutheran pastor who taught his son at home until he moved to Weikersheim as Superintendent and was able to send him to the town school. Eichhorn proved an able student and was boarded in Heilbronn in order to attend the Gymnasium, of which Schlegel was Rector. At Easter 1770 he went to Göttingen.

He was a student at Göttingen for nine semesters. During that time he heard lectures in philosophy, theology, history and classics. Towards the end of his time as a student, he began independent research into Arabic history before the time of Mohammed, the results of which he was able to present to the University of Jena for promotion to the degree of Ph.D. in May 1775. This work reflects the direct influence of two of his teachers: Michaelis, who convinced him of the necessity of studying Arabic in order to understand Hebrew better, and Schözer, like him a native of the Hohenlohe, who fostered his life-long interest in world history.

The doctorate led him, still only twenty-two years old, to be appointed professor of Oriental Languages at Jena. The same year he married the daughter of a civil servant from his home principality of Hohenlohe, with whom he was to live happily for the rest of his life. His course would seem set in oriental studies, but his true purpose was different.

At Göttingen Eichhorn had not only learnt the art of close textual criticism and linguistic criticism of oriental texts from

Michaelis, and been confirmed in an aspiration to understand the whole of the world history by Schlözer; he had also come under the spell of Heyne. From Heyne he learnt a new sort of criticism, Higher Criticism, which enabled the results of the Lower Criticism of Michaelis to be applied to the elucidation of the true course of world history. Higher Criticism was a sceptical method applied to ancient documents to penetrate behind the ostensible character of the writings, which were often pseudonymous, to their true nature. Its aim was to date the ancient documents, to discover the sources they relied on, to separate out different accounts which a later editor had combined, to distinguish later additions; above all to decide how far and in what respects the old accounts could be trusted. All this, and more, Eichhorn learnt from Heyne, and at Göttingen he had resolved to apply this method to the interpretation of Holy Scripture.

Heyne taught Eichhorn three crucial lessons: the importance of method; the necessity of scepticism; and the confidence that, when all was said and done, the best of the ancients could still speak to us.

Heyne's method in the study of classical antiquity was to date and put in order the whole mass of documents, to assign each to its proper age, to find out as much as possible about that age from contemporary accounts, to select the most important documents and moments in the unrolling of history, and to aim for a comprehensible picture of the whole subject: order, selection and the overall view.[1]

Secondly, he taught Eichhorn scepticism. Any ancient account was likely to have been altered in the telling and retelling and in the copying and recopying. There is likely to be an historical kernel, but it will have to be discovered under layers of tradition. Heyne's scepticism extended to the work of the historians of antiquity as well: too few of their statements were well-grounded in argument.

Thirdly, he taught Eichhorn to expect to find

[1] See Eberhard Sehmsdorf, *Die Prophetenauslegung bei J. G. Eichhorn* (Göttingen, 1971), p. 125 and Hermann Brauning-Oktavio, *Christian Gottlob Heynes Vorlesungen über die Kunst der Antike und ihr Einfluss auf Johann Heinrich Merck, Herder und Goethe* (Darmstadt, 1971).

enlightenment in a few choice spirits in every past age. Their ideas had to be discovered by the process of ordering a vast mass of material and by finding there what was really important and essential; these ideas were bound to be expressed in strange forms according to assumptions we no longer shared; but, once found, once discerned beneath the clothing of ancient forms of expressions, they could contribute to the education of the present age. The language, the form, the expression was very much dependent on the age; but the content of what the smaller number of enlightened thinkers in every past age had to say could still help settle our present debates.[2]

Eichhorn always insisted that the modern method of interpreting the Bible could pride itself on its brotherly relations with modern classical scholarship.[3] Heyne's lasting influence on Eichhorn is evident in every part of his voluminous writings.

Heyne taught a method, and gave influential lectures towards a systematic history of the ancient world, and a systematic history of the world, but he never produced the hoped-for books. Eichhorn, at the age of twenty-five, set out to achieve what his teachers talked about. He founded a journal: the *Repertorium für Biblische und Morgenländische Litteratur*, published in Leipzig from 1777 in eighteen parts until 1786, while Eichhorn was professor of Oriental Languages at Jena. When that journal had done its job, he published another, the *Allgemeine Bibliothek der biblischen Litteratur*, also published in Leipzig, in ten volumes, six parts to a volume, from 1787 until 1801. In 1788, Eichhorn moved back to Göttingen as professor of Philosophy, and most of the *Allgemeine Bibliothek* was written and edited from there. I say written, because Eichhorn filled most of the 1,000 pages in each volume with his own book reviews and articles, although towards the end contributions by others appeared more frequently. The reviews and articles he wrote in these years provided the basis for his three large Introductions, to

---

[2] See Heyne's preface to Dietrich Tiedemann, *System der stoischen Philosophie* (Leipzig, 1776).

[3] See, for example, *Allgemeine Bibliothek der biblischen Litteratur*, V, 2 (1793), 106–8.

the Old Testament (I, 1780; II, 1782?; III, 1783; second edition, 1787; new edition, 1795–1803; I–IV of final edition, 1823–24), to the Apocrypha (1795), and to the New Testament (I, 1804; II.1, 1810; II.2, 1811; III.1, 1812; III.2, 1814; IV–V, 1827).

The way the journals fed into his Introductions shows his conception of the historian's task. First the historian has to make his own contribution to his subject by exact and detailed studies of individual documents, studies filled with arguments for the correct placing of the document in its period of time – or for the dating of the different *parts* of the document, for most old documents are composite. Secondly, he has to work towards an overall view of the periods to which the documents bear witness, and this requires that he encourage other scholars to contribute their own special studies, and that he then summarize and criticize their work in order to advance his own overall conspectus. For this reason, Eichhorn promised in the second journal, the *Allgemeine Bibliothek*, to review all the important publications on the Bible year by year as they appeared. Thirdly, the historian has to gather up the results of his work in 'Introductions'.

Although Eichhorn saw his main purpose as being further the study of the Bible, he believed that the study of the Bible was part of the study of the progress of human culture. He saw himself as belonging to a small group of learned and perceptive men who had access to the source of truth and enlightenment; he had to discern other such men in the past and to show how they contributed to the gradual development and refinement of this truth. By tracing the history of the progress of human culture, he was to make his contribution to the perfection of human nature.[4]

So he also produced histories: a two-volume history of the French Revolution (1797), a history of the world (I, 1799; second edition, 1804; II, 1804; III–IV, 1814), a history of the last three centuries (I, 1803; II, 1804; III–V, 1803; VI, 1804) and a history of literature from its beginnings until the present

[4] See *Einleitung ins alte Testament*, vol. III (1783), p. 1; *Allgemeine Bibliothek*, V.1 (1793), pp. 172–5.

day (I, 1805; II.1, 1805; II.2, 1807; III.1, 1810; III.2, 1812; IV.1, 1807; IV.2, 1808; IV.3, 1810; IV.4, 1820; V, 1807; VI.1, 1810; VI.2, 1811). No wonder it was said that the inhabitants of Göttingen scarcely knew the famous man who lived in their midst: besides all this he also contributed to the Gotha *Gelehrte Zeitung*, the *Allgemeine deutsche Bibliothek*, the Jena *Litteraturzeitung*, and the Göttingen *Gelehrter Anzeigen*, the editorship of which he took on after Heyne's death in 1812. He lectured at least three hours a day and was always ready to receive older and younger scholars who sought his advice, but otherwise he was chained to his desk. Fortunately, he never suffered a day's illness until 1825, when he was 72. He died in 1827.

In all his immense and tireless labours he followed Heyne's three precepts: he put the documents in order; he judged them sceptically; and he held on to the Ariadne's thread to lead him out of the maze, the thread of 'enlightened ideas'. He was conscious of belonging to a new beginning to a new movement, as we can sense in this extract form a long study of Genesis 1–3 which he published anonymously in 1779 when he was twenty-six years old, though he had written it when he was twenty-three.

There still survives an ancient Pantheon, the oldest, most beautiful and simplest of all, a gift of artless nature, unshaken despite all the storms of ravaging time, bearing almost no trace of its great antiquity. A temple instinct with nature and simplicity adorns its entrance, only here and there pointed by art. A lonely tiny path leads towards it, but a path which is now overgrown and shows no trace that it was once passable, because for more than a thousand years art has been at work on making other roads which have since been constantly trod. The old path is short, but simple; the newer ways are longer, but full of vistas of complicated works of art. The old path leads straight into the temple; the new ones to pompous manors and palaces. Ever since these were begun to be built, people have lingered only around them. Very few know about the temple that lies behind, and should anyone ask for a sketch of the temple, they are usually shown a sketch of the manors.

Thou art the temple, thou holy memorial left by Moses concerning the origin of all things. The manor houses of art are the systems of theologians and natural scientists which have been piled up in front of thee. Already from afar their brightness invites the curious eye to attend, but blindness afflicts all who linger by them.

Whoever wishes to investigate the Mosaic records of the creation of all things should above everything know nothing at all of the professional opinions of others about them, in order to be able to think about them and investigate them the more impartially . . . He must forget everything he has heard spoken, or been taught, . . . by experts and non-experts, by initiates and non-initiates, by natural scientists and religious teachers — otherwise he is lost, and will sink in bogs and swamps, led on by will-o' -the-wisps like his predecessors.

Without guide, without escort, without map or guide book have I wended my way to the holy temple of God's revelations, and I abandon myself to my good fortune. I have covered the journey with great ease, without the countless difficulties that others complain about. Here is a guide book and map for my successors. Whoever wants to compare it with other maps will find it very different.[5]

The young man who wrote these words believed there was a great gulf fixed between the old dogmatics and the new historical approach. The old approach, for all his gifts as an expositor, was represented by Michaelis; the new by Heyne. Michaelis approached the Old Testament from a dogmatic point of view and recommended his results by pointing out the support they gave to certain doctrines. Eichhorn deliberately set out to forget all the dogmatics and theology he had ever learnt in order to be free and impartial in his investigation; theology had to be left alone to use his results as best she could.[6]

[5] *Repertorium für Biblische und Morgenländische Litteratur*, Leipzig, 1779, part IV.

[6] Eichhorn's review of Michaelis's Introduction to the Old Testament, *Allgemeine*

One dogmatic phrase Eichhorn borrowed from Michaelis was 'the sparseness of miracles', but their use of the test was quite different: Michaelis knew that the gullibility of men exaggerated natural events into miracles, but he nevertheless held there was good evidence for some miracles; Eichhorn argued that the Divine never actually needed to break into the natural order of things.[7]

The absoluteness of this contrast between Michaelis and Eichhorn is perfectly clear on the theoretical level – Michaelis believed in a God who acted directly by revealing himself to men and by enabling miracles to be performed, while Eichhorn thought that such a God was a childish idea.[8] At the level of actual cases, however, the contrast is not quite so clear. For example, the author of the only major modern study of Eichhorn, Eberhard Sehmsdorf, who is fully aware of Eichhorn's repeated theoretical arguments against revelation and miracle, thinks that Eichhorn, rather inconsistently and seemingly unconsciously, always affirmed the historicity of the resurrection.[9] But Sehmsdorf has not looked closely enough at what Eichhorn actually says about the resurrection, and what he says about the task of the enlightened men who guard the source of the wellspring of truth. Eichhorn always affirms the resurrection in ambiguous terms: Jesus was buried and alive *in the grave* – which may or may not mean that his body was raised.[10] The task of enlightened men is to say as much of the truth as can be received at the time. For example, he published his

---

Bibliothek, I, 3 (1787), 430–2. Michaelis had been working towards the goal of writing such an Introduction all his life, but never got down to the writing of it until spurred into action in his old age by the appearance of the first volume of his pupil Eichhorn's Introduction in 1780.

[7] Eichhorn uses the phrase 'the sparseness of miracles' in *Urgeschichte*, Repertorium iv (1779), 149. His debt to Michealis is shown by Sehmsdorf, *op. cit*, p.129, note 81.

[8] See, for example, *Allgemeine Bibliothek*, V, 2 (1793), 250 f.

[9] Sehmsdorf, *op. cit*, p. 173.

[10] *Allgemeine Bibliothek*, VII, 6 (1797), 99. In his Introduction to the New Testament he prefers to talk about 'the coming alive' of Jesus rather than 'the resurrection' of Jesus: I (1804), pp. 4, 154, 447 f; II.1 (1810), pp. 1 f. 212; III.1 (1812), p. 14; IV (1827), pp. 5 f.

Urgeschichte anonymously so that he could see how it would be received before disclosing his own authorship. In that work he only went as far in overthrowing common prejudices as he thought people could take.[11] When other writers went a little further in the same direction, he disclosed that he also had held more radical views that he felt it was prudent to express. So he treated the events in the Garden of Eden as actual happenings – there was a snake, which ate the fruit of the forbidden tree as its natural food; Adam and Eve would have been killed had they eaten too much of this fruit, but Eve supposed, from the snake's example, that the divine warning about the fruit was erroneous; she took some for herself and Adam, and the effect was like the effect of drink or drugs, arousing their passion for each other; they slept together; that evening their first experience of a thunderstorm led them to believe God was angry with them and they fled the garden for ever. As Eichhorn later confessed, he did not really believe this was an historical sequence of events; he simply thought this sort of statement was the only way to lead his contemporaries a step towards the actual truth. The truth was that the story was a saga or myth; the only way primitive people could express philosophical truth was in mythical language.[12] He justified his own lack of candour about his true beliefs on the ground that the spiritual leaders of the people had to bring all classes to the highest stage of 'edification' that was possible for them, to make each class as 'enlightened' as it could be.[13]

It was the same with his treatment of the resurrection. He first published his ideas in an anonymous article on the Fourth Gospel, which purported to be 'Letters concerning the Gospel of John by Various Authors'.[14] In this article, he argued that Jesus himself did not teach that he would rise form the dead after three days. It is true he used language that could have been misunderstood in this sense – and Matthew and the

---

[11] *Allgemeine Bibliothek*, I.6 (1788), p. 988 f.

[12] *Allgemeine Bibliothek*, I.6 (1788), 987–991; cf. II.4 (1790), 711 f.

[13] *Allgemeine Bibliothek*, V. 1 (1793), 174–7.

[14] *Allgemeine Bibliothek*, VII.6 (1797), 973–1053.

other Synoptic Gospels did misunderstand his words in this sense, and added this assertion to Jesus' actual words. But what Jesus meant was that after his death there would be a 'moral resurrection of his teaching' and that the Jewish idea of the Messiah living on an earth would be transformed into the idea that he would live on on earth through the continuance of the spirit of his teaching.[15] Eichhorn specifically cites Herder's two little tracts about the resurrection, *Ueber Auferstehung* (1794) and *Erlöser der Menschen nach den drey Evangelien* (1796), which run the line, still commonly expressed today, that the resurrection is essentially only the spiritual death, burial and rebirth to a new and living hope of the followers of Jesus.[16] However, although Jesus did not teach his own resurrection, God did in fact raise him from the dead.

Later Eichhorn returns to the question in an article on 'The Appearance of Angels at the Grave of Jesus', which he explains as simply the way silly women expressed their shock at finding the empty grave clothes.[17] This article is published over his own name, and seems not to go so far as the anonymous article on the Gospel of John. Yet the tactics are the same. There, he had said that God raised Jesus, despite Jesus not having taught his own resurrection, and the initiated reader was left free to draw the conclusion that God need not have done any such thing – and, by the law of the 'sparseness of miracles', did not. Here, he pours scorn on the notion that angels exist, and leaves the initiates to draw the conclusion that the idea that Jesus' body was raised is a similar unnecessary idea.

In other words, Eichhorn practises the 'accommodation' which he finds a standing feature of the Biblical records themselves, and which Heyne in person and Semler in his writings had taught him was a standing feature of all ancient documents. Men have had to express their ideas according to 'the spirit of the times' and to clothe their teaching in the

---

[15] *Allgemeine Bibliothek*, VII.6 (1797), 1043 f.

[16] Herder, Suphan xix, p. 97. The references to Herder in Eichhorn are to be found in *Allgemenine Bibliothek*, VII.6 (1797), 1043, 1049.

[17] *Allgemeine Bibliothek*, VIII.4 (1798), 629–640.

ways dictated by custom, speech, and convention, which changed with the times. The task of the historian was to understand these temporally conditioned circumstances so well that he could separate ideas from their husks, from their clothing.[18] The most noble thinkers of the past actually realised what they were doing and deliberately accommodated their ideas to the false ways of expressing them which were customary at the time. The greatest of the teachers of the past, like Jesus, tried to lead their hearers by way of commonly accepted ways of thinking to higher and nobler ideas; Matthew understood this, and was content to leave the reports of Jesus' ministry in their conventional clothing, confident that others, too, would realise that talk of demons, for example, was only conventional; but John decided to exclude all such misleading ways of thought.[19] John's example was a justification and spur for us (a hint Hegel and, much later, Bultmann were to take up). Philo had already made the same distinction between ideas and their clothing.[20] In other words, not only could enlightened historians make a distinction between ideas and their clothing, but on closer examination they would find that the distinction was already being made in ancient times. This was the scarlet thread to guide the historian in all his laborious and careful periodisation of the past.[21]

Eichhorn, then, had no scruple in appearing to endorse the childish notions of his less enlightened contemporaries; the enlightened would understand, and those who did not understand were not yet ready to be more fully enlightened.

What were these enlightened ideas that the past ages more or less clearly expressed in pictorial and mythical clothing? It is already obvious what they were negatively: the temporally conditioned clothing necessarily implies that all ideas of a

[18] See 'Briefe die biblische Exegese betreffend', *Allgemeine Bibliothek*, V.2 (1793), 203–298, especially the first letter, 203–222.

[19] See Vorschläge zur Hermeneutik, *Allgemeine Bibliothek*, IV.2 (1792), 330–343, especially 332–7.

[20] See *Einleitung in die apokryphischen Schriften des Alten Testaments* (Leipzig, 1795), pp. 22 ff. cited by Sehmsdorf, op. cit, p. 159.

[21] *Allgemeine Bibliothek*, V.1 (1793), 84.

God who reveals himself to men at specific times, or who comes near to them in specific places, or who acts through specific miraculous happenings are part of the husk to be discarded.

In the Bible this means that all specifically Jewish ideas are unenlightened; and in church history all the ideas of a canon or of grace as a physical power or of the articles of dogma are unenlightened: they may have been necessary to lead men to higher levels of enlightenment, but were themselves only clothing which changed with changing times.[22]

The negative part of Eichhorn's view of enlightenment is easy enough to discern, but what was its positive content?

The answer to this question is of supreme importance in understanding the history of the interpretation of the Bible in the next two hundred years, down to our own day; and not only in understanding the history of the interpretation of the Bible. German thought and, through German thought, the history of European thought, was deeply impregnated with the theme which Eichhorn lets us see for the first time with full clarity. It was a theme Eichhorn and the other brilliant and gifted young men who belonged to the Philological Seminar learnt from Heyne. It was the theme which led Eichhorn and subsequent even greater thinkers like Hegel and Nietzsche to be deeply dissatisfied with Kant. It was Stoicism. The Stoics were the thinkers of the ancient world most admired by Heyne, and it was according to Stoicism that Eichhorn interpreted the Bible and it was according to the Stoic ideal that Eichhorn interpreted the duty of enlightened scholars in his own day.

This becomes clear if we look closely at Eichhorn's interpretation of three crucial moments in Biblical history: the story of the Fall, the trials of Job, and the death of Jesus.

In the story of the Fall 'a philosopher of grey antiquity' discerned 'the basic principles of the highest wisdom', 'the source of highest peace', namely 'that longing for another state of affairs which appears to be better is the final principle

---

[22] See Eichhorn's discussion of Semler's contribution to the study of church history, *Allgemeine Bibliothek*, V.1 (1793), 93–120.

of human unhappiness'. When men became dissatisfied with
earthly food and longed for the food of the gods they lost
paradise; that longing led them to pass from the golden age
and to descend to the silver.[23]

Similarly Job did not, as ecclesiastical interpreters up to
and including Michaelis thought he did, console himself with
a belief in immortality. On a true exegesis, Job did not express
a belief in life after death. But this does nothing to shake or
to undermine the foundation of human virtue. The author of
Job taught endless resignation to whatever God sent, the
acceptance of the most severe suffering with patience and
without abandoning the worship of God and without
abandoning virtue. His teaching *could* have led to belief in life
after death, but it did not need to – and in fact did not. And
Eichhorn obviously agreed with the author of Job, without
actually saying so.[24]

Finally, Eichhorn took Jesus' death as the greatest example
of Stoic suffering. Jesus, according to Eichhorn did not expect
to be raised from the dead. 'Jesus did not definitely foresee
his resurrection; but he went towards his death with an
unshakeable firm trust in God in consciousness of his good
fate (*Sache*); that he who had given him the task, according
to his most perfect conviction, of spreading a purer religion
among his contemporaries would after his death advance the
spread of his teaching through his apostles, and would develop
his supremely beneficial plan for the human race'. Jesus was
the best possible example of 'trust in divine providence'
because he did not expect his resurrection.[25] It is true that
Eichhorn goes on to say that God did literally raise Jesus
from the dead, against Jesus' expectations, but that, as we
have seen, is merely Eichhorn's ambiguous concession to the
prejudices of his age. His real position is there for the
enlightened to see. His real position is Stoicism.

Eichhorn himself did not think that he was adopting a
specific philosophy; on the contrary, he saw himself as simply
applying the historical method to the study of the Bible. His

---

[23] *Allgemeine Bibliothek*, I.6 (1788), 987–991.
[24] 'Hiob's Hoffnungen', *Allgemeine Bibliothek*, I.3 (1787), 367 ff. at 389 f.
[25] Allgemeine Bibliothek, VII.6 (1797), 1048 f.

slogan in hermeneutics was: 'The freer, and the more liberal,
the more detached, and the more exact; the more critical,
and the more judicious, so much the better, surer, and more
satisfactory!'[26] But his historical method was entirely devoted
to discovering the actual ideas hidden beneath the popular
ideas of the time, to distinguishing the essential from the
accidental, and he did not realise that his distinction is a
distinction which has already decided what is essential and
what accidental. He prided himself on belonging to a new
theological school which had freed theology from philosophy
and had thereby reconciled theology to philosophy. He
proudly identified himself with Semler at the height of his
powers before his betrayal of liberal theology. Semler, he
said, 'was active for a full quarter century in taking off from
theological science the out-of-date and soiled garment in
which Platonism and Scholasticism had dressed her, and in
leading her back rejuvenated and equipped with new charms
to reconciliation with her sister, Philosophy, who had
threatened to reject her'.[27]

The special hermeneutical task laid on theologians who
tried to interpret the New Testament was to show that it
contained 'the teachings of a teacher who never lied, presented
and transmitted to posterity truly, genuinely and undistorted;
that at least in such passages as contain teachings, one may
find no trace of error, superstition, fanaticism; in short, that
the whole content had to be so handled that it be acceptable
to a correct and responsible reason'. The New Testament had
to be shown to be in 'harmony with a refined and sober
philosophy'.[28]

I myself have no objection to the test Eichhorn proposes,
that Jesus' teaching has to be in harmony with philosophy,
which I take to mean that his teaching must be logical and in
harmony with what we know of the universe. The difficulty
is that he assumed that there was but one correct philosophy,

---

[26] The conclusion to 'Vorschläge zur Hermeneutik', *Allgemeine Bibliothek*, IV.2
(1792), 330–343 at 343.

[27] The opening of Eichhorn's obituary of Semler, *Allgemeine Bibliothek*, V.1 (1793),
1–202, at 1 f.

[28] *Allgemeine Bibliothek*, IV.2 (1792), 331 f.

which every one agreed on, and that the distinction he was able to make between the true ideas in the New Testament and the temporally conditioned clothing was obvious. 'Independently of the New Testament one should already be led to rules as to how one can strike off the husk of Jewish thoughts from the ideas themselves, and these rules then only need to be transferred to the New Testament; and the very applicability of these rules to the New Testament further confirms their correctness and reliability.' The example he gives is the Jewish belief in angels, which he argues that even the more enlightened and nobler part of the Jews did not believe in literally.[29] The trouble is that he assumed the truth of the propositions that there is no world beyond this universe and that there is no God, a Being independent of this universe, who created the universe. Such propositions, according to Eichhorn, belonged to the Platonism and Scholasticism which had clothed Theology in her out-of-date and filthy garment. The philosophy he believed to be so obvious that it hardly needed to be called philosophy, being simply what enlightened men knew to be so, was in fact Stoicism: the belief that there is nothing beyond this world, and that this world is fated to be exactly as it is, to which the wise man submits.

If I am right about Eichhorn's true position, it is puzzling that he devoted so much energy to trying to set Kant straight when Kant published his *Religion within the Limits of Reason Alone* in 1794.[30] Eichhorn fully agreed with Kant's moral principles, and never quarrelled with Kant's religion. Why the fuss?

The simple and obvious answer is that Kant could not be bothered with the laborious detailed historical investigation

---

[29] *Allgemeine Bibliothek*, IV.2 (1792), 337 f.

[30] He cites a long passage from Kant in his first Letter Concerning Biblical Exegesis, *Allgemeine Bibliothek*, V.2, 216, the year Kant's book appeared; and returns to the question in a review of a book by J. G. Rosenmüller on Kant's exegesis of the Bible and in an article of his own on Kant's hermeneutics in the following year, *Allgemeine Bibliothek*, VI.1, 51–55 and 55–67. See Otto Kaiser, 'Eichhorn und Kant: Ein Beitrag zur Geschichte der Hermeneutik', in *Das Ferne und Nahe Wort: Festschrift Leonhard Rost*, edited by Fritz Maass (Berlin, 1967), pp. 114–23.

required to separate the enlightened ideas of Jesus and the apostles from the contemporary dress in which these ideas were expressed. He was content to leave the text of the Bible as it stood and simply to give the words an allegorical meaning which corresponded to the reasonable ideas he had arrived at by the exercise of reason alone. Eichhorn's objection is to Kant's indifference to the labours of the new historical critics of the Bible: he wanted to defend his new science.

That is a perfectly understandable aim. We who are heirs of the results Eichhorn and his collaborators were reaching about the date and authorship of the books of the Bible, about the way each of those books uses old sources and is made up of various parts and later additions, about the meaning and significance of the ideas employed and the language used, can have little to complain of in Eichhorn's defence of historical critical scholarship. But why could not Eichhorn have left Kant to go his way while Eichhorn went his? Kant must have represented a greater threat than simply to have ignored the achievements of the critical historians.

The answer must be that Eichhorn dimly perceived, but keenly felt, the possibility that Kant's ideas could nullify his attempts to make the church the instrument of ever increasing enlightenment. If the holy Bible of the church was not regarded as the archives of revealed teachings which under historical critical investigation could still yield up actual true ideas, Christians would remain chained to outworn ideas. Kant was content to leave the church in Stygian darkness while he made arbitrary allegorical use of scripture to support his own independently-won positions. Eichhorn wanted church leaders to adopt his historical-critical approach so that they would gradually lead every class of society to the stage of enlightenment of which they were capable. They must not withstand 'the stream of time', but nor must they allow individuals to upset the masses by going too far too fast: 'only that level of enlightenment can be salvific to anyone which stands in relationship to his presuppositions'. 'Wisdom and love for humanity must alone determine where teachers of the people have to stand in matters of religious enlightenment'. Every class of society must be gradually prepared to receive a higher and higher degree of enlightenment. 'A state is only safe that is so blessed by the divine'.[31]

Just as Eichhorn condemned Semler's panic-stricken attempt in his dotage to maintain subscription to the old Lutheran articles of belief, and warned radicals against disturbing the harmony of the church by their rashly expressed and untypical hypotheses, so he opposed Kant's attempt to leave Christianity where it was with its inspired canon. Eichhorn wanted Christianity itself, in its critical form, to become 'the lever of the enlightenment'.[32]

Eichhorn the Stoic was true to his Stoicism, which was the philosophy of the devoted civil servant: he saw himself as the guardian of both church and state in their great historical task of furthering the Kingdom of Truth and the perfection of human nature.[33]

So he lived, and so he died. On his deathbed, he was not attended by any minister to help him prepare to meet his Maker. Rather, after taking leave of his family, he was attended by two professorial friends who were bidden to take notes as he calmly described to them how consciousness left each part of his body in turn until he finally announced a quarter of an hour before his death that life was extinguished in his spine.[34]

---

[31] *Allgemeine Bibliothek*, V.1 (1793), 172–4, 177.

[32] *Einleitung in das Neue Testament*, vol. 1 (Leipzig, 1804), 2nd ed., (1820), p. 692.

[33] *Allgemeine Bibliothek*, V.1 (1793), 175.

[34] Albert Hune, 'Johann Gottfried Eichhorn', in *Neuer Nekrolog der Deutschen*, V.2, 1827, (Ilmenau, 1829), 637–43, at p. 640.

7

Hegel

Hegel's life is an epitome of the story about the Bible's authority this book is devoted to telling. Hegel was destined for the Lutheran ministry, but he gave up that idea and decided to devote himself to philosophy under the impact of scepticism about the historicity of the Bible and Kant's abandonment of anything but the religion of reason alone. Yet the older he became, the more firmly he appeared as a defender of traditional Lutheran orthodoxy, scourge of the rationalists and pietists alike. His mature philosophy could be taken, and was taken, as in harmony with traditional Christianity. The young Hegelians, who held another view of the matter, were nevertheless deeply influenced by a biblical view of history and they too, like Hegel, looked to a coming Kingdom of freedom on earth, a counterpart to the Biblical Kingdom of God. In Hegel's life, as in the history of his century, an attack on the Bible which might seem to have destroyed its authority for ever resulted in its attaining a new and even more exalted place in thought and in history.

Hegel was born in Stuttgart on the 27 August 1770, the same year as Beethoven, Hölderlin, and Wordsworth; the year after Napoleon. Hegel's family had settled in Schwabia as religious refugees from Roman Catholicism in the sixteenth century, and Hegel all his life despised Roman Catholicism and attacked it as a case of arrested development: stuck at the Second Person of the Trinity without going on to the Third, the Spirit.[1]

---

[1] *Vorlesungen über die Philosophie der Religion*, Third Part, *Die absolute Religion*, ed. Georg Lasson (Berlin, 1919), p. 197; see also *Über eine Anklage wegen öffentlicher*

Hegel's mother died as a result of an attack of dysentery which badly affected Hegel himself and his father; Hegel was only thirteen.[2] His mother was extremely well-educated and had put her son through the first declension Latin nouns before he was sent to school at the age of five.

At eight he was reading Shakespeare in translation. At sixteen he studied the *Iliad*, Cicero, Euripides and Epictetus. Before he was eighteen, he had read Aristotle's *Ethics*, and as he turned eighteen he read Sophocles, particularly *Antigone*.

At the age of eighteen he went to Tübingen and became a member of the still-famous Tübinger Stift, a house of studies where students for the Lutheran ministry enjoyed close companionship and common study to supplement their University courses, which consisted solely of hearing lectures. He embarked on the usual two years Philosophy and three years Theology. There he became Hölderlin's closest friend, and with Schelling they formed a conspiracy against all who would oppose the spread of Kant's ideas. Hegel neglected his formal studies in order to soak himself in Kant. His friends teased him as The Old Man. They were all enthusiastic for the French Revolution.

The Old Man was determined to become a philospher and took a post as a private tutor in Bern, where he remained for three years, from 1793 to 1796. His correspondence with Hölderlin and Schelling shows him gripped by intellectual excitement, believing that the dams of orthodoxy were about to be breached and that humanity was entering a new age. 'May the Kingdom of God come and our hands not be idle! ... Reason and freedom remain our watchword, and our rallying point the invisible Church.'[3] These phrases are all straight out of Kant's *Religion within the Limits of Reason alone*, Part One of which was published in the Berliner Monatsschrift, in 1792, perhaps to coincide with the 150th

---

Verunglimpfung der katholischen Religion, Berlin, 3 April 1826, Hegel's answer to the charge that he had publicly slandered Roman Catholic beliefs about transubstantiation.

[2] According to his sister in a letter written after his death, but perhaps she remembered wrongly, and it was 1881.

[3] Letter to Schelling, end of January 1795.

anniversary of Galileo's death.[4] Kant was nothing less than a prophet of a new world where a secret freemasonry of those to whom the Kingdom of God had come would take their appointed place and unmask the holders of power in church and state who thought by serving the visible church they were serving God. Every man had to make God for himself.[5]

Like Kant, Hegel set himself to discover the truth preserved in the superseded historical religion, and wrote for his own clarification a *Life of Jesus* and *The Positivity of the Christian Religion*.[6]

In 1796 Hölderlin found a good post for him as tutor in Frankfurt-on-Main, where he himself was tutor to Henry Gontard, a banker's nine-year-old son and heir. They would be together again. Accordingly, Hegel moved to Frankfurt in January, 1797, and remained there until late 1800, by which time his father's death and a modest legacy brought him the freedom to devote himself to an academic life. During the Frankfurt years, he shared Hölderlin's intoxication with the new world of freedom, witnessed Hölderlin's love-affair with Frau Susette Gontard, which ended in his expulsion from the Gontard household, and saw the beginnings of Hölderlin's tragic schizophrenia. Hegel learnt, in living through his friend, that love discovers life itself, but only through suffering, and suffering transcended.[7]

In 1801, with Schelling's help, he became a *Privatdozent* (lecturer) at Jena, and by 1805 Professor Extraordinary. He published a book comparing Fichte and Schelling's philosophy, and some weighty articles in *Kritisches Journal der Philosophie*. In 1806 Goebhardt in Bamberg began to print his magnum opus, the first part of a system of science, *The Phenomenology of the Spirit*. Hegel delivered the last few pages

[4] Reference to Galileo, foreword first edition, AB XV; discussion of the importance of this anniversary, Horst Renz, *Geschichtsgedanke und Christusfrage: Zur Anschauung Kants und deren Fortbildung durch Hegel . . .* (Göttingen, 1977), pp. 38–43.

[5] *Religion within the Limits of Reason alone*, Book iv, introduction; for the last statement, footnote to Book iv, part 2, 1:B 257.

[6] First published by Nohl (1907); the second translated by T. M. Knox, *On Christianity: Early Theological Writings* (Chicago, 1948, reissued New York, 1961).

[7] A fragment on Love, Nohl, pp. 378–82; Knox, pp. 302–308; this set of ideas, Nohl, p. 379; Knox, p. 305.

on the 20th October, a week after Napoleon had occupied Jena and put an end to his University career for what was to be ten years. In January 1807 he delivered the preface to the publisher, on the 5th February his landlady bore him an illegitimate son, and on the 20th he accepted a job as editor of the Bamberger Zeitung. The book was published in April, in an edition of 750 copies.

The *Phenomenology* is a book that makes the reader tread the painful road by which alone absolute knowledge can attain its proper freedom and infinity. Only if one dies inwardly can one know anything; above all, only if one dies to oneself can one know oneself. The language is religious, but religion is overcome and properly understood only by philosophy.

Hegel groaned under the business of being an editor, and in November 1808 his good friend Niethammer, in charge of a modernisation of the Bavarian school system which included introducing philosophy into the upper school, got him the post of head of the *Gymnasium* in Nürnberg. In 1811 he became engaged to Marie von Tucher whom he married on the 16th September. He was forty-one, she was twenty. In the month they were engaged he wrote a poem to her, comparing himself to a phoenix, gaining eternal youth only in his own ashes: Hegel's life and philosophy were one.[8] Their marriage was very happy. They had three children, a daughter who died soon after her birth, and two sons. When the mother of Hegel's illegitimate son died in 1817, he and his wife took the boy into their home.

During the first half-year of the marriage he wrote a 500-page book, parts I and II of his *Logic*. The third part appeared in 1816 and that same year he at last received an enthusiastic call to a chair, to Heidelberg. In Heidelberg he published an outline *Encyclopaedia* of philosophy in 477 paragraphs for use as a basis of his lectures. The *Encyclopaedia* was later enlarged to 577 paragraphs in the second and third editions published during his lifetime (1827; 1830).

[8] An Marie, 13 April 1811; text and translation in Walter Kaufmann, *Hegel: Reinterpretation, Texts, and Commentary* (1965; London, 1966), pp. 327 f.

In the third semester at Heidelberg, Hegel accepted a call from Berlin. In 1806 Hegel had welcomed the victory of Napoleon against Prussia, for Napoleon represented for him the World Spirit that had just succeeded in overthrowing the Holy Roman Empire. But now Napoleon had been defeated, and Prussia had used well the period it had been a client-kingdom in order to modernise and centralise its administration, to make itself a true nation. Part of the process of modernisation was a vigorous effort to encourage education. In November 1817 Friedrich Wilhelm III had set up a Ministry of Religion, Education, and Medicine, under Baron von Altenstein. Altenstein issued the Berlin invitation to Hegel, and backed the invitation with solid financial inducements. He encouraged his officials to attend Hegel's lectures, and Hegel did not disappoint his patron. Nationality was, for Hegel, the foundation of all living life, and Prussia now seemed destined to give Germany its nationhood, in which philosophy would at last find its home and be able to flourish.

Hegel became a popular lecturer, primarily through his lectures on the philosophy of world history. He was never an easy lecturer to follow; 'it was much more a way of thinking aloud than speech directed to listeners'.[9] Yet to many, as to Feuerbach, Hegel became a second father and Berlin their spiritual birthplace.[10] Then suddenly, when success at last seemed sure, he died. He was sixty-one (14 November, 1831).

I began the chapter by saying that how Hegel treated the Bible is a microcosm of how the Bible was treated at large in the age from Lessing to Bultmann. I now venture to go further and to suggest that the way Hegel regarded the Bible is absolutely fundamental to his philosophy. The nub of the matter is this. The Bible contained a revealed religion, and until religion was revealed human beings had not fully understood either the world or themselves. With the life, death, resurrection and ascension of Jesus Christ and the

---

[9] Letter of David Friedrich Strauss to Christian Märklin, 15 November, 1831, translated by Walter Kaufmann, *op. cit.*, p. 348.

[10] Walter Kaufmann, *op. cit.*, p. 356.

coming of the Spirit the Trinity was made known as the true doctrine of God, and world-history received its axis, the axis on which everything turned.[11] Hegel did not want to defend the authority of the Bible and the creeds as things recited and remembered for their own sake, nor would he have anything to do with those who valued the Bible as poetry that awakened deep feelings. Against both these views he fought for the good old sense of the word 'faith' that believed the Bible and the creeds on the one hand and believed with deep subjective feelings of dependence on the other hand, and united the two ways of believing to make a true religion. He was scandalized when theologians like Schleiermacher affirmed that the feeling of absolute dependence had entirely taken the place of the proofs of the existence of God in the doctrinal system. The God who existed and revealed himself in history was fundamental to his system. But belief in such a God did not come to its completion until the believer comprehended the necessity of the incarnation of God in Jesus Christ, the necessity of his death and resurrection and glorification, and the necessity of the gift of the Spirit.[12]

[11] 'God is recognized as *Spirit*, only when known as the Triune. This new principle is the axis on which the History of the World turns.' Lectures on the Philosophy of History, trans. J. Sibree (London, 1857), p. 331; *Georg Wilhelm Friedrich Hegel's Vorlesungen über die Philosophie der Geschichte*, ed. Eduard Gans, 3rd edn ed. Karl Hegel (Berlin, 1848), p. 388; *Vorlesungen über die Philosophie der Weltgeschichte*, ed. Georg Lasson (2nd ed., Leipzig, 1923), p. 722.

[12] Schleiermacher, *Der christliche Glaube, nach den Grundsätzen der evangelischen Kirche im Zusammenhang dargestellt* (1821, 2nd ed. 1830); *The Christian Faith*, English Translation of the Second German Edition edited by H. R. Mackintosh and J. S. Stewart (Edinburgh, 1928), § 32: 'The immediate feeling of absolute dependence is presupposed and actually contained in every religious and Christian self-consciousness as the only way in which, in general, our own being and the infinite Being of God can be one in self-consciousness'; § 33. Hegel's reply, *Vorrede zu Hinrichs' Religionsphilosophie*(1822): 'If a man's religion were founded merely on a feeling, this would indeed have no further determination beyond being the *feeling of this dependence*, and then the dog would be the best Christian, for he has this feeling most intensely and lives most in it'. Translation by Kaufmann, *op. cit.*, § 55, p. 239, note 18. For the theme that philosophy could not live without religion, see *Encyclopädie der philosophischen Wissenschaften im Grundrisse* (Heidelberg, 1817; 2nd ed., 1827; 3rd ed., 1830), Philosphische Bibliothek Band 33 (Hamburg, 1969), Preface to the Second Edition, p. 12. Hegel's lectures on the proofs for the existence of God, *Vorlesungen über die Beweise vom Dasein Gottes*, first lecture. *Encyclopädie*, preface to the Second

Hegel particularly emphasised the gift of the Spirit. This was his constant complaint against Roman Catholicism, that it had stuck at the Second Person of the Trinity and not gone on to the Third Person. In the ceremonies of the Roman Catholic Church Christ was objectified before the believer as the priest elevated the host, but in Lutheranism Christ is recognized as having withdrawn so that the Spirit may come. The coming of the Spirit was the necessary completion of faith, as it was the necessary completion of Hegel's philosophy. He attacked his powerful Lutheran critics who prided themselves on the exclusive possession of Christianity but who could not even drive out devils, much less perform mighty works of insight and wisdom. They busy themselves with the indifferent externals of faith, he said, and neglect the further development of doctrine. The force of spirit expanding, which thinks things right through to the end and is truly scientific, disturbs their lordly presumption that they are secure in their possession of Christianity. They do not realise that spirit is specifically distinguished in scripture from bare faith by the fact that only through this expansive force of spirit does faith develop into truth.

> 'He that believeth on me' says Christ (John 7.38), 'out of his belly shall flow *streams of living water*'. This is immediately elucidated in verse 39 ['But this spake he of the Spirit, which they that believe on him should receive: for the Holy Ghost was not yet given; because that Jesus was not yet glorified']. Verse 39 establishes

Edition, for an attack on the rationalists in particular, and for a long footnote against the pietist A. Tholuck; and the preface to the Third Edition for an attack on the pietists, followed by a brilliant brief characterisation of the rationalists. Hegel always insisted he was a Lutheran Christian, of course, but there is rightly a great deal of discussion as to whether or not he was, and whether or not he believed in God. See Bernard M. G. Reardon, *Hegel's Philosophy of Religion* (London, 1977), especially the section 'Theism or Pantheism?', pp. 100–104. The matter can only be settled by understanding his philosophy, but a preliminary indication can be gained from the fact that he would not accept *either* that God was an object *or* that everything was God; or from his insistence that philosophy had to work out the implications of the 'hard word' 'God is Dead'. *Glauben and Wissen* (1803), last paragraph; *Phänomenologie* (1807), Chapter VII, Part C, 'Die Offenbare Religion', 5th paragraph.

that not faith as faith in the temporal, sense-perceived, present personality of Christ would produce streams of living water, for it had not yet become the Truth as such. The faith of verse 38 is defined in the following verse 39 by noting that Christ spoke verse 38 concerning the Spirit those *would receive* who *believed* in him; for the Holy Spirit *was not yet present*, for Jesus was *not yet glorified*. The still-unglorified form of Christ is the form then present in time to the senses, or the personality subsequently so depicted (which has the same content), and this is the immediate object of faith. As present, Christ himself revealed to his disciples by word of mouth his eternal nature and purpose to reconcile God with himself and men with him, together with the plan of salvation and ethics; and the faith which the disciples had in him included all this. Despite that, this faith, which lacked nothing in strength of certainty, is explained to be only preliminary, only a start, a conditional foundation, only not-yet-perfected. Those who so believed do not yet have the Spirit, must yet receive the Spirit – the Spirit, truth itself, the Spirit which only comes subsequent to that earlier faith, the Spirit which leads into all truth. But [contemporary theologians] remain stuck in this sort of certainty, certainty of the preparatory type; but this certainty, itself only subjective, brings only in a conventional way the subjective fruit of *security* and then inevitably the fruit of pride, of slander, and of damnation. Contrary to scripture, they hold themselves fast only in this security against the Spirit which is the expansion of insight and not till then truth.[13]

Hegel is boldly appropriating Luther's attack on Roman Catholicism to attack contemporary orthodox Lutherans. The distinction between true faith, which is bold and reckless and expansive with the explosive power of the Spirit, and false security is fundamental to Luther, and this Hegel takes over.

[13] *Encyklopädie der philosophischen Wissenschaften im Grundrisse*, 4th ed. edited by Karl Rosenkranz (Berlin, 1845), Preface to Third Edition, p. xxvii.

The young men who listened to Hegel's slow tortured difficult lectures in Berlin in the 1820s were converted and set on fire and liberated just as joyfully as Luther's first followers had been. Hegel inspired his young men with his philosophical courage to explore everything, absolutely everything.

What was Hegel's doctrine of Spirit? The secret of his teaching is that those filled with Spirit went on an intellectual journey, the journey of Spirit itself. Spirit was capable of comprehending the realm of spirits by going out and entering into everything as though it itself, and everything it encountered, were free; but once out there, spirit discovered it was not free, and nothing was free; however, in discovering the necessity of everything, and so renouncing itself, spirit returned to itself in the highest freedom of life. When man's spirit knows itself, it participates in God's knowing himself; it participates in the inner life of the Triune God who goes out from himself into a far country and dies and returns to himself, as Father, Son, and Holy Spirit. In short, the young men who really followed Hegel's lectures were being God, and what could be more intoxicating than that? Hegel's philosophy was not a secularized subtraction from Lutheran orthodoxy but a complete appropriation of that orthodoxy in all its parts: not as a system (for true Lutheranism is no system) but as a lived life. Of course, Hegel's philosophy was not just an appropriation of old-fashioned Lutheranism: it was the appropriation of all previous philosophy as well. But that was as nothing beside the appropriation of the revealed religion of the Bible as understood in all its fulness by Luther. This full philosophical appropriation of religion was also the dethronement of religion, and that was to have far-reaching consequences, but even the dethronement has to be understood as a consequence of reading the Bible.

In Hegel's way of dealing with previous philosophies we can see how he transcends them by the use of the revealed religion of the Bible. Previous philosophies had worked on the assumption that their job was to establish what was true and what was false; the custom was to open a new book of philosophy to see what it opposed and what it supported.

Hegel's philosophy was quite different. Instead of concerning itself with such contradictions, it entered into all systems and regarded them as the progressive development of the truth. 'The bud disappears in the bursting forth of the blossom, and one could say that the bud was refuted by the blossom; in the same way, because of the fruit, the blossom could be explained as a false form of the plant — the fruit replacing the blossom as 'the truth' of the plant. These forms not only differ, but they displace one another as incompatible. But their natural flux makes these forms all moments of the organic unity, in which they not only do not contradict one another, but in which one is just as necessary as the other; and only this equal necessity displays the life of the whole.'[14] Accordingly, Hegel's philosophy is not one philosophy among many, but the only true philosophical method that enters into all nature and all history (including the history of philosophy) and sees the necessity of each successive form, and so alone comprehends the whole. Philosophy is a spiritual pilgrimage.

Not a simple journey; rather, a pilgrimage. The pilgrimage involves self-abnegation. The various forms of life the pilgrim encounters have to be really inwardly appropriated; the very errors of the stages must be taken over in order to be felt as necessary. When they are renounced, that renunciation is a sort of death. The pilgrimage of suffering leads to the only possible freedom, the freedom of self-denial to the point where the whole pilgrimage and every stage in it is seen as necessary.

Other philosophies claim to yield results and to establish truths. Only Hegel's philosophy is a philosophy that is continually expanding; only this philosophy discards nothing specific and individual in the kingdom of spirits, and rests in nothing.

It follows that Hegel's philosophy is irrrefutable. Any attempt to refute it betrays itself as not aware of the only true way to philosophise, for an attempt at refutation is an

---

[14] *Phänomenologie des Geistes*, Vorrede, second paragraph; see Walter Kaufmann's translation and commentary, *Hegel: Reinterpretation, Texts, and Commentary* (1965; London, 1966), pp. 370 f.

attempt to establish one truth over against a falsehood. Of course the attempt to establish truths over against falsehoods must be made — this is one moment in the voyage of the spirit; but to stop there is to betray ignorance about the necessity for the existence of the falsehood, and thus ignorance about the falsehood of the truth. There is no rest for the spirit. It must drive on to see the necessity of its own self-contradiction, and only thus can it return in to itself and recognise that the only freedom is that understanding of this necessity.

Philosophy, according to Hegel, no longer works by pronouncing on all the other sciences (the natural and historical sciences); philosophy enters into their domains and takes the pilgrim way of suffering through them. Consequently religion occupies a special place, for religion has the same content as philosophy; and the highest religion, Christianity in its Lutheran form, undertakes the pilgrimage philosophy has to undertake, and travels towards the same goal.

The heart of Christianity was the renunciation of all attempts to secure oneself, the abandonment of oneself entirely to God. Every believer had to undergo his own Good Friday and suffer the pain of experiencing God as dead. Only in that way could he know the resurrection. Religion objectified this movement of the spirit in the earthly Jesus, but even religion as its truest, in the New Testament, and particularly in the Gospel of St John, knew that such objectification had to be overcome. 'Spiritual expansion', Hegel's term for true Christianity, is deliberately distinguished from mere belief in scripture, and only the former is called Truth. Hegel adopts the key terms of Lutheran theology to overthrow his seemingly orthodox critics. He applies the doctrine of justification-by-faith-alone and its accompanying attack on all false certainty, all contentment with a merely historical external Jesus, to demolish his opponents. He is the true Christian; they are stuck with a purely formal external religion.

But Hegel is not simply playing polemics; he is, as always, deadly serious. The most painful abandonment of external certainty which Lutheran theology constantly preached, the self-abandonment which identified itself with Christ even in the very depths of his sufferings when he fully shared the human state of being cast off by God, all this was the only way to do philosophy. Philosophy, too, had to sacrifice all its old certainty; philosophy had to abandon itself to the same fate. Philosophy used to talk about self-sacrifice as a moral precept or about abstraction as a formal move in the game; now it must give these things a philosophical existence, embody them in its essential movement of thought. Absolute freedom could only be found in absolute suffering, the Good Friday of the intellect. Only thus could a truly comprehensive philosophy rise again to life.[15]

I have already argued that this philosophy is on its own terms irrefutable. It remains to try to explain why Hegel felt himself driven by the entire previous history of philosophy to posit a new sort of philosophy like this.

The simplest explanation is that he was convinced that Kant's antinomies were sound and that human thought reached limiting theses which could not be reconciled and which, in fact, helped to constitute the peculiar power of human thought.

In particualar, there was an irreconcilable opposition between two theses. According to (a) 'causality, according to the laws of nature, is not the only causality from which all the phenomena of the world can be deduced; in order to account for these phenomena it is necessary also to admit another causality, that of freedom'; and according to (b) 'There is no freedom, but everything in the world takes place entirely according to the laws of nature.'[16]

Kant had been content to let the matter rest there, but Hegel discerned that Kant's thought could only be maintained by a philosophy of movement, of continual pilgrimage, of expansion towards the truth. The Spirit had to move through the truth of one antinomy to its denial and to the truth of the other. Only thus could the antinomy be maintained. Just as

[15] See the final paragraph of *Glauben and Wissen* (1802).
[16] Kant, *Kritik der reinen Vernunft*, A 444 f. B 472 f.

Kant found in Lutheran orthodoxy all the doctrines he needed for religion within the limits of reason alone, so did Hegel find there the pilgrim movement by way of assertion and self-abnegation which he needed. Lutheran orthodoxy also offered a system forced by scripture to surrender all claim to free-will; Luther's most important tract was 'On the Bondage of the Will'. Everything lay to hand for a philosophy that thought itself compelled to progress from a knowledge based on freedom to a higher knowledge, a higher freedom, to be won at the cost of accepting there was no freedom.

Hegel's philosophy is on its own terms irrefutable; anyone who would refute it thereby shows that he has understood neither philosophy nor the secret of the Christian faith. To assert, without suffering the abandonment of that and every assertion, is not to live by faith.

Hegel's philosophy makes thinking depend on death and rebirth, not in the abstract, but in the concrete thinking of men who live in history and inherit a living history. Hegel had two sorts of followers, the Lutheran theologians who regarded him as immortalized and a sort of defender of the true faith, and the young Hegelians who thought he was an atheist. The Lutheran theologians effectively stemmed the tide that was running against the Bible and the church and helped to make Germany and Europe in the nineteenth century intensely religious places. The young Hegelians have perhaps had a more radical and long-lasting influence – for Karl Marx was one of them. It could be thought they helped secularize Europe and destroy the authority of the Bible, yet that would be a superficial judgement. Hegel's philosophy was so deeply grounded in the Bible that no philosophy in any way dependent on him can escape the influence of the Bible.

8

Strauss

David Friedrich Strauss was born on 27 January 1801 in Ludwigsburg, the seat of the Prince of Württenberg. After the break up of the Holy Roman Empire and the victory of Napoleon in 1806, Württemberg became a strongly reorganized kingdom and in 1815 part of the German Confederation. Strauss was the first surviving child of his parents. His father was a merchant and son of a merchant, who wished he could have been a pastor. He carried Horace, Ovid and Virgil in the original around with him on his journeys, and sat apart reading them in the garden of the inns where he put up. He wrote very easily and had a gift for poetry. He was interested in mysticism and was quick tempered. His mother was child and grandchild of Lutheran pastors. She was full of good humour, interested in the simple things of nature and of common life. In religion she was for the practical, the understandable, and the rational. She stood by Strauss when he came under fierce public attack and abuse for his *Life of Jesus*; his father did not, which made the year he had to spent at home in the wake of his dismissal from the seminary at Tübingen extremely unpleasant.

At the age of thirteen, Strauss was sent to the church boarding school in Blaubeuren on the southern slopes of the Schwabian alps. This school had been founded in a dissolved Benedictine monastery to train future pastors: there were forty seminarians and a dozen paying students. They were taught by the headmaster, two masters, and two young teachers who were immediately responsible for the daily lives of the seminarians, each overseeing two dormitories. The

whole place had recently been reopened and reorganized.
The boys got up at 5.30 in winter, 5 in summer; had prayers;
private study to 7; breakfast; four classes in the morning;
midday dinner; free to go outside till 2; two more lessons,
and then private study till another break in summer, or
straight through to supper in winter; prayers at 9 and then to
bed, or private study till 10. The head had some grasp of the
need for free activity, and gave them extra time off on
Sundays, mounted expeditions to neighbouring parts on
holidays, and in Strauss's senior years sent hiking parties off
into the countryside with one of the young teachers for
several days at a time.[1]
Strauss was taught by two remarkable men, Friedrich
Heinrich Kern and Ferdinand Christian Baur.

> Baur . . . used Herodotus to introduce us to the higher
> mythology, and Livy to introduce us to the problems
> of Niebuhrian historical criticism; and he used Tacitus
> to make us aware of the psychological art by which the
> great historian had constructed the wonderful night-
> piece, his character-sketch of Tiberius. Kern could be
> seen as Heyne's pupil for the classical poets, and as
> Herder's pupil for the Psalms and Prophets.
>
> One thing should perhaps be said: these outstanding
> men flew back and forth much too high with us who
> had scarcely become capable of flight; there was too
> much of the spirit, too little of the letter in their lessons.
> Yet that was inseparable from . . . the fact that both
> men were then still growing. Scarcely out of their
> youth, they carries us with them in their own
> development, and let us as it were join in their voyages
> of discovery. This was especially true of Baur on the
> mythological expeditions he then mounted, without yet
> possessing a proper compass; nevertheless, he still
> managed to strike many of the coasts from which he
> later brought back so rich and enduring a booty for

[1] David Friedrich Strauss, *Christian Märklin: Ein Lebens- und Charakterbild aus der Gegenwart*, (Mannheim, 1851), pp. 15–21. Märklin and Strauss (and Zimmermann, Pfizer, Vischer, Binder, Kern, Elsner) were all pupils together at Blaubeuren.

German scholarship, when he had learnt to steer a better
course.[2]

Add to the influence of Kern and Baur the influence of a
new head, Reuss, who communicated his love for the French
Revolution and for the local history of Württemberg, and
you have all the important methods and ideas necessary for
Strauss's later work: the passionate interest in history, history
as the source of living knowledge; the scepticism about the
reliability of classical historians; and the conviction that all
the important things the human race had discovered in its
dawn were expressed as myths.

When the young men who had grown together in such
close friendship in Blaubeuren went on to the University of
Tübingen, they welcomed the social freedom but found the
intellectual life dull. The only teacher who made any mark
on them was their old Blaubeuren master F. C. Baur who
came as professor in 1826 as they entered their second year of
philosophy before embarking on their three years' theology.
Baur enthused them with admiration for Schleiermacher,
whom he compared (in order to praise him) with the early
Gnostics. He also taught them that church history was the
history of the conflict between Catholicism and Protestantism, the objective and external against the subjective and
inward.[3]

Far more important than their lectures were the private
study and discussions together. They began by falling captive
to Schelling. Schelling was a pantheist, and they accordingly
became pantheists.[4]

The next step was Schleiermacher. He taught them the
move which Strauss was to make famous as the theme of his
Leben Jesu: the overcoming of both supranaturalism and
rationalism in a higher scientific standpoint.[5] God and Christ
seemed to be reintroduced into a secularized world, without
giving God the idea of personality he had lost according to

---

[2] Strauss, *Märklin*, pp. 17 f.
[3] Strauss, *Märklin*, p. 40.
[4] Strauss, *Märklin*, p. 33 f.
[5] Strauss, *Märklin*, p. 39.

the teaching of Schelling, and without giving back to Christ his supernatural prerogatives.

In their last year of theological study, Strauss, Märklin, Binder and some others began to meet once or twice a week in Binder's lodgings to work through their own position. Schleiermacher's *The Christian Faith* now dissatisfied them.[6]

So they turned again to Kant, to his *Prolegomena*, but then went on to Hegel's *Phenomenology*. This they studied like the Bible. They each read at home the section to be discussed next. When they gathered Märklin read it out aloud, which they found greatly helped their understanding. Then they discussed the passage, using Gabler's commentary. (Gabler was Eichhorn's earliest gifted student and disciple; he had already explained the miracle stories in the Gospels as myths.) Gabler they found fairly superficial, and slowly began to win a hold on Hegel for themselves. Hegel in the *Phenomenology* 'put out with his own ships and sailed around the world – an Odyssey indeed'. He displayed the power of the free philosophical spirit to cut through all obstacles – a power that, according to Strauss, markedly fell off the more famous he became.

Strauss went to Berlin in 1831–32, above all to hear Hegel. He was shattered by his sudden death. He found Schleiermacher's lectures on Jesus half-baked. When he returned to the Tübinger Stift it was as one charged with the awesome destiny of pronouncing the final word about Jesus, as an historian who would make history by bringing an historical process to its necessary end.

Strauss was twenty-five when he began to write his *Life of Jesus* and twenty-six when he published it. At twenty-five he was a promising professional theologian; at twenty-six he was finished. Those 1,400 printed pages effectively made him famous throughout Europe – George Eliot was commissioned to make an English translation, which appeared in 1848; and those 1,400 printed pages ended his career. His *Life of Jesus* spawned hundreds of Lives of Jesus for popular consumption (he even wrote one himself), so that his work more decisively

[6] Strauss, *Märklin*, p. 53: 'Nur um so lauter, weil sie [Schleiermachers Dogmatik] es verschwieg, wies diese überall auf Kant, auf Spinoza zurück . . .' (Schneckenburger drew their attention to the importance of Spinoza).

affected the authority of the Bible at a popular level than that of anyone else in the nineteenth century, for to write a Life of Jesus rather than a commentary on the sacred Gospels of Matthew, Mark, Luke and John is to treat Jesus as one more hero whose life will be of interest to the reading public.[7]

Strauss's first *Life of Jesus* was not itself cast in the form of a biography. It was, rather, a long and detailed discussion of every aspect of the recorded stories about Jesus and the recorded teaching of Jesus in which he compared the accounts in all four Gospels and tried to sort out what actually happened (if anything) and how the resultant records came into being. For example, he discusses the cleansing of the Temple and asks whether it was more likely to have occurred early in Jesus' ministry (as John says) or late in Jesus' ministry (as Mattthew, Mark and Luke say). He canvasses the idea that the whole story is impossible and perhaps grew out of a saying of Jesus because no one man could have done what he is supposed to have done and not been stopped – and he notes that Origen in the third century had this doubt about the historicity of the incident. But in the end Strauss thinks Jesus did do something like what was recorded.

On the feeding of the multitude he is convinced the event did not happen. There is no possible natural explanation that will explain the production of so much bread and fish in a short time – wheat might multiply very fast, but this story is about bread, an artificial man-made product. There is no indication that the bread multiplied because other members

[7] Strauss has been well studied recently. Gotthold Müller, *Identität und Immanenz: Zur Genese der Theologie von David Friedrich Strauss: Eine theologie- und philosophiegeschichtliche Studie.* (Die philosophischen Voraussetzungen der Theologie von D.F.S., dargestellt aus seiner Jugend- und Frühgeschichte *vor* dem Erscheinen des 'Lebens Jesu' . . .) (Zurich, 1968). Peter C. Hodgson, Introduction to a new edition of George Eliot's translation of Strauss's *The Life of Jesus Critically Examined* (Philadelphia, 1972; London, 1973). Jörg F. Sandberger, *David Friedrich Strauss als theologischer Hegelianer* (Göttingen, 1972). Horton Harris, *David Friedrich Strauss and his Theology* (Cambridge, 1973). Leander E. Keck, Introduction to his translation of Strauss's *The Christ of Faith and the Jesus of History: A Critique of Schleiermacher's Life of Jesus* (Philadelphia, 1977). Hans Frei, 'David Friedrich Strauss', in *Nineteenth Century Religious Thought in the West*, edited by Ninian Smart, John Clayton, Steven T. Katz and Patrick Sherry, vol. 1 (Cambridge, 1985), pp. 215–260.

of the crowd copied Jesus' generosity and distributed their own supplies. The origin of the story lies in the old myth of the feeding of the Jewish people by Moses in the wilderness. That is not quite sufficient, however, to explain the story of Jesus, because in the case of Moses the food comes out of nothing and in the case of Jesus the food is already present and the miracle lies in its multiplication. The bridge between the story of Moses and the story of Jesus is Elijah's multiplying the widow's meal and oil in 1 Kings 17 and Elisha's feeding a hundred men with twenty loaves in 2 Kings 4. There are also rabbinic stories of a holy man who made a small quantity of shew-bread more than suffice for a great number of priests.

Strauss deals with every alleged moment in the life of Jesus from his conception to his ascension and argues that a supernatural explanation is impossible, and a naturalistic explanation (such as the explanation that the Gospel writers mistook the generosity Jesus awakened in the crowd for a miracle of the multiplication of the loaves and the fishes) is highly unlikely. The true cause of the Gospels is the power of myth, the belief current at the time that God intervened in history in miraculous ways.

> It appeared to the author of the work . . . that it was time to substitute a new mode of considering the life of Jesus, in the place of the antiquated systems of supranaturalism and naturalism . . .
>
> The new point of view, which must take the place of the above, is the mythical. This theory is not brought to bear on the evangelical history for the first time in the present work: it has long been applied to particular parts of that history, and is here only extended to its entire tenor. It is not by any means meant that the whole history of Jesus is to be represented as mythical, but only that every part of it is to be subjected to a critical examination, to ascertain whether it has not some admixture of the mythical.
>
> The exegesis of the ancient church set out from the double presupposition: first, that the gospels contained a history, and secondly, that this history was a

supernatural one. Rationalism rejected the latter of these presuppositions, but only to cling the more tenaciously to the former . . . the inquiry must first be made whether in fact, and to what extent, the ground on which we stand in the gospels is historical. This is the natural course of things, and thus far the appearance of a work like the present is not only justifiable, but even necessary . . .[8]

Here is a young man who had the energy and skill to master the whole of a vast technical literature on the Gospels and the courage to answer his dozens of critics in a large three-part volume, and then to do two large-scale revisions of the original *Life*. If that were not enough, he went on to find the energy to write a two-volume *Doctrine of the Christian Faith*, 739 pages long, all before he turned thirty-four. This *Doctrine of the Christian Faith* was no abstract system of doctrine but a thorough and relentless history of doctrine, with an accomplished history of modern philosophy since Leibniz thrown in. Although Strauss was thoroughly grounded in philosophy he had no interest in doing philsophy or in doing theology. He thought history had brought the church and theology to its present moment, and all that had to be done to see the consequences was to examine the history. In the history of Christian dogma all the reasons for the rise of the beliefs and all the possible criticisms of the beliefs are made *in history* by the various ecclesiastical parties to the debate and by the heretics who criticised the decisions of councils and synods. There is no need to philosophise about Christian doctrine: 'the true criticism of the dogma is its history.'[9]

This is also the clue to Strauss's massive attack on the authority of the Bible. For all his debt to Hegel in giving

---

[8] *Das Leben Jesu, kritisch bearbeitet* (Tübingen, 1835. 4th ed. 1840). English translation by Marian Evans (George Eliot), 1846. Edited with an Introduction by Peter C. Hodgson, 1972; London, 1973. From the preface to the first German edition.

[9] *Die christliche Glaubenslehre in ihrer geschichtlichen Entwicklung und im Kampfe mit der modernen Wissenschaft*, 2 volumes (Tübingen & Stuttgart, 1840–1841), i. 71.

him the sense that his immense literary work was necessary
(that is, the inevitable next stage in world history), Strauss
was really an honest historian who was impatient with
theoretical quibbles. He had attempted to show at the end of
his *Life of Jesus* that the destruction of belief in the historicity
of Jesus' miraculous conception, his miracles, and his
resurrection and ascension left the inner kernel of the
Christian faith untouched as 'eternal truths', but he soon
abandoned that position and at the end of his life argued that
modern man had a completely new faith based on Darwin's
principle of the struggle for life, with literature and the music
of Mozart and Beethoven replacing the church. He discarded
belief in personal life after death before he began his Life of
Jesus. 'My belief is unchanging that the inexorable discarding
of the view of personal life after death must be the stone on
which we shatter and crucify our own and others'
unphilosophical, trivial consciousness, in order to be able to
ascend in the concept'.[10] Thenceforth he was to be the
practical historian, patiently explaining illusion on the basis
of a careful history of illusion. 'What is the point of the
tricks?', he wrote. 'Why the pretending to others and to
oneself? Why not come out into the open with speech?'[11]

There is something refreshingly honest and open about
Strauss. George Eliot only met him many years after she had
accomplished the tedious task of translating his long *Life of
Jesus* into English. What struck her then was that 'he speaks
with very choice words, like a man strictly truthful in the use
of language'.[12] I like that. If the authority of the Bible is to
be maintained, it has to be maintained by showing that
Strauss's rejection of its authority misread the history, and
that Strauss's assumption that there was no personal existence
after death is unlikely to be true. Like Strauss, we should not

---

[10] Strauss to Binder, Ascension Day 1832, published by Theobold Ziegler, *Deutsche
Revue* 30 (1905), ii.205; see Horton Harris, *David Friedrich Strauss and his Theology*
(Cambridge, 1973), p. 38.

[11] Cited by Eduard Zeller, *David Friedrich Strauss in seinem Leben und seinen Schriften*
(Bonn, 1874), p. 84.

[12] J. W. Cross, *George Eliot's Life as Related in her Letters and Journals*, new edition
(Edinburgh and London, n.d.), p. 252.

be too patient with philosophies or theologies that fudge the issues he confronted. The true criticism of any dogma is its history, and the dogma that there is no God and no personal survival, and the dogma that no miracles occur are dogmas that also have their histories. Like Strauss we have to call in the evidence and to be strictly truthful in our use of language to express our results.

Strauss made little impact on the professional theologians after the initial controversy caused by his *Life of Jesus* died down. His work lacked technical brilliance, and did not decisively address itself to the Synoptic Problem (the literary relation of Matthew, Mark and Luke as interdependent documents) or to the nature of the Fourth Gospel, although he had many sensible and perceptive remarks to make on the way. He was ignored and, being excluded from university life, had to live by writing popular biographies. But, although his chief effect was on the popular mind, he was an honest scholar tackling the right issues.

2

F. C. Baur

When Strauss was buried, on the 11 February, 1874, he had expressly forbidden the ringing of church bells, and had directed that no minister of the church should speak at his grave; indeed, that no one should speak, except perhaps to announce that the silent solemnity was finished, to stop an unauthorised person saying anything. There were no church bells; there was no minister; but the friends had to sing a hymn because the words of Strauss's own song had been mislaid, and Gustav Binder made a speech.[1]

When Ferdinand Christian Baur was buried, on the 5th December 1860, there were full church ceremonies and a number of memorial meetings at which leading theologians spoke − conservatives as well as liberals. Louis Georgii, a pupil of Baur's and a friend of Strauss's, said at his grave what an influence for blessing he was in the church as a preacher of the gospel; how he loved to observe church regulations; to serve the interests of church life and see others do so too.[2]

Baur always prided himself on being 'positive' in his critical work and deprecated Strauss's 'negativity'. Strauss thought

[1] Horton Harris, *David Friedrich Strauss and his Theology* (Cambridge, 1973), prints for the first time Strauss's 'Last Will and Testimony with Regard to My Burial', 22 June, 1873, to be found among his letters to Kuno Fischer in the Heidelberg University Library; Harris, 256 ff., with a description of the funeral.

[2] See Ernst Barnikol, *Ferdinand Christian Baur als rationalistisch-kirchlicher Theologe*, (Berlin, 1970), pp. 8 f. Barnikol's very title poses the problem I am concerned with. Peter C. Hodgson, *The Formation of Historical Theology: A Study of Ferdinand Christian Baur* (New York, 1966), makes use of Baur's sermons in manuscript.

this a bit thick, and in 1844 made up a witty little aphorism
for Baur to say on the subject of negative and positive
criticism:

> Strauss and I are like No and Yes,
> Like storm and rainbow:
> He says, 'It is not true';
> I say, 'It is simulated'.[3]

Strauss's bitterness is understandable. Baur had been his
teacher at the seminary school of Blaubeuren in the
Schwabian alps: Baur the thirty-two years old teacher began
to publish his first book, on symbolism and mythology, the
nature religion of antiquity, in 1824, the year his pupil Strauss
turned sixteen. When Strauss went to Tübingen to study
philosophy and theology, Baur soon followed as a young
professor. Baur's inaugural lecture praised Schleiermacher's
theology as similar to Gnosticism and in 1835, the year
Strauss's *Life of Jesus* was published, Baur brought out a book
on Gnosis as the forerunner of the modern philosophy of
religion perfected by Hegel. This philosophy showed there
was no need to retain the idea that God was living, personal
and separate from the world; no reason to hold the
immortality of the soul; and no reason to think that Christ as
God-man was an isolated individual since the incarnation is
nothing but belief in man in his universality.[4]

Baur and Strauss thus perfectly agreed on their fundamental
religious beliefs, and Baur always acknowledged the service
to the age Strauss's *Life of Jesus* performed by drawing
together the results of hundreds of critical monographs and
making the necessary conclusions.[5] Yet when the young
Strauss was dismissed from his junior post in the Tübinger

[3] Strauss, *Poetisches Gedenkbuch: Gedichte aus dem Nachlasse*, ed. Eduard Zeller
(Bonn, 1877), p. 21, (written about 1844).
[4] *Die christliche Gnosis oder die Religions-Philosophie in ihrer geschichtlichen
Entwicklung* (Tübingen, 1835), pp. 705 f.; pp. 706–10, note 30; p. 715.
[5] See his introduction to *Paulus, der Apostel Jesu Christi ... Ein Beitrag zu einer
kritischen Geschichte des Urchristenthums* (Stuttgart, 1845; 2nd ed. Leipzig, 1866–7).
English translation, vol. i (London & Edinburgh, 1873; 2nd ed., revised by A.
Menzies, 1876).

Stift, his teacher and professor stood by and did nothing. Why? Of course he had a young and growing family to think of, but there was more to Baur's prudent silence than that. He differed from his pupil on one cardinal point.

Baur had a far different estimate of the church from that of Strauss. For Baur 'protestantism *is* ceaseless progress'.[6]

> Thought has now, after the laborious toil of many centuries, emancipated itself and cast away its crutches, and it naturally turns its gaze back into the Past. The spirit, at rest in itself in the assurance of its own self-consciousness, stands for the first time on a vantage-ground, from which it can look back upon the paths along which it has passed, as circumstances shaped its course; it retraces those paths not as at first, when it yielded unconsciously to surrounding influences, but as recognising the inner necessity in obedience to which it has grown up to its present form . . . Where can it be of greater importance than where the Present is linked with the Past by the strictest and closest ties, and where this union has its roots in the deepest interests of our spiritual being?
>
> Christianity is on the one hand the great spiritual power which determines all the belief and thought of the present age, the absolute principle on which the self-consciousness of the spirit is supported and maintained, so that, unless it were essentially Christian, it would have no stability or firmness in itself at all.
>
> On the other hand, the essential nature of Christianity is a purely historical question, whose solution lies only in that Past in which Christianity itself had its origin; it is a problem which can only be solved by that critical attitude of thought which the consciousness of the present age assumes towards the Past.[7]

---

[6] *Kirchengeschichte des neunzehnten Jahrhunderts*, posthumously edited by Eduard Zeller (1862; 2nd ed. 1877), p. 335, cited by Wolfgang Geiger, *Spekulation und Kritik: Die Geschichtstheologie Ferdinand Christian Baurs* (Munich, 1964, p. 231); see his whole discussion.

[7] From the introduction to his book on Paul; see note 5 above.

Long before he became a professor in Tübingen and read Hegel, Baur believed that world history was a revelation of divinity. Just as an individual develops in consciousness, so does world history develop. History developing is Spirit developing, revealing itself in different forces and activities.[8] Spirit develops by negating every temporal form and taking those negated preceding moments into itself as its necessary condition. The aim of Spirit is the autonomy of self-consciousness. But this aim of Spirit is precisely the principle of Protestantism, the freeing of consciousness from every authority it cannot recognise as its own self-determination.[9] It is no accident that Baur's early years as a professor were partly taken up with a series of defences of protestantism against the criticisms of his colleague in the Catholic faculty, Johann Adam Möhler. Baur argued the Möhler in his heaping-up of authority on authority had missed the clue to history. Christianity had in its early history taken over many features of the religion it superseded, but the subsequent history of Christianity was its progressive overcoming of these restrictions. Paul (and behind him, Jesus) had expressed this essentially inward religious view, which was immediately attacked by the continuing spirit of Judaism; Marcion tried to oppose these tendencies in the church, but eventually catholicism produced a compromise. At the Reformation, true inward religion made a powerful advance, but the Reformation itself in turn hardened, until the modern philosophy of religion arose finally to challenge all external authority and establish complete inward self-determination. Baur was a protestant and remained a protestant because he thus allied himself with the continual forward movement of Spirit.

This picture of the development of Christianity undoubtedly goes back to Semler and, behind Semler, to

---

[8] *Symbolik und Mythologie oder die Naturreligion des Alterthums*, part I (Stuttgart, 1824), preface p. vf.

[9] *Die christliche Lehre von der Versöhnung in ihrer geschichtlichen Entwicklung von der ältesten Zeit bis auf die neueste* (Tübingen, 1838), Foreword, pp. vif; *Vorlesungen über die christliche Dogmengeschichte*, edited by F. F. Baur, vol. iii (Leipzig, 1867), pp. 356–9.

Thomas Morgan. Baur, like Eichhorn before him, criticised Semler for not standing back from history and periodising the great forward movements marked off from each other by crises like the Reformation. But Baur's key move came straight out of Semler, and he did little more than harvest the critical results Semler's successors had produced.

Baur regarded the New Testament collection of books no longer as an objective authoritative canon for the Christian church. Rather, the individual books were the deposit left by the struggle that took place early in the life of the church between Paul, the true representative of the religion of Jesus, and Peter, the representative of Judaism. Paul argued for the universalism of Christianity while Peter was for Jewish privilege.

Baur's debt to Semler is clear. In 1830 or 1831 Baur gave a course of lectures on 1 Corinthians. Out of that course came a curious article on 'The Christ-Party in the Corinthian Church; the Opposition of Petrine and Pauline Christianity in the Earliest Church; the Apostle Peter in Rome'.[10] He began with a short section in support of J. E. C. Schmidt's suggestion that 'I am of Paul; and I of Apollos' in 1 Corinthians 1.12 referred to Paul's party, and 'I of Cephas; and I of Christ' referred to Peter's party, who prided themselves on being connected with the earthly Jesus, the Jesus of the flesh, through the chief of the apostles, Cephas (Peter), and despised Paul who had not been with Jesus during his ministry. Then the rest of the article is taken up with a long exposition of 2 Corinthians 5.16, a long section on a body of writings called the Pseudo-Clementines, and then an even longer section, of 70 pages, almost half the article, on denying that Peter had ever been at Rome. The point of the section on the Pseudo-Clementines is to argue that a church party in the second century had used a legendary account of Peter's attack on an obscure heretic to launch an attack an Paul. The point of the denial that Peter had ever been in Rome was to argue that Peter's later followers made up the

[10] *Tübinger Zeitschrift für Theologie* (1831), no. 4, pp. 61–206; reprinted in Klaus Scholder, Baur's selected works, vol. 1 (Tübingen, 1963).

story in order to raise Peter to the same level as Paul, who had been martyred in Rome.

The article is grotesquely disjointed: long scholarly treatments with the briefest of connecting notes. The reason is, I believe, that Baur had simply worked up three brief but linked observations Semler had made in his paraphrase of Galatians (1772). At the end of § 5 and in § 6 Semler had made three points: the early church was divided into two, the disciples of Paul against the followers of Peter and James and other Palestinians; the Judaizers whom Paul opposed invented a Roman history for Peter, modelled on the history of Paul; most of these books of the Judaizers have perished, for the church at large dropped the abuse and preserved the idea of the two apostles working side-by-side, but the Recognitions and Homilies of Clement have survived. The general interpretation of Paul as a preacher of an internal religion against the external religion with its ceremonies and institutions is found throughout Semler, but is neatly expressed on the third page of the Preface to the same paraphrase of Galatians.[11]

Baur took Semler's ideas and worked them up as they stood into his long scholarly article. Over the next fifteen years he mastered a mass of learned contributions to the critical study of the New Testament made by Semler's successors in order to put flesh on this basic thesis. Baur never claimed originality for his work; all he did was done as a service which the education of the age distinctly called for. By dint of getting up every morning, winter and summer, at 4 o'clock and by preparing his lectures so that they were written and constantly revised with an eye on publication, he was able to dominate the field. The Tübingen School was his creation, and everyone else working on the New Testament in his generation was either a follower, an ex-follower − a growing band as time went on − or an opponent.

Baur lived at the end of a great period of scholarship when the traditional authorship of every book of the New

---

[11]J. S. Semler, *Paraphrasis epistolae ad Galatas cum Prolegomenis, Notis et Varietate Lectionis Latinae* (Halle, 1772), pp. 23–27.

Testament was questioned. The books were seen, one by one, as reflecting the controversies that were going òn in the early church; the books were seen as having a part in history as well as recording a history; the 'tendency' of the book showed its place in the story.

In the study of the first three Gospels, the Synoptic Gospels, the great Dutch scholar Hugo Grotius had argued, following a hint of Augustine's, that Matthew was used by Mark, and Matthew and Mark by Luke. A Welshman, Henry Owen, published a variant on this theory in 1744: Matthew was written first, for Jewish converts; Luke second, using Matthew, for Gentile converts; and Mark third, using both Matthew and Luke, an epitome, for Christians at large. This theory was taken over by Johann Jakob Griesbach, a pupil of Semler's, and adopted in turn by Baur.

Until the end of the eighteenth century no one questioned the traditional authorship of the Fourth Gospel by the Apostle John, but as soon as it was questioned by Edward Evanson in *The Dissonance of the Four Generally Received Evangelists, and the Evidence of their Respective Authenticity Examined* (Ipswich, 1792; 2nd ed. Gloucester, 1805) the floodgates opened, and by 1826 W. M. L. de Wette in his *Introduction to the New Testament* said, in his moderate way, that the authenticity of the Gospel was not beyond doubt, and by 1847 Baur could rely on Strauss, Bruno Bauer and E. K. J. Lützelberger for his extremely late dating of the Gospel about AD 170.

The same sort of radical conclusions were argued for most of the rest of the New Testament. Baur did not accept an attempt by a German critic G. L. Oeder, which had been taken up by Semler, to place the Apocalypse or Revelation of John in the second century as the work of a Montanist fanatic. He needed the traditional authorship of John to provide him with a typical product of the Jewish party of Peter in the early church. Nor did he take up Evanson's suggestion in the book on the Gospels already mentioned that Romans was not by Paul, for Romans, with 1 and 2 Corinthians and Galatians were to provide him with documents on the other side, genuine writings of Paul, the apostle of universalism. But Baur was able to regard all the rest of the New Testament books as inauthentic and to place them each as polemical writings playing a part in the history of the church.

His picture was as follows. The Christian church began with an outright clash between Paul, who represented the true position of Jesus, and Peter and James, who represented the Judaizers. Paul wrote the four chief epistles to defend his law-free gospel; Revelation represents the Jewish particularist position.

The initial clash inevitably led to attempts to reconcile the two opposed positions. Hebrews, which had long been seen as not by Paul, was an attempt to persuade Christian Judaizers, from the Pauline side, to adopt a much freer form of Judaism lest they fall back into Judaism proper.

The Pauline authorship of Ephesians had been denied by Usteri and de Wette and that of Colossians by Mayerhoff. Baur regarded them as a pair, written on the assumption that Christianity was substantially Judaism enlarged into universalism by the death of Christ so as to embrace the Gentiles as well. Philippians was denied to Paul by de Wette, and Baur argued that it was an attempt from the side of the Petrine party to show that Paul had played his part in establishing the unified church of Rome under Clement.

The Epistle of James was suspected not to be by James as early as the third century, and Luther was sure it could not have been by an apostle. Baur regarded James as a late attempt from the Jewish Christian side to reconcile the two parties, just as 1 Peter, the authenticity of which had been denied by Semler, Eichhorn, Cludius and de Wette, was a late attempt from the Pauline side to do the same.

Philemon, which perhaps Baur was the first to deny to Paul, was a little Christian romance about reconciliation; I and II Thessalonians, whose authenticity had been denied by Schrader and J. E. C. Schmidt, were late tracts to express an idea about the coming of Christ drawn from 1 Corinthians 15.51; and the Pastoral Epistles, denied to Paul by Eichhorn, were late reactions to the flourishing of Gnosticism. All these epistles belonged to the time in the life of the church when the opposition between the two parties had been overcome and an institutionalized unity attained. Baur's picture of the early church was based on a beautifully clear idea that two starkly opposed positions, one right and the other wrong, were gradually brought together to a compromise position by lesser mortals who naturally worked for unity. The beautifully simple idea was then provided with a dense elaboration based on Baur's reading of dozens of brilliant detailed monographs. In this way progressive protestantism was given a simple ideology, and its priests were the immensely learned and diligent university professors who argued endlessly over the details and formed schools to advance their own particular modification of this detail or that. Baur's view of the Gospels soon came in for serious criticism, as we shall see, and Philippians, Philemon and 1 Thessalonians were reclaimed for Paul, but his general theory, that catholic Christianity was the compromise reconciliation of two world views originally opposed to one another, has remained the dominant view in protestant scholarship ever since his day. The authority of the Bible has been replaced by the authority of a story about history. The story had built into it a hostility to Judaism which provided too good a soil for the resurgence of hostility to Jews. And the story itself, for all its appealing simplicity is, to my mind, highly unlikely.

Ferdinand Christian Baur was an epigone who gloried in that fact; an epigone who summed up a great creative period in New Testament scholarship and triggered off more good work, but whose greatest influence was on the church he loved to see progress: for 'protestantism is ceaseless progress'.

10

Weisse

Weisse, like Strauss, was born in the first decade of the nineteenth century and so was privileged to come to maturity and live his life in the period of peace and reconstruction that followed the collapse of the Napoleonic Empire in 1815. Despite times of hunger and unrest it was generally an age when the population of Europe could grow unchecked and when the level of prosperity of the poorest people began to rise. What a Europe the children born under the shadow of Napoleon were to create: John Henry Newman, born the same year as Weisse, 1801; Charles Darwin, 1809; Charles Dickens, 1812; Wagner and Kierkegaard, 1813; and Bismark, 1815. It was a pious Europe, by and large, and if the Bible had lost its old authority, it was still treasured and retold as story. Christianity came to be valued on aesthetic grounds among educated people, and Weisse is a good example of this approach. But he is something more; he is the gifted amateur who is able, by his detachment, to make important contributions to the large technical problems as well. There are three key technical problems anyone who studies the New Testament today must master: the Synoptic Problem (the problem of the literary relationship between the first three Gospels); the Johannine Problem (the problem of the origin of the discourses of Jesus that are peculiar to the Fourth Gospel); and the problem of the authenticity of the Epistles of Paul (the problem of which epistles, and what parts of which epistles were written by Paul himself). Weisse made striking suggestions in all three fields and his solutions are still debated and discussed.

Christian Hermann Weisse was a university professor's son, of a well-to-do family, and related to a number of writers and philosophers, the most famous of whom was his grandfather Christian Felix Weisse, Lessing's friend and early collaborator, who wrote poetry, plays, and operettas, and who was famous as the editor of the children's paper Der Kinderfreund. He studied his father's subject, jurisprudence, at his father's desire, but then turned from this mainly historical study to philosophy, art, and literature. He often said that he was driven to philosophy by his interest in aesthetics and history, and that his passion in life was to understand art and history in the light of divine eternity.[1]

Before he turned thirty, Weisse had published a book on Homer and mythology and another on Greek mythology in general, a review of Goethe's *Faust* Part II Act I as soon as it was published (1828), a book on the difference between Plato and Aristotle, and a book in which he announced his departure from Hegel on the grounds that Hegel only posited the possible as possible, it being left to experience to recognise reality – the That of existence and the How of that That.[2] He had also become Associate Professor of Philosophy at Leipzig, got married, and published the first volume of a three-part philosophical system, the part to do with aesthetics.

In 1831 Hegel died, and in 1832 Weisse produced a popular work on philosophy after Hegel. Strauss visited Weisse on his way back from Berlin to Tübingen, and was annoyed to hear Weisse say that Schelling was a better philosopher than Hegel.[3] In 1833, Weisse produced the second part of his system, the *Idea of Divinity*, in which he argued for a kind of trinity in the divinity, a trinity of Reason, Imagination, and Will, or Truth, Beauty, and Goodness. He published a philosophical justification for a reinterpreted immortality, and two popular booklets (one of them in verse on the same theme) under the name of Nicodemus.

[1] Rudolf Seydel, 'Nekrolog: Christian Hermann Weisse', *Zeitschrift für Philosophie und philosophische Kritik*, neue Folge, 50 (Halle, 1867), 154–168 at 156. See also Heinze, *Allgemeine Deutsche Biographie*, 41 (Leipzig, 1896), 590–94.

[2] Seydel, 'Nekrolog', p. 157.

[3] Strauss's letter to Vatke, 18 August, 1832.

In 1837 he applied for a full chair, which he did not get
because he refused to conform to the reigning philosophical
system (that of Herbart, a Kantian moralist and educational
philosopher), and he retired from academic life to his estates
at Stotteritz. That year he published a book on Goethe's
Faust with an appendix on Goethe's morality.

In 1838 he published a two-volume work on the *Gospel
History treated critically and philosophically* in which he argued
that our Gospel of Mark was the actual source used by the
compilers of our Gospels of Matthew and Luke, and that our
Gospels of Matthew and Luke also used a sayings-collection,
the work of the genuine Matthew, and therefore older and
more reliable than Mark's Gospel, the author of whom had
to rely on oral tradition. Weisse thus laid down the great
simplification of the Synoptic Problem that has ruled Gospel
criticism ever since.

The idea that Mark was an epitome of Matthew and Luke,
the theory of Henry Owen, taken over by Griesbach and
adopted by F. C. Baur, had been attacked in 1782 by J. B.
Koppe. Gottlob Christian Storr, a Tübingen professor of an
older generation than Baur, who also had his own Tübingen
school, had concluded that Mark was the first Gospel, that
Matthew used Mark, and that Luke used both the other two
(1786, 1794). Herder followed Storr. Eichhorn saw it was
more likely Luke and Matthew used another common source
than that Luke used Matthew, and so the basic work needed
in order to produce Weisse's form of the theory was already
done. Weisse relied mainly on an 1835 article by a classical
philologist, Karl Konrad Friedrich Wilhelm Lachmann on
the order of the narratives in the Synoptic Gospels.[4]

[4] Gottlob Christian Storr, Ueber den Zweck der evangelischen Geschichte und
der Briefe Johannis (Tübingen, 1786; 2nd ed., 1810), 58, 59, 61; Herder, *Vom Erlöser
der Menschen* (1796), section 4; *Regel der Zusammenstimmung unsrer Evangelien aus ihrer
Entstehung und Ordnung* (1797), Suphan xix. 380–424; Christian Gottlob Wilke,
'Ueber die Parabel von den Arbeitern im Weinberge', *Zeitschrift für wissenschaftliche
Theologie*, i (1826), 71–109; *Der Urevangelist oder exegetische kritische Untersuchung über
das Verwandtschaftsverhältnis der drei ersten Evangelien* (Dresden & Leipzig, 1838). Karl
Konrad Friedrich Wilhelm Lachmann (1793–1851), 'De ordine narrationum in
evangeliis synopticis', *Theologische Studien und Kritiken*, viii (1835), 570–90;
reprinted in his *Novvm Testamentvm Graece et Latine*, vol. ii (Berlin, 1850), pp. xiii–

... Once one has given up belief in the verbal inspiration of the Biblical writings in the old form, there will be no individual theologian who will not have found it necessary to explain the relationship [between Matthew's Gospel and Mark's Gospel] in some way or other: either by pushing back to the common source of tradition, or by assuming that Matthew's Gospel was used by Mark (the necessary choice of those who still cling to the belief that the Apostle Matthew had committed to writing an actual historical narrative). However, we maintain concerning this assumption as well that its falsity can be made evident from a more rigorous examination of the two related Gospels. In full consciousness of the trustworthiness of what the evidence itself bore witness to, Lachmann said [that, while no one could still hold that Matthew's Gospel was either more accurate than the others in chronology or written by an apostle, the view was even less probable that Mark was 'a bungling dilettante who blundered around, arbitrarily tossed between selecting from Matthew and Luke, now by boredom, another time by partiality, then by negligence, and lastly by an irrational diligence'. Those who held this view were surely deceived by 'a certain monograph of Griesbach's which looks diligent and subtle, but which is at best ingenious, and in fact totally trivial and insignificant'].[5] However bold these words might appear to some people, even perhaps presumptuous, we do not for a moment hesitate to subscribe to them with absolute conviction. When we now dare with the same assurance to *extend* Lachmann's assertion in two respects, namely (1) by

---

xxv; English translation of the most important sections, N. H. Palmer, 'Lachmann's Argument', *New Testament Studies*, 13 (1966–67), 368–78. See Werner Georg Kümmel, *Das Neue Testament: Geschichte der Erforschung seiner Probleme* (Munich, 1958), chapter 3, section 2, 'The Literary Questions'; English translation (London, 1978). See also, C. M. Tuckett, 'The Griesbach Hypothesis in the 19th Century', *Journal for the Study of the New Testament*, 3 (April, 1979), 29–60.

[5] Lachmann's words in inverted commas come from p. 577 of his original article (cf. p. 372 of Palmer's article) and were cited by Weisse on p. 39, note.

affirming that the very same evidence which caused us confidently to conclude that the Gospel which had the 'logia' ['sayings'] as one of its originally independent basic components, also convinced us that the narrative by which the 'logia' were enlarged was taken in all its main respects from Mark, from the same Mark which we now possess as an independent Gospel; and (2) by affirming furthermore that, as far as Mark itself is concerned, not only is there no weighty evidence that Mark was in turn composed out of somewhat corresponding parts, or that Mark was dependent on Matthew or some other document otherwise unknown[6] to us, but that this same evidence speaks entirely in favour of the work's having originated *at one casting*, not depending on any written predecessors; when we now dare affirm these two propositions, we can at least do so in the full assurance that we are driven to this conclusion completely independent of all preconceived opinions, purely on the basis of a study of the documents themselves.[7]

Weisse had the gift for generalizing and simplifying. He could spot a crucial problem – the literary relationship between the Synoptic Gospels had, after all, been troubling thoughtful men at least since Owen wrote *Observations on the Four Gospels* in 1764. Not only could he see what needed attention; he could paint a plausible picture in broad strokes and did not bother with the great difficulty Lachmann would not overlook – the difficulty that although a comparison of the *order* of events in the first three Gospels strongly favoured the view that Matthew and Luke were following a fixed order that was Mark's, they could scarcely be copying Mark's actual Greek *wording*. Weisse simply assumed that Matthew and Luke felt perfectly free to alter Mark's wording, and left it at that.[8] Not for Weisse the long and tedious detailed

[6] Weisse prints 'otherwise known to us', a slip.

[7] Christian Hermann Weisse, *Die evangelische Geschichte kritisch und philosophisch bearbeitet*, vol. i (Leipzig, 1838), pp. 39 f., 54 f. The emphases are mine.

[8] *Die evangelische Geschichte*, vol. i (1838), p. 66.

＂＂＂＂

discussion we find in his contemporary Wilke, who tried to show case by case how Mark's wording was changed.[9]

Weisse was an aristocrat, a man of means, and regarded his technical solution of the problem as simply a necessary part of a much larger task. As a layman he saw himself in an ideal position to recommend a revised Christianity to his educated contemporaries. His solution of the Synoptic Problem was just another piece of evidence to show that first of all tradition and then ecclesiastical dogma had overlaid the simple positive truth of the significance of Jesus.[10]

The theory is scarcely argued; rather it is assumed. The work consists of a broad treatment of the life of Jesus: the discussion of the sources of the Gospel history takes up only 138 pages, and includes a section on John's Gospel as well as on the other three, and the rest of the two volumes treat the sagas of the childhood of the Lord, an overall sketch of the history of Jesus until his death, a brief commentary on Mark, a commentary on Matthew and Luke, a commentary on John, a discussion of the resurrection and the ascension, and a final hundred or so pages of philosophical conclusions on the significance of the personality of Jesus and the Gospel tradition.

He argued that the idea that Jesus' actual body was raised never even occurred to the early disciples, and that the dominant Catholic belief which was carried over into Lutheranism (and which was opposed by Calvinism), that Jesus' risen body was transfigured, should now be extended to denying that Jesus' resurrection had anything to do with 'outward corporeity'. In saying this, Weisse simply carries on the tradition of Semler; he rightly cites Spinoza and Hegel in his support.[11] He has an ingenious argument that none of the early disciples seriously believed Jesus' body had been raised because none of them ever discussed whether or not he had really died, which they would have done had they supposed

[9] Christan Gottlob Wilke published his large book on Mark as the original evangelist in the same year as Weisse. See note 4 above. By 1838 Wilke had ceased to be a Lutheran pastor and he later became a Roman Catholic.

[10] *Die evangelische Geschichte*, vol. i (1938), Vorwort, pp. iii, viii.

[11] *Die evangelische Geschichte*, vol. i (1838), pp. 339 ff., especially p. 340.

he rose bodily from the grave. This will scarcely do as an
argument, since there are traditions that Pilate ensured Jesus
was dead; and, in any case, the early disciples must have been
in no doubt that by talking of resurrection they meant bodily
resurrection, for the dispute between the Pharisees and the
Sadducees turned on bodily resurrection (Acts 23.6–8). But at
least Weisse thinks he was obliged to produce arguments
based on evidence.

Weisse opposed both ecclesiastical Christianity and
rationalistic attacks on Christianity on the grounds that they
ignored the mysterious aesthetic moment in human life which
expressed itself in myths of divine revelation. His programme
for a philosophical reconstruction of Christianity was called
for in order to preserve these aesthetic moments.

In 1841 Weisse returned to the University of Leipzig as a
lecturer; he became an Associate Professor again in 1844 and
a full professor in 1845. Ten years later he published the first
volume of a three-volume *Philosophical Dogmatics*, and the
next year, 1856, a survey of current Gospel criticism. The
philosophy of the *Philosophical Dogmatics* is of little interest,
except perhaps for those would like to trace back Bultmann's
distinction between 'Historie', outward objectively observed
events, and 'Geschichte', moments of pressing present
existential import; they will find it all there, without the
spurious verbal distinction, in §§149 and 151, on the thesis
'the divine revelation is history'. The most interesting part of
the *Philosophical Dogmatics* is the close-printed section on the
Epistles of Paul. Here Weisse again shows his sure touch in
seizing on an urgent historical problem.

The problem was this. F. C. Baur had argued that only
four of the Epistles ascribed to Paul were actually written by
him: Romans, 1 and 2 Corinthians, and Galatians. Bruno
Bauer, as we shall see, went on to ask why even those should
be ascribed to Paul. Weisse recognised that there were
spiritual or aesthetically recognisable differences in tone
between various parts of the four epistles F. C. Baur regarded
as genuine, and he argued that Paul's original letters had been
combined and interpolated with other material, at first even
with Paul's approval.

This thesis of Weisse's did not exert very much influence; in fact Bruno Bauer's idea that none of the epistles was genuine enjoyed much greater popularity for a time in the 1880s. Loisy worked on similar lines to Weisse in Romans and the Corinthian correspondence, with great insight, but the whole question has been almost forgotten. Yet, on intrinsic grounds, Weisse is likely to be right, since no other Biblical documents, apart from the Epistles of Paul, are now regarded as anything but composite, made up of parts from the hands of different writers or different traditions.

Weisse's other striking thesis of these years has fared much better. He suggested that the Prologue of St John's Gospel and the discourse of Jesus in John 3.31–36 came from an independent written source. This theory has been extended to the other discourse material, most notably by Rudolf Bultmann in his great commentary on John's Gospel completed in 1941, and remains the most important advance in the study of the Fourth Gospel in modern times.

Weisse died of cholera in 1866 at the age of sixty-five, just when he was thinking of retiring from academic life to go and live in Italy.

He is a signal example of the gifted amateur who has a feel for the problem. He was right that 'experience' (his favourite term) showed the rationalistic dismissal of religion unlikely to be true, but his attempt to give a positive tone to his theodicy scarcely succeeded in carrying conviction, although he had a few disciples. His strategy was to use all the great terms like 'freedom' and 'revelation' and 'the Kingdom of God' in another sense, a spiritual and inward sense. 'Freedom' is the insistence that we feel we choose and so share divine choice, when we actually cannot choose; 'revelation' is the religious experience of a people expressed as myth; and 'the Kingdom of God' is the approaching development of the highest good in the human race.[12] It cannot be said that this strategy failed, as it remains in use today, but it is not very convincing.

[12] Philosophische Dogmatik oder Philosophie des Christenthums, vol. i (Leipzig, 1855): 'Freedom', §§654 ff.; 'Revelation', §§118 ff. *et passim*; 'The Kingdom of God', §§131 ff.

His emphasis on actual historical experience, however, made him interested in the history of ideas as expressed in ancient documents. In this field, his relaxed approach and his sense for the texture of the documents led him to make three advances in New Testament criticism: to fix the present-day solution to the Synoptic Problem; to raise the question of the nature of the Pauline Epistles; and to see the outlines of the distinctive source of the Fourth Gospel.

In this field he over-simplified, but that was the defect of his strength. He could see the wood for the trees. He divined that there should be a 'clarity and simplicity' and 'an inner probability' in hypotheses concerning living human documents.[13]

---

[13] *Die evangelische Geschichte*, vol. i (1838), Vorwort, p.v.

11

Ewald

Heinrich Ewald, like his hero Herder, came from a humble family background. He was the son of a cloth weaver and was born in 1803 at 56 Lange Geismarstrasse, Göttingen. He had typhus as a schoolboy. He was so brilliant at school and university that he qualified as a university teacher by the time he was nineteen, in a dissertation devoted not only to denying the hypothesis that Genesis was made up of a number of disconnected fragments, but also to denying the existence of parallel strands of narrative (a position he recanted before he was thirty).[1] This dissertation had been prepared while he was teaching at the Gymnasium at Wolfenbüttel. He had access to the Duke's Library, of which Lessing had been librarian, and he busied himself copying Arabic manuscripts. In 1824 J. G. Eichhorn got him an academic post in Göttingen as Repetent in the Theological Seminary. In 1825 he produced a study of the metre of Arabic poetry and in 1826 he dedicated a work on the Song of Songs, which expounded it as a dramatic poem, to Eichhorn. When Eichhorn died in 1827, Ewald became an Associate Professor to fill the gap. The chair was in the Arts Faculty not in Theology, though later in Tübingen and on his return to Göttingen he was a member of the Faculty of Theology. Nevertheless he wasn't

---

[1] *Die Komposition der Genesis kritisch untersucht* (Braunschweig, 1823). See Julius Wellhausen, 'Heinrich Ewald' in *Festschrift zur Feier des hundertfünfzigjährigen Bestehens der Königlichen Gesellschaft der Wissenschaften zu Göttingen* (Berlin, 1901), pp. 63–88; reprinted in *Julius Wellhausen: Grundrisse zum Alten Testament*, ed. Rudolf Smend (Munich, 1965), pp. 120–138. Page references to original edition. These references, pp. 65, 72.

a minister although he dressed like one, wearing a splendid white cravat of clerical cut with an elegant knot.[2]

In his twenty-third year he wrote a *Critical Grammar of Hebrew* in which he modestly but firmly claimed to have 'sought to elucidate the laws of Hebrew speech, I think not entirely in vain; there is no greater satisfaction than to see light and coherence where before it was dark'. Julius Wellhausen judged that he pretty well founded Hebrew syntax as a discipline. His gift was that of digesting all the material and arranging every part so that it appeared naturally and in its proper place. He had an amazing ability to bring order out of chaos. He found simplicity in apparent confusion, the root beneath the luxuriant growth. He was interested in *sentences* rather than words.[3] In 1830 he married the daughter of Johann Karl Friedrich Gauss, the great mathematician and natural scientist, who made Göttingen the place where the secret of the atom was to be discovered. They had one daughter, Minna. Wellhausen illustrates Ewald's childlikeness and unpretentiousness by recalling that at Minna's baptism he played ball on the grass with his father-in-law Gauss and Wilhelm Weber, the great physicist.[4]

For all his simplicity, Ewald was a formidable figure, with a quick temper and easily upset. Wellhausen, an old student and friend, was shown the door in 1870 when he refused to say Bismarck was a scoundrel. 'One visited him with great trepidation, was shy in his presence, and marvelled how his little daughter clung so trustingly to the lion.'[5]

Ewald was an outstanding teacher, having the gift of kindling enthusiasm in young students who gave themselves to him. Foreign students began to come to Göttingen for his sake, and he deeply stamped his mark on T. K. Cheyne of Oxford and the two great Scottish Old Testament scholars,

---

[2] Wellhausen, 'Heinrich Ewald', p. 72. See the photograph, Frontispiece, T. Witton Davies, *Heinrich Ewald, Orientalist & Theologian 1803–1903, A Centenary Appreciation* (London, 1903).

[3] *Kritische Grammatik der hebräischen Sprache ausführlich bearbeitet* (Leipzig, 1827). Wellhausen, 'Heinrich Ewald', p. 72.

[4] Wellhausen, 'Heinrich Ewald', pp. 80 f.

[5] Wellhausen, 'Heinrich Ewald', p. 80.

W. Robertson Smith and Adam Welch. Robertson Smith, it is true, lost his job for teaching critical views of the Old Testament, but that does not alter the fact that critical Old Testament scholarship was soon seen in Britain as building up the life of the church, and this was largely the result of Ewald's influence.

Ewald had a thin high voice, and there were long pauses between his sentences when he lectured. He preached rather than instructed, and he announced his results without giving the reasons on which they were based. His more effective teaching was done with small groups of students in his own house, where he made them translate passages of the bible in his study bare of books, under the portraits of his heroes Herder and Eichhorn.[6] His comments were masterly, but everything he said he put forward as certain and necessarily true.

This was no accidental trait. He spoke like that and taught like that because he believed the highest truth came by direct divine revelation and could only be expressed and heard in brief oracular sentences. Prophetic oracles were the originating power behind the Hebrew destiny to be the one nation that discovered true religion.

> The oracle expresses something as from God, therefore as irrefutably and beyond doubt true. What is beyond doubt true is able to compress itself, must compress itself to be as brief and pointed as possible. This means that clear and forceful brevity belongs to the nature of the oracle. The purer and more self-confident, yes the more perfect the oracle is, the more it loves and the more it attains this concise brevity of expression.[7]

Ewald had a passionate longing to restore certainty to

[6] T. K. Cheyne, 'The Life and Works of Heinrich Ewald', Inaugural Lecture, Oxford, June, 1886, reprinted in *Founders of Old Testament Criticism* (London, 1893), pp. 66–118 at p. 71; *Works* vol. iv, pp. 241–80 at pp. 244 f.

[7] Heinrich Ewald, 'Uber die kürze des Bibelwortes', *Jahrbücher der Biblischen wissenschaft*, Erstes Jahrbuch, 1848 (Göttingen, 1849), 154–60 at 157. Ewald adopted the spelling reform advocated by Jakob Grimm and did not put capital letters to nouns; *ibid.*, p. 1, note.

German Protestantism. As he looked back on the thirty-three years that had elapsed since the brief time when Germany had stirred itself and come together to resist Napoleon he saw nothing but lassitude and pitiable unmanliness. The Pope and his Jesuits were making great strides because of the indifference of Protestants, and many German courts were succumbing to their wiles.

He had always tried to awaken Germany to the danger, and in 1837, at the age of thirty-three, he suffered for his pains. When the union between England and Hannover was dissolved with the accession of a Queen to the throne of England on the 20th June that year, Ernest August, George III's fifth son, became King of Hannover. He was an extreme Tory, and immediately dissolved the liberal constitution of 1833. Ewald and six other Göttingen professors protested: W. E. Weber, the physicist already mentioned, the brothers Grimm, and the historians Gervinus and Dahlmann, who both later became members of the Frankfurt National Assembly in 1848. They were dismissed from their chairs as a result and became famous as 'The Göttingen Seven'. Ewald went on a journey to England and then returned to take up a chair at Tübingen.

In Tübingen he found fresh evidence of the decline of certainty in religion, for he saw theology in the grip of the new Tübingen school, first represented by David Friedrich Strauss and Friedrich Vischer (young men who knew nothing, who denied the beyond, and desecrated the Holy) and later led by Ferdinand Christian Baur (a new Gnostic). Ewald despised their scholarship and their lack of earnestness. But their opponents, led by the conservative Old Testament scholar Ernst Wilhelm Hengstenberg, were no better. Neither party had genuine awe, 'a deep unease of the heart seeking the truth of things-in-themselves according to their infinite height and breadth. They prefer one or two endlessly repeated scholastic catch-phrases to any more accurate knowledge.'[8]

While in Tübingen Ewald started his monumental *History*

---

[8] Ewald, *Ueber einige wissenschaftliche Erscheinungen neuester Zeit auf der Universität Tübingen* (Stuttgart, 1846), pp. 18 f.

of the People of Israel down to [and including] Christ. But he made so many enemies and was so contemptuous of the way the University was run ('Tübingen is even in danger of becoming a second Oxford' – a degree factory rather than a centre of pure and vigorous scholarship)[9] that he was glad to return to Göttingen when the adoption of a new constitution in 1847 made that possible. Early in his exile from Göttingen his wife had died, and a softening influence was removed from his life.[10]

The year he returned, 1848, was the year in which the events in Paris set off revolutions all over Europe. Ewald was disappointed at the ineffectiveness of the Frankfurt National Assembly, and proceeded to found his own journal to further the only two things which, hand in hand, could lead to a revival of Germany and of Europe: active Christianity and the scientific study of the Bible.[11]

By active Christianity he meant the sort of Christianity represented by Oliver Cromwell, a Christianity that was not confined to family life or the conscience, but concerned itself with the whole nation, that did not allow the church to swallow the state, as Hengstenberg and the conservatives wanted, not the state to swallow the church, as Hegelians preferred.[12]

By a scientific study of the Bible he meant treating the Bible as any other literature, not as 'holy scripture'. False confidence in scripture should disappear from the Evangelical Church (the Lutheran Church) and, instead, the truths which existed independently of scripture should be discovered; 'one should only count scripture as holy in order correctly to find in it its special excellences and truths, and only treasure it as holy because one applies scripture to the sanctifying of one's own life and discovers that, with scripture, nothing ever fails'.[13]

[9] Ewald, *Ueber einige wissenschaftliche Erscheinungen* (Stuttgart, 1846), p. 10.
[10] Cheyne, 'The Life and Works of Heinrich Ewald', pp. 263 f.
[11] Ewald, 'Uber den jetzigen zustand der Biblischen wissenschaft ... Absicht und entwurf dieser zeitschrift etc', *Jahrbücher der Biblischen wissenschaft*, Erstes Jahrbuch: 1848 (Göttingen, 1849), pp. 1–34.
[12] Ewald, *Ueber einige wissenschaftliche Erscheinungen* (Stuttgart, 1846), p. 20.
[13] Ewald, 'Uber die kurze des Bibelwortes', *Jahrbücher der Biblischen wissenschaft*, Erstes Jahrbuch: 1848 (Göttingen, 1849), 159 f.

The heart of true religion was the sovereignty of God: the Kingdom of God on the one hand, and men's duties on the other hand. God's kingdom revealed and men's fear react on each other to move the history of revelation forward.

> The true religion [theocracy], from the time it began to exist and to operate upon the earth, naturally always sought a higher form ... and demanded its own consummation, simply because it was not yet the perfect religion, nor had as yet appeared perfectly in even one single man. Everything that contains an immortal germ of pure eternal truth seeks, by transcending itself, to reach a higher perfection ... So theocracy in Israel always had the ineradicably firm consciousness of its own lasting duration and divine indestructability: as much at the very beginning, in the swelling longings and hopes of genuine prophecy and amidst the hosannas of the earliest establishment of theocracy, as at the high noon of its brightest splendour, when it was most mighty and powerful among its neighbours.
>
> And even from beneath the thick veil of priestocracy, theocracy still looks out into the world with a dimmed eye but a throbbing heart, in the same ever-youthful trust. Yet every longing that Jahve would some day subject the whole human world to himself as he had hitherto subjected Israel, every desire (even in the earliest times) that Israel should rule over her neighbours was a striving to consummate the divine work thus begun, and a more or less clear expression of a feeling that the very continuance of theocracy on earth could only be secured by its wider spread.[14]

The true religion of theocracy in Isreal went through three stages: original prophetic purity; monarchy; and the third

[14] *Geschichte des volkes Israel bis Christus*, vol. v: *Geschichte Christus' und seiner zeit* (2nd ed., Göttingen, 1857), pp. 72 f. Cf. *The History of Israel*, vol. vi, *The Life and Times of Christ*, translated by J. Frederick Smith (London, 1883), pp. 96 f.

debased state, priestocracy. At the end of this third period theocracy had either to be revived and made universal or perish. This Jesus saw clearly and he discovered and lived out the higher truth that the Kingdom of God was both present with him, the only man who fully and completely submitted to God's rule, and would come in the future with him, as the power that he released inevitably spread.

As soon as Jesus began to operate as the Messiah, impelled by the Baptist's acclaim and his own consciousness, he was completely free to choose his own way to the goal, unconfused by any special advice or wish of the Baptist or of any other living being – that follows from the very concept of Messiah. Now he had only One over him, in all that concerned his special calling, whose word, whose deepest meaning and slightest hint had to be to him a command: God himself. God in all his truth and glory had in particular laid this unique vocation on him; God who wanted to see the consummation of his Kingdom of true religion attained through Jesus . . .

Now the choice of the right way will itself in turn be determined only by a clear conception of what has to be attained: in this case, the Kingdom of God in its consummation. Everything depended on what conception concerning this hung as a steady picture before Jesus' spiritual eye. Indeed, the correct conception of the Kingdom had to form here nothing less than the inviolable foundation upon which all true action could begin to arise.

All the living force of Jesus' speaking and thinking about the consummated Kingdom of God turns on the inner unity and certainty of two propositions: that the Kingdom was already present on earth with himself, and that the Kingdom would come with himself. These two propositions appear at first sight irreconcilable, yet he unquestionably held fast to them both, from the very beginning of his public Messianic activity. The whole great new truth which he brought into the world lay in the inner unity of these two propositions . . .

Jesus is the first to recognize that the Kingdom of God, like every other spiritual good, can always be as easily present to any one as it is future, according to the extent to which a man relates himself to it. The most perfect Kingdom of God that is conceivable and possible would really already be present if it only actually held sway in the narrowest space on earth; and conversely, this perfect Kingdom would never come and never be able to extend itself until it was at least already present and perfectly active in the narrowest space. For then when it was really present as the perfect Kingdom it would necessarily, because of its inner glory and power, automatically extend itself further and attain its final goal. This is the creative basic idea which already includes everything else in itself: like immediately joins itself to like.

It follows that the consummated Kingdom of God can never really come except first in the narrowest space: but what is already perfectly adequate to be this narrowest space is just one single spirit, active in a weak human body. If there is only on earth just *one* in whose life the perfect true religion unfolds its complete effectiveness, so there is here given this highest conceivable conjunction of the divine and the human spirit. Then God has at least *one* on earth who is completely his own, *one* who follows only his voice in everything. And then there enters reality a perfect cooperation between man and God which will already be the full beginning of the totally true and therefore perfect Kingdom of God. Not until this beginning is livingly present, indestructible and fully active, can the outward completion of the perfect Kingdom of God follow on – and it will certainly come when, as a result of the steady progress of that action, its time is come . . .

So here everything conspired together. And even though it only then required one clear vision and sound perception for any truly enlightened man to recognize all this in its divinely ordained necessity, yet it was still only Jesus who did recognize it and who thereby laid the only correct basis for his activity as Christ.

Here we see in this brief space the complete conjunction of the creative foundational thoughts, thoughts which must have lain closely woven in Christ's spirit from the first moment of his public activity onwards, and out of which alone the whole true nature of his activity reveals itself.[15]

Ewald sees a clear line of continuity between the Old Testament and the New. The idea of the Kingdom of God was fundamental to both. True, the original purity of vision in the time of the prophets was obscured by the triumph of priestcraft, but even the threatened disappearance of the vision made it abundantly clear that there was only one way forward: a single individual had to realize the Kingdom in himself by becoming completely submissive and obedient to the word of God and his righteous will. This one man's certainty that the Kingdom was present and would eventually also come in all its fulness when everyone would do God's will would be enough to realize the Kingdom; once one man submitted, everyone would be kindled by the same spark until the whole of humanity was on fire.

Ewald had learnt this theology from Herder. By Ewald's influence the idea of 'realized eschatology' became popular as a way of interpreting Jesus' message and significance. Jesus was supposed to have taught that the Kingdom of God was present supremely in himself and that it could be present in those who were also kindled by the spirit; in this way he also looked forward to the complete coming of the Kingdom on earth.

It is clear that something strange is going on. Ewald emphasized, as no theologian since Herder or before Barth has done, the sovereignty of God. He is always talking about revelation: the oracular utterances of the prophets from above

---

[15] *Geschichte des volkes Israel bis Christus*, v. 195, 196, 202 f., 207; cf. English translation, pp. 200, 201, 206 f., 210.

and the fear of the Lord from below. Humanity from the earliest times, as the history of speech shows, was instinct with the possibility of receiving revelation, tinder waiting for the oracular spark. Once that spark falls, all is clear, certain and sure. The thing to notice in Ewald is that 'the word' is everything, and human words on both sides, the revelation side as well as the fear-of-the-Lord side. There are no miraculous deeds, as two contemporary sharp-sighted witnesses observed. Ewald 'is always talking about miracles and doesn't believe in them.'[16]

Christ, we see, is not God's gift to mankind of his Son but the role Jesus takes on himself when he sees the solution to the problem posed by his people's betrayal of the vision of the Kingdom: he must become the place of its presence. Jesus possessed 'the inner certainty of the spirit which over against the world reveals itself in its truth.'[17] That is a dark saying, but it looks as though the imminent transcendence of the spirit of the universe is being invoked rather than a living God who acts as well as speaks.

Ewald's long-term influence in retaining and strengthening a love for the Bible and an obedience to its moral demands cannot be doubted, however suspicious we may be of the means he employed. He also had two more particular effects on how the Bible was regarded, the first on how the Old Testament was read, and the second on how the Synoptic Gospels were read.

The great discovery that was made in Old Testament scholarship in Ewald's day was that the Law, the first five books of the Bible, was not the earliest part of the Bible but a relatively late collection of documents, put together under priestly influence at the time of the Babylonian exile when the loss of the Temple and the Temple religion spurred the priests to put some other means of preserving the national identity in the place of sacrifice. This discovery was the work

---

[16] Wellhausen, 'Heinrich Ewald', p. 76; R. A. Lipsius to F. C. Baur, 23 December 1858, cited by Horton Harris, *The Tübingen School* (Oxford, 1975), pp. 252–4. Lipsius's letter puts C. H. Weisse in the same boat, except that he is more honest than Ewald in openly acknowledging his rejection of the possibility of miracles.

[17] Ewald, *Die lehre vom Worte Gottes* (Leipzig, 1871), p. 139.

of de Wette and Vatke and was taken up by Wellhausen, as we shall see, to become the cornerstone of a far-reaching new interpretation of the place of the Biblical books in the long and varied history of Israel. Ewald knew about these suggestions. At first he ignored them, and then he rejected the whole theory. In Wellhausen's eyes Ewald was 'the great bar to progress'.[18]

It is true that Ewald did hinder progress and he was wrong not to acknowledge that the Babylonian exile saw the written formulation of the Law and the combination of the strands that make up the Pentateuch into our present canonical books. However, by emphasizing the apodictic declaratory form of the earliest prophetic oracles in the Law, he strikingly anticipated Albrecht Alt's conclusion in our century that this was the most primitive and distinctive form of Israelite law, which the Israelites brought with them into Canaan and eventually combined with the native Canaanite casuistic law. Ewald was wrong on one point, but he rightly hung on to an insight which it took over fifty years to rediscover and establish again as an important feature of Israel's earliest religion.[19]

Ewald's second contribution to scholarship was to exercise a decisive influence in establishing the now generally accepted view of the Synoptic Problem. In the journal he began to publish on his return to Göttingen from Tübingen he printed what he claimed to be a new theory, that Mark and a Sayings Collection were the two sources used by Matthew and Luke. It was Ewald's article and book on the subject that helped one of the ablest and most influential members of the Tübingen School, Albrecht Ritschl, to abandon the theory that Mark's Gospel was an epitome of Matthew and Luke.[20]

Ewald claimed to be original, but was he? We have seen

---

[18] Wellhausen, 'Heinrich Ewald', pp. 73 f.

[19] Albrecht Alt, *Die Ursprünge des Israelitischen Rechts* (Leipzig, 1934), translated by R. A. Wilson in *Essays on Old Testament History and Religion* (Oxford, 1966), pp. 79–132.

[20] Ritschl to his father, 24 January, 1851, cited in Horton Harris, *The Tübingen School* (Oxford, 1975), p. 228; Ritschl, *Tübinger Theologische Jahrbücher* (1851), 480 ff. referred to by Wellhausen, 'Heinrich Ewald', p. 76.

that Weisse put forward a similar view in 1838, but Ewald
did not derive his theory from Weisse, whose work on the
Synoptic Problem he did not read until the end of 1855.[21]
Not did it come from Wilke or Lachmann, since Wilke lacks
the idea that a sayings-source lay behind Matthew's Gospel
and Mark's Gospel, and Lachmann is solely concerned with
the argument from order, which plays little part in Ewald's
theory. Ewald honestly believed that his theory simply
corresponded to the obvious truth of the matter when
examined with a pure moral scientific earnestness, but a man
who keeps his books in another room from his study is not
thereby saved from dependence on books. A comparison
between Ewald's theory of the history of the formation of
our Gospels and Herder's theory makes it fairly plain that
Ewald's leading ideas came straight from Herder.[22] [See
Appendix].

Deeply influential though Ewald's ideas were among
scholars, on one point his German admirers refused to follow
him. For Ewald the Bible was the source of a moral revelation
that had political consequences, and few of Ewald's successors
in University teaching, with the honourable exception of
Harnack, took any interest or part in politics; to most it was
unthinkable that a cultured German should have a political
position.

Ewald was always politically active as his protest against
the suspension of the Hannoverian constitution has already
shown. The older he grew, the more his interest and activity
increased, in church politics as well as state politics. In 1862
he played a leading part in the reform of the Hannoverian
Church, and in 1863 he was one of the founders of the
Protestant Union. The aims of the Union were to oppose the
power of State consistories and to foster congregational

[21] Ewald, review of Ch.H. Weisse, *Die Evangelienfrage* (1856) in *Jahrbücher der Biblischen wissenschaft*, Achtes Jahrbuch: 1856 (Göttingen, 1857), 186–191 at 187.

[22] Ewald, 'Ursprung und wesen der Evangelien' especially the sections 'Die anfänge des Evangelischen schriftthumes' and 'Die weite ausbildung des Evangelischen schriftthumes', *Jahrbücher der Biblischen wissenschaft*, Zweites Jahrbuch: 1849 (Göttingen, 1850), 190–224. Herder, *Regel der Zusammenstimmung unsrer Evangelien, aus ihrer Entstehung und Ordnung* (1797), Suphan xix. 380–424.

freedom, to welcome the results of modern Biblical research, to oppose materialism and any anarchy from either above or below, to work for the completion of the Reformation by helping German Catholics to break with the Pope, and to promote an organic union of the individual state churches as well as mutual recognition between different confessional bodies.[23]

In 1866 the Kingdom of Hannover was forcibly incorporated into the Kingdom of Prussia. Ewald protested and refused to swear an oath to the King of Prussia. He could no longer go to public worship because he would not join in public prayer for the King of Prussia. He had to pay for his stand by being expelled from the Theological Faculty, though he could still teach and draw his salary. But then he went further and wrote a fierce pamphlet against the Prussian policy of annexing German-speaking territories that had no desire to become part of the Prussian State – first Schleswig-Holstein, and shortly Alsace-Lorraine. He wrote, 'if Prussia persists, nothing but evil can ensue, and eventually the total disintegration of Germany. The ancient peoples felt, and rightly, that every serious transgression for which the people did not atone must be effaced like a blood stain with the greatest awe and care. The unatoned guilt of Germany created the indescribable misery in which we find ourselves today. If this misery is not righted and if this transgression is not atoned for, then the German Reich and the German people must perish'.[24] This pamphlet led the government to withdraw his salary and his right to teach. He was sixty-four.

Ewald became a member for Hannover of the North German Reichstag and then of the German Reichstag, ironically as an ally of the conservative churchmen he had previously attacked.

In 1874 at the age of seventy-one he was put in prison for three weeks for comparing Bismarck to Frederick II in having

---

[23] The constitution is quoted in Ewald, 'Der Deutsche Protestantenverein', *Jahrbücher der Biblischen wissenschaft*, Zwolftes Jahrbuch: 1861–1865, Erste hälfte (Göttingen, 1865), 124–143 at 129–131.

[24] Ewald, *Lob des Königs und des Volkes* (1968), cited by Hans Kohn, *The Mind of Germany: The Education of a Nation* (1960, reprinted with corrections 1962, London), p. 179.

waged an unrighteous war against Austria, and to Napoleon III for 'picking out the best possible time for robbery and plunder'.[25] He died on the 4 May 1875.

There was a large funeral, but no one in Germany preached a memorial sermon to Ewald, only Dean Stanley in England.[26]

Appendix

Herder	*Ewald*
I A Common Gospel, Aramaic, orally transmitted.	I The Oldest Gospel, Hebrew (Philip the author?).
II The Gospel of the Hebrews, to prove Jesus' Messiahship, Hebrew. Known by translation in our Matthew and, more freely, in our Luke.	II The Sayings-Collection, Matthew's 'logia', at first in Hebrew.
III The Gospel of Mark, probably the first Greek Gospel, follows I, with a few explanations for foreigners.	III The Gospel of Mark, the first account of the whole life and work of Christ, originally shorter than our Mark; as used by our Matthew and, slightly longer, by our Luke.
	IV The Book of the Higher History based on I but including the Temptations and some spiritual history as found in Matthew and Luke.

[25] Kohn, *The Mind of Germany*, p. 179.
[26] 'Professor Wellhausen ... told me that Dean Stanley was the only man he knew of who preached a memorial sermon for Ewald after his passing away.' T. Witton Davies, *Heinrich Ewald* (London, 1903), p. 66.

IV Our Luke, the first Christ-history, for Hellenists, by a companion of Paul, spurred into writing by Mark's Gospel, using II and III.

V Our Matthew, used I–IV, especially II and III, plus an Infancy Narrative, written before the Fall of Jerusalem.

VI Three later works,
VII found mainly in Luke
VIII (VIII is Luke's Infancy Narrative).

V Our Matthew, free Greek translation of II with omissions and probably additions, after the Fall of Jerusalem.

IX Our Luke, by a companion of Paul.

VI Our John, written by an Apostle who thought Hebrew and wrote Greek, long after the others, at the end of the century.

X Our John, quite different from the rest, written by the Apostle John somewhere between AD80–90.

12

Bruno Bauer

Bruno Bauer was the son of an artist, and himself a great artist with words. His father was a skilled porcelain painter who moved with his family from Eisenberg near Weimar to Berlin-Charlottenberg when Bruno, born 1809, was five years old. Bruno's mother was daughter of a Judge Avocate General in an Infantry Regiment. Bruno said of his family background, 'I honour my mother that I was born in beautiful wooded Thuringia; I value it as good fortune that through the migration of my father I came to the hot sand, the keen wind off the steppes of Mark Brandenburg, and the cruel history of Prussia; above all I am proud of my Saxon blood, the source of my freedom and my independence'.[1]

Bruno Bauer received an excellent education, first at the Charlottenberg school, and then at the Friedrich-Wilhelm-Gymnasium in Berlin. He went to the university in 1828 to study theology. He was 19. He fell completely under the spell of Hegel. All this religious doubts vanished in peace and certainty. 'He seemed to dispense the simple truth in such a way that I thought I heard nothing new, but simply the explanation of those things the knowledge of which is inborn in everybody. How great was this man's simplicity and disinterestedness in discovering the truth, how sacred his

---

[1] A reminiscence of 1858 quoted by E. Schläger, *Internationale Monatsschrift. Zeitschrift für allgemeine und nationale Kultur und deren Literatur*, i (Chemnitz, 1882), 387 f.; cited by Ernst Barnikol, *Bruno Bauer: Studien und Materialien, aus dem Nachlass ausgewählt und zusammengestellt von Peter Reimer und Hans-Martin Sass* (Assen, 1972), p. 6 note 1.

indignation when he told how the pillars of the church were broken down by the very people who were appointed teachers and shepherds of the church, and how great was the passion of his spirit when he showed how the moderns had no wish either to despise or deny the dogmas, and when he displayed their eternal truth.'[2]

Hegel died at the beginning of Bauer's last year at the university. From 1832 to 1834 he worked on a dissertation under Marheineke, the right-wing Hegelian theologian, and Schleiermacher's death in 1834 left the way open for him to receive his licence to teach. In 1836 he started his own theological journal, the *Journal for Speculative Theology*, to which all the leading Hegelians contributed (except Strauss). Strauss wouldn't join the board because Bauer attacked his *Life of Jesus*, and showed that the miracles were all necessary, from the Virgin Birth onwards. In his last semester as a lecturer in Berlin, the Summer Semester of 1839, Karl Marx heard him lecture on Isaiah; they were already fast friends. He was twenty-nine and Marx twenty-one.

Bauer was working on a new edition of Hegel's lectures on the Philosophy of Religion. The new edition was made necessary by the coming to light of good notes of the first set of lectures in 1821 (in addition to the notes of 1824, 1827 and 1831 previously used) and of Hegel's own preparatory manuscript.[3] Bauer had already seen that Hegel's system was basically pantheistic, and in an early article had coolly accused both the rationalists and the supranaturalists of being pantheistic themselves, though that was the charge they levelled against Hegel. The rationalists did not realise that Kant's God, who was only a *theoretical* object, was a dead God about whom they had dead thoughts – pantheism. The supranaturalists preached a God who was not accessible to reason and, since the relation of the human spirit to the divine spirit was immanent, they too were pantheists. Both parties should recognise they shared in the guilt of modern

---

[2] Bauer's *curriculum vitae*, 9 November, 1839, when applying for a lectureship at Bonn; cited by Ernst Barnikol, *Bruno Bauer*, pp. 515–8 at p. 516 f.

[3] Barnikol, *Bruno Bauer*, pp. 193 ff.

consciousness; only when they confessed their guilt would the guilt be overcome.[4]

Bauer was still a right-wing Hegelian in Berlin, a Privatdozent in search of a more permanent post. He planned a 3- volume *Critique of the History of Revelation* and produced the first 2 volumes, *The Religion of the Old Testament in the Historical Development of its Principles*, in 1838. He also wrote a bitter brilliant attack on E. W. Hengstenberg's book on the authenticity of the Pentateuch. Hengstenberg lacked method and was an opportunist gathering arguments from all the ends of the earth.[5] In 1839 Bauer went to Bonn as a privatdozent, with the possibility of a chair. There, in peace, he finally broke with Christianity.

The more he studied Hegel the more clearly he saw that Hegel, for all his high-sounding defence of the orthodox doctrines of the Christian faith which he defended against people like Schleiermacher, was actually an atheist, in that he did not believe in a God who created the universe and was independent of the universe.

Bauer, as he came to see the truth about Hegel, which was for him simply the truth, took in hand the writing of a Hegelian history of the process of reflexion by which the human spirit produced Christianity. He started from the latest of the four Gospels, the Gospel of John, and argued that this Gospel was not an historical account at all but an expression of the developed faith of the church. This theme of Bauer's was taken up by F. C. Baur in 1844 and became very quickly the ruling orthodoxy, despite the rearguard action of people like Ewald.

Here is Bauer's comment on John 1.29, John the Baptist's words to his followers about Jesus, 'Behold the Lamb of God, who takes away the sin of the world.' Bauer begins by laughing at the commentators who 'explain' John the Baptist's words on the basis of a conjecture that, at the moment John saw Jesus, he also happened to see some lambs being driven up to Jerusalem for use in the Passover sacrifices.

---

[4] Bruno Bauer, 'Der Pantheismus innerhalb des Rationalismus und Supranaturalismus', *Zeitschrift für spekulative Theologie*, i (Berlin, 1836), 267–276.

[5] Joachim Mehlhausen, *Dialektik, Selbstbewusstsein und Offenbarung: Die Grundlagen der spekulativen Orthodoxie Bruno Bauers in ihrem Zusammenhang mit der Geschichte der theologischen Hegelschule* (Bonn, 1965), p. 74.

Thousands of Paschal Lambs could have been driven past the eyes of the Baptist and his companions, but it would have been impossible either for him to call Jesus the Lamb of God in this typical sense, or for his companions to understand him, unless there were belief that the Messiah was to suffer sacrificial death for the sins of the world. Since this popular belief was not present, the Baptist could not have spoken in terms of this belief nor, had he so spoken, could he have been understood by his companions; so there remains only one basis upon which this belief could have arisen: the Christian church's perception.

This church was first led to that typical description of the Messiah through the coincidence of the death of Christ with the Feast of the Passover; she was also able to bring the prophecy (fulfilled in the Lord) of the suffering servant who bears the sin of the world into connection with the typical description: in short, only under these historical conditions could such a formula have been constructed and been immediately understood the moment it existed, a formula that gathered up in the image of the Paschal Lamb the self-sacrificing love of the Saviour and that love's manifestations as they reach their highest pitch.

The Baptist bears witness to Christ like a Christian who has been redeemed by the sacrificial death of the Saviour. The Evangelist does not know how to make any distinction between unbelief and complete belief, and can allow the forerunner to bear witness in no other way than as one to whom he attributes the developed perception of the later church.[6]

This is brilliantly done, and in fact most commentators today accept that no Jewish theology of a Messiah who dies as the Lamb of God to bear the sins of the world was to hand. Most commentators accordingly ascribe the theology not to John the Baptist but to the creative work of the church. I myself have tried to show that in fact there did

[6] *Kritik der evangelischen Geschichte des Johannes* (Bremen, 1840), pp. 31 f.

exist a well-worked-out Jewish theology of the Messiah as the Lamb of God bearing the sins of the world. The evidence is to be found in the Testament of the Twelve Patriarchs, a collection of documents published in the thirteenth century by Bishop Grosseteste as a genuine Jewish writing, but condemned by post-Reformation scholars as a Christian forgery. Had Bauer deigned to mention it, as he mentioned other Jewish writings from the period between the Old and New Testaments in his long excursus to volume i of his Synoptic commentary, he would no doubt have condemned the references to Christian themes as Christian interpolations. That is still today the standard way of treating these alleged forerunners of a suffering Messiah who would die for the sins of the world.[7] In this case I think the evidence runs the other way, but clearly Bauer's position is not to be despised. Here, as on so many other questions, his bold radical hypotheses have slowly come to be accepted as platitudes by scholars who pride themselves on being modern supporters of the Christian faith.

In 1841 and 1842 Bauer (in cahoots with Karl Marx) produced two brilliant pamphlets anonymously, which announced their discoveries about Hegel to the world. The pamphlets took the form of cries of outrage from a pious Lutheran pastor, the tone of which is nicely conveyed in their titles: *The Trumpet of the Last Judgment against Hegel the Atheist & Antichrist: An Ultimatum*, and *Hegel's Teaching about Religion & Art Judged from the Standpoint of Faith*.[8] The aim of these books was to carry through what Bauer saw as Hegel's true intention. The horrible kernel of Hegel's system, according to the pretended outraged pastor, is the perception

---

[7] Bauer's discussion of alleged Jewish antecedents to Christian themes, appendix to volume i of *Kritik der evangelischen Geschichte der Synoptiker* (Leipzig, 1841), pp. 391–416: 'Die messianischen Erwartungen der Juden zur Zeit Jesu'. My article on 'The Lamb of God in the Testaments of the Twelve Patriarchs' is in *Journal for the Study of the New Testament*, Issue 2 (January, 1979), 2–30.

[8] *Die Posaune des jüngsten Gerichts über Hegel den Atheisten und Antichristen. Ein Ultimatem* (Leipzig, 1841, reprinted Aalen, 1969); *Hegel's Lehre von der Religion und Kunst von dem Standpuncte des Glaubens aus beurtheilt* (Leipzig, 1842).

of the religious relationship as nothing but the inner relationship of self-consciousness to itself.

> The man who has tasted this kernel is dead to God because he holds God for dead; the man who eats this kernel is fallen further than Eve when she ate the apple and Adam was led astray by her; for Adam hoped to become like God, but the adherent of Hegel's system lacks even that pride – sinful though it be. He no longer wants to be like God; he wants only to be I – I; he wants only to attain and enjoy the blasphemous eternity, freedom, and self-satisfaction of self-consciousness. This philosophy wants no God, not even gods like the heathen; this philosophy wants only men, only self-consciousness; everything for it is nothing but self-consciousness.[9]

The I has made a mirror image of itself and for thousands of years worshipped this image of God. 'The wrath of God and his chastising righteousness is nothing but the I clenching its own fist and threatening itself in the mirror; the grace and mercy of God is again nothing but that I offering its hand to its image in the mirror.'[10]

Bauer worked out this theme in his brilliant commentary on the Synoptic Gospels. Strauss had shown that the Gospels were the product of a tradition, but had left the nature of the tradition mysterious, attributing everything in the Gospels to the result of reflection on the Old Testament. Weisse had shown that this was not likely (at least in the Birth Narratives), and he had also shown that Mark was the earliest Gospel and that Mark, together with a sayings-source, was used by Matthew and Luke. Wilke, at the same time, made the brilliant remark that Mark was 'an artistic composition'.[11] The task of Gospel criticism was now to show how not just the form of Mark was an artistic composition, but also its

---

[9] *Die Posaune des jüngsten Gerichts*, pp. 48 f.

[10] *Die Posaune des jüngsten Gerichts*, p. 148.

[11] C. G. Wilke, *Der Urevangelist* (Dresden and Leipzig, 1838), pp. 671, 684, cited by Bauer, *Kritik der evangelischen Geschichte der Synoptiker*, vol. i (Leipzig, 1841), Vorrede of March 1841, p.xiii.

content.[12] The earliest written Gospel was the creation of the human spirit come to self-consciousness.

Take Jesus' entry into Jerusalem as an example. The whole thing would have been ridiculous, as Calvin saw, were it not a reference to Zechariah 9.9: 'Rejoice greatly, O daughter of Zion; shout, O daughter of Jerusalem: behold, thy King cometh unto thee: he is just, and having salvation; lowly, and riding upon an ass, and upon a colt the foal of an ass.' But, as Calvin also pointed out, Jesus' contemporaries would not have understood the reference (because they were not looking for a Messiah, says Bauer). Calvin said Jesus was thinking ahead to the needs of later Christians. 'We must rather say, This story first happend there where it was first understood: in the later church, in Mark's head.'[13]

Bauer's decisive move was to assert that there did not exist a Jewish christology to produce the Gospels, as Strauss had assumed. Christianity, for all its dependence on the Old Testament, was a decisive break with the folk-spirit of Judaism. In Christianity the I reigned supreme and alone.

Both Strauss's Tradition Hypothesis and the earlier orthodox views of the origins of Christianity

> asserted that the Jews at the time Jesus appeared had not only long expected 'The Messiah' but had constructed a complete christology – which must certainly have been the case on the assumption they were expecting the Messiah ... Historical criticism consistently carried through comes at last to the point where it pronounces on the death and life of this hypothesis, and where its final fate is decided. It can be proved that before Jesus' appearing and before the development of the church the reflective idea of 'The Messiah' did not hold sway, that consequently there was no Jewish christology which the Gospel christology could have copied. This is the sentence that first emancipates Biblical criticism, breaks down the bridges, and burns the ships which maintained

[12] Bauer, *Kritik der evangelischen Geschichte der Synoptiker*, vol. i, pp. xvi f.

[13] *Kritik der evangelischen Geschichte der Synoptiker und des Johannes*, 3rd and final volume (Braunschweig, 1842), p. 108.

its communication with the earlier orthodox point of view. This is the sentence that deprives Biblical criticism of the last hold it had on unrecognized positivity; this sentence transposes it into the free element of self-consciousness, to which alone it now must hold fast, and in which it has to orientate itself. With this sentence Biblical criticism and its subject-matter is led back into its true and proper homeland. The fasting-cure will have worked.[14]

Bauer has still not decided whether or not Jesus actually existed and can write: 'Jesus, if he really existed . . .'[15]

At the end of volume III Bauer wrote a magnificent polemical passage which laid down the lines of his future literary work.

He had set himself to unmask theology by showing it as the last necessary stage of suffering the self-consciousness had to go through before it could itself rebuild nature and art, family, the people and the state on the basis of its terrible self-knowledge alone. He saw history as a series of stages in which the I of self-consciousness made its self-alienation bearable by various religious devices. The religions of antiquity enchained the human spirit, but the chains were decked with flowers. Christianity had to arise so that the I could realize its universal scope, not tied to one nation or people. This I, conscious of its universal power, could not bear this knowledge, and so had to objectify itself; it did so by creating Christ. Christianity thus became the worst alienation the I had yet suffered. Now, in the nineteenth century, the I was at last thoroughly conscious that it was the only power in the universe; it could throw off Christianity, if necessary in battle, and begin to create humanity in total freedom.

---

[14] *Kritik der evangelischen Geschichte der Synoptiker*, vol. i (Leipzig, 1841), pp.xvii f.

[15] See Albert Schweitzer's judgment in his brilliant chapter on Bruno Bauer in *Von Reimarus zu Wrede*. 'If a man of the name of Jesus has existed' . . . *Kritik der evangelischen Geschichte der Synoptiker und des Johannes*, (Braunschweig, 1842), pp. 314 f.

The result of our criticism, which states that the Christian religion is the abstract religion, is the disclosure of the mystery of Christianity. The religions of antiquity had as their principal powers nature, the family-spirit, and the folk-spirit. The world-rule of Rome and philosophy represented the stirrings of a universal power which sought to raise itself above the limits of the hitherto existing life of nature and folk-life and to become their lord — lord of humanity and of self-consciousness. This triumph of freedom and humanity for the universal consciousness . . . could not yet be adduced in the form of free self-consciousness and pure theory because religion was still a universal power, and it was first necessary that the universal revolution inside religion itself should occur . . . In the religions of antiquity, the essential interests hide and disguise the depth and the horror of the alienation. The intuition of nature enchants, the family bond has a sweet charm, folk-concerns give the religious spirit a burning zeal for the powers of its worship: the chains that the human spirit wore in the service of these religions were decorated with flowers; like a sacrificial animal bravely and festively arrayed, man offered himself as a sacrifice to his religious powers; his chains themselves deceived him over the hardness of his service.

As the flowers faded in the course of history, the chains were broken by Roman might; the vampire of intellectual abstraction finished the work. Sap and strength, blood and life did this vampire drain out of humanity, right to the last drop. Nature and art, family, people and state were sucked dry, and on the ruins of the submerged world remained over the impoverished I by itself: a power, but the only power. After the immense loss, the I itself could not yet immediately recreate nature and art, people and state out of its own depth and universality; the great and terrible thing that now come to pass, the only deed that it was busy with, was rather the absorption of everything that had hitherto lived in the world. It was now everything, this I — and yet it was empty. It had now become the universal power, and yet it had to be appalled before itself on the ruins of the world, and to despair at the loss. The empty all-devouring I was dismayed at itself. It did not dare to conceive of itself as 'the all' and as the universal power – that is, it still remained the religious spirit and completed its alienation in that it confronted its universal power as something strange to itself, and in the face of this power worked for its own preservation and blessedness in fear and trembling. It saw the surety for its preservation in the Messiah who only represented to it the same thing that it itself basically was, namely itself as the universal power. This universal power was just what the I was, the power in which were swallowed up all perception of nature, the customary rules of family-spirit and folk-spirit and state life, as well as all perception of art.

The historical starting point for this revolution was given in Jewish folk life, because not only were nature and art already completely strangled in Jewish religious consciousness . . . but the folk-spirit in the most varied forms . . . had already had to enter into a dialectic with the idea of a highter universality. The defect in this dialectic lay only in the fact that at its end the folk-spirit yet again made itself the centre of the universe. Christianity removed this defect by making the pure I universal. The Gospels carried out this transformation in their own way, that is by the way they presented history: although entirely dependent on the Old Testament and little else than a copy of it, they have allowed the power of the folk-spirit to be consumed by the almighty power of the pure unadulterated I that is yet alienated from true humanity.

If we look at the Gospels in this way . . . we must be absolutely astonished that humanity could be busied with them for all the eighteen centuries – and so be busied with them that their secret was not discovered. For in none of them, not even in the smallest paragraph, are there lacking notions which injure, offend, and revolt humanity . . .

Did humanity have to torment itself for a millennium and a half with such things? Yes, she had to, since the great immense step could only be taken after such torments and exertions, if it were no longer to be taken in vain, and if it were to be valued for its true meaning and importance. Self consciousness had to do with *itself* in the Gospels – even if with itself in its alienation; indeed, with a fearful parody of itself; yet with itself. That is why the magic spell humanity adopted put her in chains and, so long as she had not yet found herself, forced her to give up everything in order to preserve her own image of herself; yes, to prefer it to all other and to count all other as dung in comparison with it, as the Apostle did [Philippians 3.8]. Mankind was brought up in bondage to her own image so that she would prepare for freedom all the more thoroughly and would embrace freedom more inwardly and more fiercely when it was at last won. The deepest and most terrible alienation had to mediate the freedom that was to be won for all time – to mediate it, to prepare it and to make it valued, perhaps even make it valued also because of the battle that slavery and stupidity would mount against it. Odysseus has returned to his home, but not by favour of the gods; not asleep but awake; thinking, and in his own strength. Perhaps he will also have to battle with the suitors who have squandered his own possessions and who want to withhold from him his dearest one. Yet Odysseus still knows how to bend the bow . . .

And then a few pages later:

The historical Christ is the man whom religious consciousness has raised into heaven, that is, the man who then, when he comes down to earth to do miracles, to teach and to suffer, is no longer a true man. The Son of Man of religion in his very role as Reconciler is man alienated from himself. He is not like a man, does not live like a man in human relationships, and does not die like a man. This historical Christ, the 'I' ascended into heaven, the 'I' that has become God has overthrown antiquity, and defeated the world by sucking it dry. It has fulfilled its historical destiny when, by the immense disorder into which it has thrown the true Spirit, it has compelled this Spirit to recognise itself and to become conscious of itself with a thoroughness and a decisiveness of which naive antiquity was not capable.[16]

In 1842, Bauer's right to teach was withdrawn by the Ministry in Berlin, for now that the Minister Karl, Baron von Stein zum Altenstein, who had appointed and supported Hegel was dead (May, 1840) and Friedrich Wilhelm III had been succeeded by Wilhelm IV (June, 1840) there was little hope that a blatantly atheist theologian would be allowed to continue teaching in any of the Prussian universities. He was thirty-two.

He had already begun to work on the French Revolution and the eighteenth century before his dismissal, and by 1843 he was able to publish the first volume of a *History of the Politics, Culture and Enlightenment of the Eighteenth Century* which was published by his brother, after great difficulties with the censor, in the years 1843–5. Bruno Bauer argued, among other things, that pietism was the forerunner of secularism and that the music of Bach and Handel transformed the entire stuff of religious feeling: architecture and painting had already freed hand and eye, and now music freed voice and hearing, and there occurred the first cry of jubilation of humanity for its rewon freedom.[17]

The Enlightenment was not the beginning of a new age, but the culmination of the old system. The chief dogma of the Enlightenment was universal and everlasting immaturity. One blow put an end to it, the French

---

[16] *Kritik der evangelischen Geschichte der Synoptiker und des Johannes*, vol. iii (Braunschweig, 1842), pp. 309–312, 313 f.

[17] Bruno Bauer, *Geschichte der Politik, Cultur und Aufklärung des achtzehnten Jahrhunderts. Erster Band: Deutschland während der ersten vierzig Jahre des achtzehnten Jahrhunderts* (Charlottenberg, 1843: Verlag von Egbert Bauer), Pietism, §§ 10–12; Bach and Handel, § 21, especially p. 320.

Revolution.[18] In reaction to the French Revolution England made the pure egoism of nationality and privilege triumph, but the triumph would be temporary. Germany, a country without a united people and without a society, laid the foundation of the perfect theory of human life in the philosophy of Hegel: it was Germany's destiny to perfect that theory. Purity of theory would be happy and salvific because unspotted by egoism.[19]

As far as I can see, Bruno Bauer is talking about the end of human alienation and the triumph of communism, like his friend Karl Marx, but a triumph of a conservative version of communism, brought about not by the dictatorship of the proletariat but by Prussian might – a might all the more terrifying for being disinterested. Both Marx and Bauer are driven by a strictly atheist vision of future revolution when man's alienation from himself will be finally and perfectly reversed.

Marx criticised Bauer as the critical critic who appropriated criticism as his own private possession. He wrote of his friend Bauer: 'The religious saviour of the world is finally realised in the critical saviour of the world, Herr Bauer'.[20] Bruno Bauer was, by all accounts, a far nicer person than Karl Marx, but niceness is not the issue. Each must be held responsible, I think, for the consequences of their own ideas, and each, it seems, provoked a triumph of the egoism they thought they had risen above. The triumph of Prussia and the triumph of communism are both terrible.

In 1850–52 Bauer finished his analysis of the New Testament with a book on Acts and a three-part work on the Epistles of Paul.

F. C. Baur had taken up the theories of Karl Schrader

---

[18] *Geschichte der Politik, Cultur und Aufklärung des achtzehnten Jahrhunderts.* Fortsetzung, Erste Abtheilung (1844), pp. 6 f.

[19] *Geschichte der Politik, Cultur und Aufklärung des achtzehnten Jahrhunderts.* Erster Band (1843), p.xii.

[20] Karl Marx, *Die heilige Familie, oder Kritik der kritischen Kritik: Gegen Bruno Bauer und Consorten* (Frankfurt, 1845), pp. 226 f.; cited in Joachim Mehlhausen, *Dialektik, Selbstbewusstsein und Offenbarung* (Bonn, 1965), pp. 439 f.

(1836) and argued that Acts was an irenic attempt to make Paul appear as Petrine and Peter as Pauline as possible.[21] Bruno Bauer argued, with a much sharper insight, that 'when Acts was written the tensions of parties had collapsed, the opposition was veiled, the difference was obliterated and peace had already been concluded. The Acts is not a proposal of peace, but the expression and consummation of peace and toleration'.[22]

In this book appears Bauer's thesis about the Judaism of his own time which he was to work out in a series of antisemitic articles for Herrmann Wagener's 23-volume conservative encyclopedia *Staats- und Gesellschafts-Lexikon* (Berlin 1859–1867), which Bauer himself largely edited.[23] The Judaism which he argued had taken over the church and fastened the church to the Jewish world was not the Jewish Christianity F. C. Baur and the Tübingen School were talking about, but a Judaism which fully accepted the freedom of Gentile Christians and the universality of the church. 'We mean by Judaism the conservative, conciliatory, anti-revolutionary spirit which, at the same time, conserves the gains of the revolution.'[24]

Bauer's estimate of Acts has now become a commonplace, and may be said to have advanced the study of Acts; the tragedy was that his attacks on what he called 'Judaism' as 'a power that has asserted its supremacy, even though in changing forms, down to our own time'[25] gained wide popular currency in Wagener's *Staats-Lexikon* and fed antisemitism by the thesis that 'Judaism' was working against the coming revolution when humanity would attain its freedom.

[21] Karl Schrader, *Der Apostel Paulus* (1836); F. C. Baur, 'Über den Ursprung des Episcopats in der christlichen Kirche', *Tübinger Zeitschrift für Theologie* (1838) Heft III, 1–185 at pp. 142 ff; see A. C. McGiffert, 'The Historical Criticism of Acts in Germany' in F. J. Foakes Jackson & Kirsopp Lake, *The Beginnings of Christianity. Part I: The Acts of the Apostles*, vol, ii (London, 1922), pp. 363–395.

[22] Bruno Bauer, *Die Apostelgeschichte, eine Ausgleichung des Paulinismus und des Judenthums innherhalb der christlichen Kirche* (Berlin, 1850), cited by McGiffert.

[23] Barnikol, *Bruno Bauer: Studien und Materialien* (Assen, 1972), p. 395.

[24] Bruno Bauer, *Die Apostelgeschichte* (1850), p. 12.; cited by McGiffert, p. 379.

[25] Bruno Bauer, *Die Apostelgeschichte*, p. 123.

Bauer's *Criticism of the Pauline Epistles* argued that none of the books attributed to Paul in the New Testament could have been written by him. They are all fictions written in the second century, and the question is which parts were written before Acts and which after. Bauer's shrewdest point is that Galatians 1.13, for example, speaks of 'Judaism' as though it were a closed, antiquated, foreign world, and 'Judaism' had not become that in relation to 'Christianity' until long after the time of the historical Paul.[26]

Bauer's thesis was revived by some Dutch scholars in the 1880s and most fully by a Swiss scholar, Rudolf Steck (1842–1924), but is now all but forgotten. Christian Hermann Weisse took the charge seriously a few years after Bauer's book appeared, and argued that not all of the four chief epistles of Paul (Romans, 1 & 2 Corinthians, Galatians) could have come from his pen, and that thesis of Weisse's, like his theory about the origin of the discourses in St John's Gospel, seems to me to be a signal advance.

In 1852 Bauer published another work on the Gospels, which as far as I can see merely elaborated his general position as outlined in the foreword to *Criticism of the Gospel History of the Synoptics* in 1842. All New Testament documents have now been firmly planted in the second century. A late work, *Christ and the Caesars: The Origin of Christianity from Roman Hellenism* alleges that Christianity was really the creation of the Roman emperors and the philosophy of the Stoic Seneca. Christianity got its spirit from Graeco-Roman civilization and its bones from Judaism.[27]

Bruno Bauer's eccentricities should not blind us to how typical a figure he was. He expressed views that are now generally accepted, but in a fierce, extreme and unbalanced way; yet he stood where his contemporaries and successors

[26] Bruno Bauer, *Kritik der paulinischen Briefe*, Erste Abtheilung: *Der Ursprung des Galaterbriefs* (Berlin, 1850); Zweite Abtheilung: *Der Ursprung des ersten Korintherbriefes* (1851); Dritte und letzte Abtheilung (2 Corinthians, Romans, the Pastorals, 1&2 Thessalonians, Ephesians and Colossians, Philippians) (1852); reprinted (Aalen 1972); these references vol. i, pp. 4, 14.

[27] *Christus und die Caesaren: Der Ursprung des Christenthums aus dem römischen Griechenthum* (Berlin, 1877).

stand. He established firmly the view that John's Gospel was a work of theological reflection; he accepted the priority of Mark among the Synoptics, but established that Mark, too, was a theological book, and that every paragraph preached a theology; above all, he drove deep the point that, although Christianity copied Jewish ideas, it was quite distinct from Judaism. These are all simplifications, and they are all in my view questionable, but they have become the generally accepted assumptions of most subsequent New Testament scholarship.

Bruno Bauer is a great historian of ideas; above all, he is a master of the small portrait, with a sharp eye for detail and a gift for hitting off character. But he is always trying to see significant patterns in history, and too often his patterns run out into absurdity and, in the case of his antisemitism, into fatefully dangerous absurdity. The brilliant Semler biography he wrote for the *Lexikon* was reissued as part of a book called *Influence of English Quakerism on German Culture and on the English-Russian Project for a World Church* (Berlin, 1878). Bauer thought he himself was the I that reached full self-consciousness and could discern the future of the world – and look what he thought he saw: a British plot to bring together the Church of England and the Orthodox church to form an alliance between Britain and Russia to destroy Germany. And yet, on the way, he has argued an important historical thesis, that Quakerism from England took over German theological scholarship. That seems to me a true thesis, and accounts for the general inability of modern New Testament scholars to recognise hierarchy, order and dogma in the New Testament, even when it stares them in the face. We have become crypto-Quakers.

Bruno Bauer and Karl Marx were both of them humble and disinterested egoists, and each helped spawn his own historical monster: beasts that kill and destroy in the name of disinterested theory. To 'Das gottgewordene Ich' cruelty became a duty, on the ground of strict theory and principle.

Bauer boasted – rightly boasted – that he had rescued the true authority of the Bible from the Christian apologists, who had killed it. He discerned in the letter of the Bible the source of its power.[28] He ascribed this power, of course, not to God but to the I that had become God, to pure self-consciousness. Bauer needed the Bible with all the absolute claims to speak of the incarnation of God the Son that orthodoxy saw in the Bible and which the modern apologists were weakening. Only the full authoritative Bible with its absolute claims was enough for him because he thought these absolute claims belonged properly to himself and those like him who were completely selfconscious. Modern scholarship has taken over many of Bauer's theses about how the New Testament came into its present form as the result of reflection. Few scholars will go as far as Bauer; but why not?[29] If we are not to follow Bauer the whole way, we need to pit ourselves against his brilliant and acute historical work on detail, as well as to tackle the riddle that human self-consciousness, for all its power and creative insight, can hardly have created what it discerns.

[28] See the brilliant comment on the Apologists' attempt to handle Jesus' answers to the question of why John the Baptist's disciples fasted while his did not; *Kritik der evangelischen Geschichte der Synoptiker*, vol, ii (Leipzig, 1841), p. 117.

[29] See William Wrede's tribute to Bauer in the appendix to his *Messiasgeheimnis* (1901); English translation (Cambridge, 1971), pp. 281–3.

13

Kähler

Martin Kähler was born in 1835, the year David Friedrich Strauss published his *Life of Jesus* and made Biblical criticism a burning public question. Kähler seemed to the Halle students who drank in his lectures and to the earnest Bible-reading laymen and women who flocked to congresses to hear him speak to have reestablished the authority of the Bible once and for all. He was immensely learned, but he always spoke very simply. 'The theologian's highest aim must be to teach in such a way that his fellow-believers find his teaching completely obvious.'[1] He devoted his life to winning for himself and others a dependable relationship to the Bible. Only in the Bible could one arrive at unmediated access to the revelations of God, independent of the vicissitudes of any theology.

Kähler based his system on the complete acceptance of Lessing's dictum that 'accidental truths of history can never become the proof of necessary truths of reason'; he held that 'the keen pursuit of historical science has of late for the general public only broadened and deepened the ditch which according to Lessing, separates facts and the truths of reason'.[2] He agreed with Kant that faith and history (in the ordinary sense of facts about the past) repel each other like oil and water. So he attacked the books that pretended to offer

[1] *Dogmatische Zeitfragen. Alte und neue Ausführungen zur Wissenschaft der christlichen Lehre*, Vol. 1, *Zur Bibelfrage*, 2nd enlarged ed. (Leipzig, 1907), p. 118; introduction to part 3 of the essay, 'Jesus und das Alte Testament'.

[2] *Zur Bibelfrage* (Leipzig, 1907), p. 344; introduction to part 3 of the long essay, 'Geschichte der Bibel in ihrer Wirkung auf die Kirche'.

modern readers the historical Jesus, and he presented instead the Biblical Christ who was 'historic' in another sense. He relies on a supposed distinction between the two German adjectives 'historisch' and 'geschichtlich'.

My warning cry I am able to summarize and I want to summarize in a truly striking way, in the judgement: *the historical Jesus of modern writers conceals the living Christ from us.* The Jesus of the 'Life of Jesus' is merely a modern variety of the products of human creative art, no better than the infamous dogmatic Christ of Byzantine christology; they are both equally far removed from the true Christ. Historicism is at this point just as arbitrary, just as humanly haughty, just as pert, and as 'faithlessly gnostic' as the dogmatism which in its own day was also modern . . .

We are well used to hearing it said that today the 'Life of Jesus' has either supplanted the dogma about Christ, or ought to take its place. Then we are offered a mass or an apparent totality of facts, which to rights remain the subject of endless scholarly investigation – offered them as incontestable truths of faith, or if we find that more correct, as incontestable experiences of faith. And the consequence must be and will be an uncertainty, a postponement in the formation of convictions, a reserving of judgement, doubt precisely in those who delve more deeply, which attacks the root of the faith of Christians. Yet it hits you in the eye about these very presentations of the Life of Jesus that they are only attempts on a large scale or in detail to grasp the past. They have to enter into discussion, point by point, with other equally diligent and honest attempts. Or, when they don't do that, they win the appearance of certainty by a temporary lapse of memory or concealment; and this deception can't long maintain itself. If this sort of work claims 'to lay a foundation' that which there is no other [cf. I Corinthians 3.11], it will in so doing only make clear that this foundation is incapable of bearing any weight. For historical facts that scholarship has first to make clear cannot *as such* become experiences of faith. And for that reason the history of Jesus on the one hand and Christian faith on the other flow apart like oil and water as soon as the magic of enthusiastic and enrapturing description loses its power.

Nevertheless, when we ponder the relation of faith to its subject-matter, then there appears to be really no essential difference to be made as to whether this subject-matter comprises just simply the content of the Biblical report or the picture of Jesus arrived at by scholarly research. Consequently, the discussion runs up against the quite undecidable choice between either subjectivism or a faith dictated by authority, whether the authority be ascribed to the Bible or to contemporary theology. Let us not make ourselves cross-eyed by staring at this either-or. Let us look away from it for the moment, and investigate simply the position of a naive Christian . . .[3]

The position of a naive Christian who reads his Bible and believes is admirable, and it seems to me legitimate for a person untrained in theology and unread in modern discussions about the authority of the Bible to defend a lifelong certainty by a simple appeal to a lifelong experience. This is a way of gathering together and summing up thousands of incidents in a life and the reflections that accompanied those incidents and presenting the result of observation and reflection to the questioning sceptic. It is not irrational to hold on to this sort of certainty while conceding the overwhelming weight of argument on the other side. This is the point of Samuel Johnson's remark that all theory is against the freedom of the will; all experience for it (April 15, 1778).

[3] *Der sogenannte historische Jesus und der geschichtliche, biblische Christus* (Leipzig, 1892), pp. 4, 26 f.; second enlarged edition (1896), pp. 73 f. The first edition together with parts of the second edition has been edited by E. Wolf (Munich, 1956, 1961). Most of these parts of the second edition and the whole of the original address in its lightly revised second-edition form are given in *The So-Called Historical Jesus and the Historic, Biblical Christ*, translated and edited, and with an introduction by Carl E. Braaten, foreword by Paul Tillich (Philadelphia, 1964), pp. 43, 73 f.

If there is force in the appeal to the position of the naive Christian, however, the duty of the scholar is to show the Christian is justified or not justified by the evidence and the arguments that can be based on evidence. It is doubtful if the scholar can be content himself to rest in the naive Christian's position.

Furthermore, Kähler's exposition of the Biblical 'historic' Christ must, it would seem, have a content. Kähler himself is offering yet one more figure, the Biblical Christ, as the object of belief, and presumably his Christ is someone discovered in the Bible and presented to modern man, and therefore as open to doubt as any other modern product. What makes Kähler's Biblical Christ immune from the criticism he directs against the modern historical Jesuses presented in the lives of Jesus?

The answer he gives is that the Biblical Christ alone is the one figure in history to be surrendered to with certainty, the Christ whose image it is forbidden to discuss, the one to whom surrender is the only response.

We must distinguish between the offer of a content for faith and the reason that motivates us to grasp the content in the faith. And it will hold for every evangelical Christian, indeed for every living Christian who depends with true and childlike trust on his Saviour, that this motivating reason in the last resort lies in the experiences he quietly enters on in surrendering to his Saviour. Yet the Saviour with whom he lives is not merely a felt Saviour or a Saviour self-fabricated; the Saviour with whom he lives is rather the one preached to him; the Saviour with whom he lives is above all – clearly or obscurely – yet in the last resort always the Christ of scripture . . .

So it remains unalterably the case: whoever comes to agree with this judgement about the image of Christ that encounters us will also acknowledge the miracle that Christ made it possible, in the simple course of a fallible tradition left to itself, to make his figure decisive and alive for the driving forward of the further development of humanity. And is it a deficiency when the origin of this image remains obscure? No one saw the loaves prepared or multiplied which at Jesus' prayer of thanksgiving satisfied the thousands; there they were, and they were real genuine loaves. So it is with all the miraculous deeds of our God: what we see and possess belongs to this world; we do not know the origin; but what we sense, that we tell to be from beyond.[4]

There is a little sleight of hand in Kähler's position. He seems to be condemning lock stock and barrel the modern lives of Jesus. It is true he tells his audience that it need not be either confused by the variety of their pictures of Jesus or deterred from believing in Christ by their negative criticisms of the reliability of the Gospels. But that is not quite the denial of their truth the unwary listener might have expected from Kähler's wholesale denunciation of the class of literature, the lives of Jesus.

If we read Kähler attentively, we find that he held as proven eight specific historical facts about the New Testament's picture of Jesus. These are, of course, controversial and as little certain as any other historical conclusions, but Kähler held them, and held them certainly enough to make them part of his theology.

First, he held that the christology of the fourth and fifth century creeds of Nicaea and Chalcedon is false to the Christology of the New Testament. We can gather this from an aside at the beginning of his famous lecture on the historical Jesus and the Biblical historic Christ quoted above. He attacks the modern attempts to reconstruct the life of the historical Jesus for being just as arbitrary, just as humanly arrogant, just as presumptuous and faithlessly gnostic as the dogmatism (as he calls it) of the Byzantine christology. This attack in itself does not brand the Byzantine creeds as untrue to the Bible, although it clearly gains much of its emotional force by appealing to a prejudice in his audience against the statements of the Byzantine Creeds. But the case is clinched

[4] *Der sogenannte historische Jesus* (Leipzig, 1892), pp. 28 f., 42; 2nd ed. (1896), pp. 76, 90; English translation, pp. 76, 91.

by another aside a few pages later: the 'Life of Jesus movement' is right in so far as it sets the Bible against 'abstract dogmatism'.[5]

Secondly, he argued that the Fourth Gospel and the Synoptic Gospels were written about the same time, not by apostles, and that the disagreements between them in historical detail showed that the authors were careless of historical accuracy.[6]

Thirdly, he held that the Infancy Narratives were not true, for nothing else but this follows from his remark that the story of the twelve-year-old in the Temple is not to be trusted because it belongs with the Infancy Narrative in Luke.[7]

Fourthly, he assumed that the body of Jesus that died was not raised from the dead. This follows from his assertion that the risen Christ is the preached Christ, and only the preached Christ: the resurrection marks the end of the historical Jesus.[8]

Fifthly, Kähler attributed the spread of Christianity to the Gentiles to the work of the Apostle Paul and allows no part to the original disciples: 'The small band of Nazarenes is of no importance to contemporary Judaism. The rest of the world would have never bothered about Jesus, had not Saul of Tarsus assembled a community for him, that giant tree which grew out of the mustard seed, under whose shade the birds of heaven build their nests'.[9]

Sixthly, Kähler assumed that contemporary Jewish teaching about the resurrection of the dead and the judgement of all mankind by Christ was purely pictorial and a misleading way of expressing Jesus' own view of his significance. 'We

[5] *Der sogenannte historische Jesus*, 1st ed. (Leipzig, 1892), pp. 4 f; 2nd ed., pp. 44 and 47; English translation, pp. 43 and 46.

[6] *Der sogenannte historische Jesus*, 1st ed. (Leipzig, 1892), pp. 39 ff.; cf. note on pp. 8 f.; 2nd ed. (1896), pp. 87 ff.; cf. note on pp. 50 f.; English translation, pp. 88 ff.; cf. note on pp. 50 f.

[7] *Der sogenannte historische Jesus*, 1st ed. (Leipzig, 1892), p. 9; 2nd ed. (1896), p. 51; English translation, p. 50.

[8] *Der sogenannte historische Jesus*, 1st ed. (Leipzig, 1892), pp. 20 ff.; 2nd ed. pp. 64 ff.; English translation, pp. 64 ff. See Kähler's reply to Otto Ritschl in the 2nd ed., p. 185, reproduced in Wolf's ed., p. 41.

[9] *Der sogenannte historische Jesus*, 1st ed. (Leipzig, 1892), p. 20; 2nd ed. (1896), p. 64; English translation, p. 64.

surely know how vigorously the unpretentious Rabbi [Jesus] had to contend with the terrestrial hopes for a splendiferous Son of David who was to lay the kingdoms of this world, in all their glory, at the feet of his people. Those images and metaphors from Jewish eschatology which Christians drew upon in painting their vivid pictures of the Christian hope still constitute the stumbling block which is apt to betray the hope of faith into denial of itself.[10]

Seventhly, Kähler denied that the death of Jesus was meant by Jesus or by Paul or by the New Testament as a whole to be a sacrifice offered to the Father for the sins of others.[11]

Finally, the most important point, Kähler assumed that Jesus' teaching and the events of his life were completely unexpected according to the contemporary Jewish ideas of the Messiah. When we compare Jesus with Paul, says Kähler, we discover Paul to be a Jew of his day and Jesus to be quite different: D. F. Strauss found something Hellenistic in Jesus – certainly nothing related to late Judaism; and Kähler himself thought Jesus was like someone who lived in the unhistorical time of the patriarchs. Any sayings of Jesus that could also be found in scripture or on the lips of pious Jews before him were quite different in his mouth. The Christian confession that Jesus is Messiah is in complete opposition to the official idea of a Messiah, and in complete opposition to what would be expected of him. Christ completely contradicted the expectations his contemporaries held about the Messiah.[12]

These eight historical propositions are, of course, fallible and subject to revision and therefore not, according to Kähler, a proper foundation for faith. But they are propositions Kähler holds to be true, and we cannot fail to observe that some of them entail the conclusion that at points the Bible is

[10] *The So-Called Historical Jesus and the Historic, Biblical Christ*, translated by Carl E. Braaten (Philadelphia, 1964), p. 64; German, 1st ed. (Leipzig, 1892), p. 20; 2nd ed. (1896), p. 64.

[11] See the article 'Offenbarung', Herzog-Hauck (3rd ed.); vol. xiv (1904), p. 341; *Die Versöhnung durch Christum in ihrer Bedeutung für das christliche Glauben und Leben* (Leipzig, 1907), p. 34.

[12] *Der sogenannte historische Jesus*, 1st ed. (Leipzig, 1892), pp. 12, 16, 21; 2nd ed. (1896) pp. 54 f., 59, 64 f.; English translation, pp. 54, 59, 65.

wrong. The Bible is an unreliable guide to the facts about Jesus.

We must conclude that Kähler, in order to defend the authority of the Bible, had to reject the relevance of historical investigation of the Bible as a possible support for the authority of the Bible because historical investigation of the Bible showed the Bible to be unreliable. Kähler, like every author of the lives of Jesus he criticizes, had his own historical Jesus and he built his theology on the clear contrast between his Jesus and the Jesus of the Bible or the creeds.

Who, then, was the Biblical historic Christ who is obscured from us by the various historical Jesuses of modern research?

So far, the only thing we can say about this Biblical Christ is that he and he alone is certain; that is the crucial difference between him and the various images of the historical Jesus. Kähler's personal and intellectual problem was the search for certainty, and he claimed that this search for certainty was also the problem of the age in which he lived. 'There is no doubt that Frank, with his 'System of Christian Certainty', expressed what we might call the watchword of this time; for everywhere the question was the same, the question of how one became certain of faith in Christianity. Hofmann asks it just as much as Frank; the modern Hegelians ask it; Lipsius and Ritschl ask it; the neo-Kantians ask it.'[13] Lessing had said that if God offered him a choice between all truth in his right hand, and in his left hand the everlasting striving after truth so that he should always and everlatingly be mistaken, and said, Choose, he would choose the left hand. Kähler replied that Christians needed a surer foundation. They needed a 'storm-free area' which nothing could disturb.[14] But this 'storm-free area' was not even possibly the result of increased knowledge, for knowledge was always of the past

[13] Martin Kähler, *Geschichte der protestantische Dogmatik im 19. Jahrhundert*, edited by Ernst Kähler (Munich, 1962), p. 85. The reference is to F. H. Reinhold Frank (1827–1894), *System*, 1870–73.

[14] 'Das Offenbarungsansehen der Bibel' (1903), *Aufsätze zur Bibelfrage*', edited by Ernst Kähler (Munich, 1967), p. 96. See also *Der sogenannte historische Jesus*, 2nd ed. (Leipzig, 1896, reprinted 1928), pp. 200 f. Lessing's famous remark is in *Eine Replik* (1778), ed. Lachmann, xiii. 24.

and was always questionable. Kähler had never studied for curiosity's sake, always in order to win through to convictions.[15] He was one of the most learned and widely-read theologians of his age but he deliberately denied the value of any scholarly discussion for establishing the certainty he desired. Historical investigation never led to certainty; scholarly exegesis of the New Testament text in practice only persuaded students that they could never come to a *certain* understanding of the words; philosophical discussion was of *no* help in giving content to morality.[16]

Anything discovered by examination is inherently uncertain. We find what we expect to find, so that what we expect to find is always available as an explanation of what we find; a psychological explanation of our experience is always possible. We examine historical records with all the techniques at our disposal and to do so we must be very learned and very clever, and yet our results are always open to revision; if the records we examine are ancient, they are found to be more or less trustworthy, and it is always possible that they are untrustworthy. Whether we look within to our own experience, or outside to the Bible as an historical document we find uncertainty.

The only possible basis of certainty, according to the line of reasoning that Kähler is following, is a revelation from beyond which we receive not as something to be examined and approved but as something implicitly believed. Now we look differently: outside, not for historical records but for 'facts' or revelation; inside, not for subjective impressions but for faith. Kähler criticized the old orthodox view of the Bible which tried to establish the inerrancy of all the details in scripture in order to safeguard the one main point. The old orthodox 'thought that only an inerrancy in respect of any and every arbitrarily chosen matter would guarantee the trustworthiness [of scripture] in the one essential main point

[15] *Theologe und Christ: Erinnerungen und Bekenntnisse von Martin Kähler*, edited by Anna Kähler (Berlin, 1926), p. 133.

[16] See for example, *Der sogenannte historische Jesus*, 1st ed. (Leipzig, 1892), long note on pp. 22–25; taken into the text of the 2nd ed. (1896), pp. 69–71; English translation, pp. 67–71; *Theologe und Christ*, pp. 186, 224.

– and forgot that this main point was the *the one great exception* which, come what may, refuses to turn the grace of God adrift to the mercy of human fallibility'.[17] The one great exception, the one main point is a revelation which possesses a trustworthiness that was provable in no other way than by faith, so that it was open to no scientific or scholarly test whatsoever. All ideas about God were subjective; only the living God himself as encountered and believed could give objectivity.

Who is this living God who alone gives the certainty Kähler sought and believed he had found? He is Christ, the Biblical historic Christ, for Kähler's other favourite description of Christ is that he is 'der offenbare Gott', the open, accessible, manifest, evident God.[18] This evident God is the gracious one who is immune from uncertainty. Uncertainty is the perennial human problem and the Messiah, the Biblical Christ is the one who has supra-historical meaning for the whole of humanity.[19] Faith in Christ is the way to certainty; certainty is humanity's final essential need; and humanity finds in Christ its salvation. Jesus represents the 'humanity of God'.[20] In so far as individuals receive the humanity they need by believing and trusting the Biblical Christ, they grow towards true humanity. They find themselves part of a company of members of the true humanity and they devote themselves to serving the unity of all men and their history.[21]

For anyone to whom being drawn to God is the

[17] 'Besteht der Wert der Bibel für den Christen hauptsächlich darin, dass sie geschichtliche Urkunden enthält?' part I of the 2nd ed. of *Der sogenannte historische Jesus* (Leipzig, 1896), p. 13; cf. English translation, p. 114; my italics.

[18] For example, *Der sogenannte historische Jesus*, 1st ed. (Leipzig, 1892), pp. 17, 30, 41,; 2nd ed. (1896), pp. 61, 77, 90; English translation pp. 61, 77, 90. (Braaten understandably translates 'the revealed God', but that is not quite accurate).

[19] *Der sogenannte historische Jesus*, 1st ed. (Leipzig, 1892), p. 21; 2nd ed. (1896), p. 64; English translation, p. 65.

[20] *Der Schriftbeweis: Ein Theologischer Versuch*, Erste Hälfte (Nordlingen, 1852), pp. 7 f. et passim. Kähler preferred the phrase 'der offenbare Gott', but used 'die Menschheit Gottes' in *Die Bibel, das Buch der Menschheit* (Berlin, 1904), offprint, p. 37.

[21] *Die Bibel, das Buch der Menschheit* (Berlin, 1904), offprint, p. 35.

heart-beat of human life, the Bible will also be humanity's book. It is because of the Bible that we have the concept of the unity of our race is its origin and goal; more than that, it is because of the Bible that we have faith in that unity. And that is exactly the one important result which this educative book of humanity has exerted and goes on exerting in the process of educating towards genuine human humanity.[22]

Christianity had brought to light the worth and equality of man by teaching him he was destined for eternity; Christianity planted eternal life in his heart. This was the origin of the idea of human progress and the guarantee that human progress would reach its goal.[23]

As far as I can see, Kähler is preaching faith that humanity could progress so long as it had faith. The Bible is read not for historical details it conveys but because it is a paradigm for the unfolding of humanity; as the gospel spreads by the preaching of faith, so will humanity. The variety of human experience in the Bible 'presents the unfolding of humanity in its length and breadth'. All is unified, in the Bible and in the progress of humanity, by 'the Spirit of Faith which steadily mounts upwards despite all its wanderings'. 'Humanity thanks the Bible for its consciousness that it is humanity.'[24]

The Biblical Christ, the manifest God who is beyond doubt and beyond question, turns out to be the point of focus for humanity seeking certainty. The certainty it finds is faith in its own unity and its own progress – so long as it has faith.

Kähler was no exclusively theoretical theologian. All his

[22] The article 'Bibel' in Herzog-Hauck, 3rd ed., vol. 2 (1897), p. 691.

[23] See the lecture on 'The Progress of Humanity and the Eternity of Man' published in *Dogmatische Zeitfragen: Alte und neue Ausführungen zur Wissenschaft der christlichen Lehre* (Leipzig, 1898), pp. 16–45; also in *Zeit und Ewigkeit, Der Dogmatischen Zeitfragen* III. Bd. (Leipzig, 1913), pp. 116–195. 'The Bible, Book of Humanity', centenary lecture for the British and Foreign Bible Society; there is a copy of the original lecture in the Westminster College, Cambridge, Library, and the enlarged version is most accessible in *Zur Bibelfrage* (Gutersloh, 1937), pp. 219–265.

[24] *Die Bibel, das Buch der Menschheit* (Berlin, 1904), offprint, p. 35 and p. 19.

life since his student conversion he wrestled in private with students who sought certainty in the midst of uncertainty. He wrestled to bring them to a point of decision about the Biblical Christ, and then he committed them to one of the network of Bible study groups, often under lay leadership, where this certainty could be nourished. Those of his students who themselves became theologians were freed from anxiety in all their theological and Biblical studies. Kähler's position allowed them to engage freely in showing the trustworthiness or not of the Biblical accounts without that examination having any bearing whatsoever on their faith: faith had to be in principle certain and, as historical conclusions were in principle undertain, historical conclusions could not in principle bear on faith at all. In fact, it could even be argued that the greater the uncertainty of the results and the greater the untrustworthiness of the evidence, the better for faith; faith would stand out more clearly as that which it was, untestable certainty.

Kähler saved the authority of the Bible for countless men and women of his generation, but only at the cost of planting a gigantic irrational faith in faith at the centre of their lives: a belief that was completely certain, and completely untestable, and a belief that was only sustained by the belief they had which marked them out as truly human and as part of the humanity progressing to the goal of unity. The trouble was that the Christ of Kähler's system could just as well be replaced by another world figure, and Kähler's system precluded the rational preference of Christ to this other figure, for this Christ was the Biblical preached Christ, not the Jesus whose life one could examine and test and prefer.

14

Overbeck

Franz Overbeck's field of scholarship was the history of the church. He held a chair of theology specially set up in Basel by a party of liberal reformers, where he gave strictly philological lectures on books of the New Testament and historical lectures on early and medieval church history. He published one controversial book, *On whether or not our contemporary theology is Christian* (which was almost completely ignored by contemporary theologians), an inaugural lecture, a new edition of an old commentary on Acts, seventeen articles on early church history and the history of the canon, and about ninety book reviews. He decided very early in his teaching career that it was impossible both to believe a religion and to study a religion as a scholar. As he wanted to devote his life to studying the history of Christianity, he could not therefore be a Christian theologian. His only theological function was to pronounce the Last Judgement on Christianity.[1] He never did this openly as a theological teacher, although his best students understood his basic position: 'We knew right enough that there stood a paradox at the end of Professor Overbeck's method, the paradox that scholarship and religion are mutually destructive'.[2] Most of them went on to be pastors who lived with the paradox; one or two drew Overbeck's own conclusion and dropped out of being either pastors or

[1] Franz Overbeck, *Selbstbekenntnisse herausgegeben und eingeleitet von Eberhard Vischer* (Basel, 1941) reprinted with an introduction by Jacob Taubes (Franfurt 1966), p. 105.

[2] Pastor B. Hartmann, Basler Jahrbücher (1906), 183, cited by Walter Nigg, *Franz Overbeck, Versuch einer Würdigung* (Munich, 1931), p. 62, note.

180

theologians. The problem is, why did Overbeck himself go on as an ostensible Professor of Theology?

He did once think of becoming a librarian, like Lessing, I suppose; but Overbeck was already a professional scholar with an ambition to write a history of the church, for which project he had an enormous amount to learn. The only practical way to learn was to take a job as a university teacher, and the only job where church history could be learnt was as a theological professor.[3]

Scholarship of the quality of Overbeck's is rare. He combined an exact knowledge of the evidence with good judgement about the proper reading of the facts. Such scholarship needs time, diligence, and the sovereign simplicity which knows that 'Profound Thinking is many times the Cause of shallow Thought' — to quote the tag from Shaftesbury that Overbeck loved to repeat.[4] A philosopher colleague said of Overbeck at his death, 'He was a strict scholar, the like of which perhaps there never was; who went endlessly deep in research; who would never be ready, because he could never get himself to do enough; a self-mortifying monk of scholarship'.[5] That was how it appeared, but he was all the time actually writing down conclusions in the form of aphorisms and shorter or longer essays. He arranged the material under subject-headings like 'Christianity (Development)', 'Christianity (Eschatology) General', 'Miracles (Recognition of) Recent Apologetics', 'Miracles (Miscellaneous)', 'Monasticism (Rejection of the World, Misanthropy)', 'Monasticism (General Estimates)', 'Origins of Monasticism', 'Shaftesbury (Letter concerning Enthusiasm)', 'Shaftesbury (Miscellaneous Reflections)'. The subject headings he kept on cards from the very beginning of his

[3] Overbeck's note of 12 December 1900, *Selbstbekenntnisse*, p. 135.

[4] Anthony Ashley Cooper, Third Earl of Shaftesbury, *Characteristicks of Men, Manners, Opinions, Times*, vol. iii (London 1714), p. 226, cited by Overbeck, W. M. L. de Wette, *Kurze Erklärung der Apostelgeschichte*, 4th ed., edited and greatly enlarged by him (Leipzig, 1870), p. xiv; Nachlass A270; A237, p. 8, according to Arnold Pfeiffer, *Franz Overbecks Kritik des Christentums* (Göttingen, 1975), p. 127.

[5] Karl Joël, Die neue Rundschau (1906), September issue, cited by Walter Nigg, *Franz Overbeck: Versuch einer Würdigung* (Munich, 1931) pp. 15 f.

time as a teacher, and he inserted 6″ × 4″ sheets – notes of what others said, evidence, and his own reflections – on these subjects in that order into cartons. There were two series, Exegetical and Historical, and by his death they comprised thirty-nine cartons and a dozen more boxes; each carton contained about 300 loose sheets. All this went to the University Library in Basel, and still the books on Overbeck come, the most interesting part of which is always the set of quotations, the longer the better, from these remains. Overbeck's historical judgement has stood the test of time better than that of any of his contemporaries.

There was more to Overbeck's decision to stick at theology than his desire to be a student of church history. He was a shy man and a sickly boy and man, who came from an extraordinarily happy home where he was expected, in a quite irreligious way, to become a theologian and a scholar. He loved and honoured his family and the culture they represented, a culture that could be quite conventionally Christian, a culture which in its conventional religion preserved some of the finest human virtues and produced some of the most admirable people, but a culture which was fast disappearing, overwhelmed by boring and superficial modernity.

Franz Camille Overbeck was an eldest child, born in Petersburg in 1837. The birth was difficult, and left a red mark on his forehead. His mother was a Catholic; both her parents were French, but they too were born in Russia. His father had grown up in England in a prosperous German trading family under the patronage of the Duke of Sussex, a fellow-Freemason. The business failed in 1817 and the family eventually settled in Russia. Franz spoke Russian to the servants, and French in the family until his youngest sister was born when his mother was forty-seven and they were all permanently settled back in Germany – but his weekly letters to his mother up to her death in 1876 remained in French. He also spoke fluent English, for English was the language of the cultured in Petersburg.[6] Of course he could speak German, and had to speak German to his pious Lutheran grandmother,

[6] *Selbstbekenntnisse*, pp. 55 f.; 79.

who had insisted that the children be not brought up as
Catholics – but who herself died troubled in her faith. But he
only spoke German irregularly during his first twelve years.
When the mother and children were at last settled in Dresden
his parents employed a private tutor to help him, and only
then did he attain really accomplished mastery of German;
it was this tutor who opened to him the portals of German
classical literature.[7] He always wrote German as a stylist
who was self-consciously trying to say the thing well and
exactly.

The move of the family back to Germany was partly for
the mother's health, but also for Franz's education. His father
had always wanted to be an academic himself, and saw how
able Franz was. The young boy had said he wanted to be a
pastor, and so they settled in Dresden so that he could study
'pour la carrière à laquelle il se destinera'.[8] It was his father
who gave Franz at eighteen or nineteen a history of recent
theology which he had seen recommended in a periodical.
From this history, Franz early imbibed a coolly critical view
of contemporary theological scholarship, and a high estimate
of Ferdinand Christian Baur.[9]

Overbeck started theology at the University of Leipzig in
Easter 1856, when he was not yet nineteen. He moved to
Göttingen and Berlin before returning to Leipzig in spring
1861 to join the circle of his old school-friend Heinrich von
Treitschke, whom he later named his 'educator in
Unchristianity'. Yet he drew back in horror from abandoning
Christianity entirely and, full of scruples, decided to prepare
to be a University teacher in New Testament. He was
attracted to Jena by Karl Hase (1800–90) where he found
'that noble and wise tranquillity which even Theology can
allow herself to be cheated out of only through illusion –
only through illusion could she come not to value tran-

---

[7] *Selbstkekenntnisse*, pp. 80 f.

[8] *Selbstbekenntnisse*, pp. 74 f.

[9] Karl Schwarz, *Zur Geschichte der neuesten Theologie*, reprinted in the year of
publication (1856). See Arnold Pfeiffer, *Franz Overbecks Kritik des Christentums*
(Göttingen, 1975), pp. 101–12. For Overbeck's mature judgement of Baur see *Über
die Christlichkeit unserer heutigen Theologie*, 2nd ed. (Leipzig, 1903), pp. 6 f.

quillity as the best mood we can maintain in all human concerns.[10] In the happy years between his twenty-six birthday and his thirty-second birthday, when he received a call to Basel, Overbeck worked out the main lines of his history of Christianity. He had long given up preaching, and he simply enjoyed the tranquil investigation of Christianity as 'a miracle that arises naturally out of the human world.'[11]

He observed that Christianity still had the power to produce noble and significant characters even in his own day – but not among theologians. 'How beautiful' he thought as he walked home after reading the *Histoire d'un Amour Chrétien* he had seen reviewed in a periodical; 'How beautiful is this deep, pure, sure piety that has no occasion to stray beyond the limits of feeling, that never falls into contradiction by trying to meet the demands of understanding. And still there are men of note in this respect who so believe. How seldom such faith among theologians, who under the circumstances can scarcely avoid that conflict. While in the former case, faith shows their nobility of soul, in the case of theologians their faith only proves to us their narrowness; what elevates and ennobles those, lowers these and makes them brutish'.[12]

Overbeck's history of Christianity was grounded in a deep and thorough study of the Acts of the Apostles, which was published in 1870 as a revision of de Wette's commentary. It is a curious book, which shows Overbeck's modesty and his eirenic temper, as well as his mastery of a complicated problem. De Wette, a friend and admirer of Herder, had done important work both on the Old Testament, preparing the way for Wellhausen's solution to the problem of the sources of the Pentateuch, and on the New Testament. He published an influential *Introduction* and wrote commentaries

[10] Franz Overbeck, *Zur Geschichte des Kanons* (Chemnitz, 1880, reprinted Darmstadt, 1965), dedicatory epistle.

[11] Nachlass, A272, cited by Arnold Pfeiffer, *Franz Overbecks Kritik des Christentums* (Göttingen, 1975), p. 143.

[12] A remark written in 1866, Nachlass A272, cited by Arnold Pfeiffer, *Franz Overbecks Kritik des Christentums*, p. 125.

on every book in the New Testament canon. In his commentary on Acts he made many learned notes on details but dismissed with contempt F. C. Baur's attempt to show that Acts was written in the second century by a Paulinist. Overbeck though it not right to jettison de Wette's notes, but he saw himself working very much on the lines of Baur and Baur's follower and son-in-law, Eduard Zeller. His solution was to reprint most of de Wette's commentary, add his own notes in single inverted commas, and preface the whole with a new introduction. In this introduction he restated Baur and Zeller's position, and then moved significantly beyond it in the spirit of Bruno Bauer.

F. C. Baur and Zeller had argued that the author of Acts was a Paulinist who offered peace to the Jewish Christians by portraying Peter and Paul as having agreed and worked in harmony in the early years of the church's life. Acts turned Peter into a universalist and Paul into a friend of Jewish Christianity. Zeller had argued that the book of Acts had a further purpose in that the author tried to work on his own party, the Paulinists, to make concessions to the Jewish Christians. Overbeck saw the author of Acts as far less aware of what he was doing; he was no party-man with a thesis to establish, but rather a Gentile Christian, writing at a time when Gentile Christianity had become dominant, looking back and trying to see how the Christianity he lived in had come into being from the work of Peter and Paul. He did not understand Paul's distinctive theology and retained nothing of it save Paul's universalism. His own church life was deeply influenced by Judaism and he portrayed the church as developing organically out of Judaism, although he saw that development as at every turn the result of the unbelief and guilt of the Jews.

Overbeck places the composition of Acts not earlier than the age of Trajan (who died in AD 117) and regarded as 'an immediate forerunner of the apologetic literature that flourished in the time of the Antonines'. The author was, like the Apologists, especially concerned with the relationship between the church and the Roman state.[13] This late dating

---

[13] W. M. L. de Wette, *Kurze Erklärung der Apostelgeschichte*, revised and greatly

of Acts has found little favour, although I myself think it is likely to be right. The great difficulty it must meet is that the author of Acts, had he written so late, could hardly not have used Paul's letters (and Overbeck assumed he did use Paul's letters, particularly Galatians, and deliberately contradicted Paul's picture of events). Yet Acts does not read like a deliberate answer to Paul's letters and betrays no interest in Paul as a letter-writer, as Overbeck observed. There is a genuine historical puzzle here which we are still working on, although most scholars still take the easy way out, a way barred against them by Overbeck, of trying to date Acts in the first century.[14]

However much the author of Acts might make up events, like the quarrel between the 'Hellenists' and the 'Hebrews' in Acts 6, Overbeck saw him as only just emerging as an independent author. Acts like the Gospels, even the Gospel of John, still belonged to the period of pre-literature-proper. For the first hundred years or so of its life the church produced effortlessly unreflecting works in which religion was alive and the myths potent. Acts was still a saga. Some of this writing was separated off from the rest of the literature of this primitive time to become the 'canon' of holy scripture, but there were other writings which bore the same stamp. The crucial moment in the history of the church was when Christians began to try to write literature according to the standards of world-wide literature, which would be 'an acquisition for all ages,' according to Thucydides' definition. The first person to do this was Clement of Alexandria, who wrote in the middle of the second century and who not only recommended Christianity to the educated public of the Roman Empire and wrote a catechesis for Christians, but also attempted to equip the church with a theology by showing the truth of the Christian faith and the wisdom of Christian knowledge. Clement took the fateful step of trying

enlarged by Franz Overbeck (Leipzig, 1870); preface translated by J. Dare in E. Zeller, *The Content and Origin of The Acts of the Apostles critically investigated*, vol. I (1875), pp. 2–81.

[14]J. C. O'Neill, *The Theology of Acts in its Historical Setting*, 2nd revised and enlarged ed. (London, 1970).

to make Christianity possible in a world which it properly denied.[15]

The attempt to justify itself by providing itself with a theology was doomed from the beginning because the very search for a theology was the sign that the old myths were no longer self-sustaining. Yet the attempt did succeed in one respect: Christianity managed to capture the Roman Empire – or so it seemed. In reality true Christianity had at last succumbed to what remained of the ancient world.

Nothing more would have been heard of Christianity had not an extraordinary reaction within Christianity itself enabled Christianity to survive. Just as the classical world was about to triumph, hermits appeared and monasticism arose. The hermits and monks, no more than modern believers, could not recover the original impulse in Christianity, but they were able to transpose that original idea into something else: real martyrdom was closed to them, but the daily martyrdom of the solitary life or of the constant mortification of community life under discipline seemed to be a substitute. Even this was impossible to achieve, but nevertheless monasticism had an important part to play in western history. 'For though we have to say that Christianity in the East was never anything but the tomb of an old and disappearing culture, and monasticism could do nothing to alter that, yet Christianity in the West was the cradle for a young and newly arising culture, and in this monasticism had a very substantial part to play'.[16]

Christianity's role of helping to cradle a new culture ended with the Reformation when Luther replaced the productive self-mortification, which monasticism had preserved, with a facile optimism, justification by faith alone.[17]

[15] 'Über die Anfänge der patristischen Literatur', *Historische Zeitschrift*, 48 (1882), 417–72; reprint (Basel, 1959?).

[16] Overbeck's 'Rosenvortrag', 'On the Origins of Monasticism', Jena, 6 February 1867, Nachlass A77, p. 15, cited by Arnold Pfeiffer, *Franz Overbecks Kritik des Christentums* (Gottingen, 1975), p. 147. Overbeck's lecture on receiving permission to teach (his Habilitationsvorlesung), Jena, 21 October 1864, was on the same subject.

[17] Franz Overbeck, *Über die Christlichkeit unserer heutigen Theologie*, 1873, 2nd ed. (Leipzig, 1903), p. 84. This is pure Schopenhauer.

Overbeck, like Lessing and Schopenhauer before him, believed that the history of civilisations was like the history of an individual, with birth, youth, maturity, old age and death following each other as a natural matter of course. He also believed that the Copernican revolution inaugurated a new age in which it was no longer possible to believe in miracles. From this it followed that any historical examination of Christianity was the examination of an irrecoverable past set of beliefs that no modern critic could possibly share. As historian, the past was past for Overbeck. He puts the point rather neatly in the observation, 'The absoluteness of the ecclesiastical view of Christianity is destroyed (a) by natural science (the Copernican world system, among other things); (b) by history – namely just by the division of history into ancient, medieval, and modern, which taken strictly already excludes the possibility that Christ was, in the ecclesiastical sense, a 'turning point of the ages'. In fact the Reformation is a so much deeper break with preceding history, because it compels us to concede that a new period began, the period of the decaying church or the period of the diminishing absoluteness of Christianity.'[18]

Overbeck's historical 'touch' his judgement of the significant facts about great events in the past, was unrivalled. He saw clearly in the 1860s that Christianity began as a movement looking forward to the end of our sort of human history and the coming of the Kingdom of God, a point of view that gained little scholarly support until the work of Hermann Gunkel, Johannes Weiss, and Richard Kabisch in the late 1880s and 1890s, which was gathered up by Albert Schweitzer in the early years of this century.[19] Although

---

[18] Overbeck's Nachlass, A272, cited by Arnold Pfeiffer, *Franz Overbecks Kritik des Christentums* (Göttingen, 1975), p. 143.

[19] Hermann Gunkel, Habilitationsvorlesung, Göttingen, 16 October 1888; see Werner Klatt, *Hermann Gunkel, Zu seiner Theologie der Religionsgeschichte und zur Entstehung der form-geschichtlichen Methode* (Göttingen, 1969), p. 16 *et passim*. Johannes Weiss, *Die Predigt Jesu vom Reiche Gottes* (1892), translated, edited and with an Introduction by R. H. Hiers and D. L. Holland (London, 1971). Richard Kabisch, *Die Eschatologie des Paulus in ihren Zusammenhängen mit dem Gesamtbegriff des Paulinismus* (Göttingen, 1893) (I possess William Wrede's review copy; see Theologische Literaturzeitung, 1893).

there are still some scholars who try to deny this conclusion, they do not, in my view, make a very convincing case. Similarly, his judgement that western monasticism preserved Christianity and made possible the medieval and renaissance flowering of European culture is surely right.

As historian, Overbeck can still be read with pleasure and profit; he is full of unpretentious insight. What leaves me dissatisfied is the philosophical move he took over from Shaftesbury, the absolute dichotomy between Faith and Knowledge, a dichotomy which Lutheranism and pietism helped to reinforce. This dichotomy was quite general; the irreconcilablilty of Christianity and Theology was only a special case of a universal rule. Scholarship is designed to pronounce a kind of Last Judgement on things. Things cannot be represented by anything else; they live as themselves – and they only die because of the seeds of their own destruction which they contain. It is a riddle why things have to live. When we ask why, then they are dying. Nothing we can do will keep them alive: scholarship certainly cannot construct a living representation of what was once alive.[20]

This seems to me true of some past ideas and theories, namely, of false ideas and theories. But if there were any true ideas and theories in the past then scholarly investigation could discover them and find them to be true. There is only a contradiction between scholarly and belief in the case of false beliefs; and the fact that beliefs are old does not inevitably prove, as Overbeck seemed to think, that they are false.

Overbeck's picture of a completely unreflective Christianity is an illusion itself. Paul was a reflective theologian who weighed arguments and observed evidence before he was converted, and after his conversion he defended Christianity against the counter-arguments of his fellow-Jews. It is true that he and his opponents shared beliefs in what God could do in relation to Israel that Overbeck's age denied, but there were philosophers in Paul's day who were also

---

[20] Franz Overbeck, *Selbstbekenntinisse*, ed. Jacob Taubes (Frankfurt am Main, 1966), pp. 104 f.; 111 f.

atheists and determinists whose arguments were well known. We today live in the age of Frege and Gödel and Wittgenstein in which determinism has come under severe criticism and in which the possibility that there is a God who could think the universe and act on the universe in a way analogous to our own thinking of the universe as entity and to our own acting on the universe cannot be so easily ruled out as Overbeck thought.

One of the lynch-pins of Overbeck's argument was that monasticism arose in the third century and managed to revive Christianity by providing a surrogate for the old apocalyptic dream of the end of the world. According to Overbeck monasticism did not succeed completely in reproducing the true early Christianity, because love for neighbour was still only a duty and not a spontaneous growth. I wish to argue that, far from originating in the third century, monasticism was always a part of Christianity and that Christian monasticism was a continuation of Jewish Essene monasticism such as we have evidence of in the Deed Sea Scrolls. Just as the Essenses had married communities and monastic communities side by side, so did the church from the beginning.[21] If I am right, Jesus and the church, although looking for the speedy end of the world, also saw the necessity of two sorts of Christians, monks and nuns who denied themselves marriage and property, and married Christians who took part in the usual affairs of the world. Overbeck's idealised picture of an entirely other-worldly primitive Christianity may be only half right, and his standard strictures on monasticism may be judging the institution by criteria foreign to primitive Christianity itself.

Yet Overbeck was right to see that all attempts to demythologize old beliefs were doomed to failure. He rightly condemned the facile optimistic liberal theology of his day for completely missing the point about Christianity. He saw that primitive Christianity was a whole: miracles, eschatology,

---

[21] I argue the case in the Festschrift for Henry Chadwick: *The Making of Orthodoxy: Essays in Honour of Henry Chadwick*, ed. Rowan Williams (Cambridge, 1989), pp. 270–87.

the use of allegory to interpret scripture, and the formation of a sacred canon, all belonged indissolubly to the religion. In that, I believe, he was right. If scholarly investigation cannot allow these things to be in general true and intellectually defensible, Christianity cannot be sustained. But the activity of investigating the facts about primitive Christianity and the activity of testing the truth of what Jesus and the Apostles held to be true cannot in itself spell the death of these things. Scholarship as such does not kill – which Overbeck himself saw; but the exercise of historical and critical scholarship on any living thing does not automatically signal that the thing is dying. The thing may yet, under examination, prove to be still alive, because still true.

15

Nietzsche

Friedrich Nietzsche was born in 1844, the eldest son of a Lutheran pastor of a small village in Thuringian Saxony, since 1815 part of Prussia. His father died when Nietzsche was five years old, and his mother took him and his one surviving sister Elisabeth to live with his paternal grandmother and two aunts in Naumberg. He won a scholarship to the famous boarding-school of Pforta near Naumberg, where Klopstock, Fichte and Ranke had been pupils. At twenty he went to the University of Bonn to study theology and philology, and then followed his teacher of classical philology to Leipzig. He was appointed associate professor of classical philology at Basel in 1869, at the age of twenty-four, even before he had completed his dissertation. He was already a devoted follower of Richard Wagner. He lodged in the same house as Franz Overbeck, his truest friend and most perceptive critic. On taking Swiss citizenship, he was made a full professor in 1870. In the France-Prussian war he volunteered as a medical orderly with the Prussian army, but after a month he returned to Basel, seriously ill with dysentery and diphtheria. He was often ill. By 1878 he had broken with Wagner. In 1879 he resigned his chair and received a generous pension. From henceforth he lived a solitary life and poured out a mass of short aphoristic books, culminating in a great flood of masterpieces in 1888. He finally lost his reason in January 1889 and died in 1900.

Within twenty-five years of the time Nietzsche ceased to be able to write coherently, his sister and disciple Elisabeth had collected and arranged aphorisms he had written in the

1880s, made them into a book, and begun to give that book canonical status. The authority that had hitherto belonged to the Bible was now for the first time transferred to another collection; every German soldier who went to the front in 1914 was given a copy of *Wille zur Macht, The Will to Power*, in his knapsack.

Elisabeth Nietzsche-Förster, it is true, abbreviated and falsified her brother's aphorisms, and modern Nietzsche scholars warn us not to accept *The Will to Power* as an actual book of Nietzsche's, but her popularisation of Nietzsche's teaching was not far off his intention. He saw himself as breaking humanity's history into two: there is life before him (just as there was life Before Christ, BC) and life after him (Just as there was life after Christ, in the years of our Lord, AD).[1] His early book *Thus Spake Zarathustra* was a new Sermon on the Mount, and the style was the aphoristic style of the original model.

Nietzsche's fantastic claim would seem to be completely justified – if indeed he succeeded in establishing what he claimed, namely the lack of value of all values. Establish that, and you establish that Christianity was a lie, for Christianity is at least based on the assumption that all values lead up to a supreme value, the love of God, and that this supreme value is worth dying for. Establish that, and you also establish that the large body of intelligent people in Nietzsche's day, who had given up Christianity but who had not given up the search for values outside themselves, were indeed decadent, not able to face up to the cost of the utter lack of value of all values. Establish that, and you have a case for saying that history has indeed come to a new division of the ages which will make the old BC–AD division pale into insignificance.

The heart of the matter is the nature of Christian morality. Christian morality for Nietzsche is not a special problem in moral philosophy; the English (like George Eliot) may think that morality can exist despite their denial of the existence of God, but Nietzsche is much too profound a thinker to fall

---

[1] *Ecce Homo*, xiv 'Warum ich ein Schicksal bin (Why I am a Fate)', 8.

into *that* trap.[2] Morality is by nature Christian, and the whole enterprise stands and falls with a decision about the existence of the Christian God. Once it is understood that God is dead, much more follows than anyone before in history had had the 'hardness' to assert.

The test case is truth. Hitherto humanity had been driven by the will to truth. This drive to discover truth had led to the assertion that only atheism was a tenable position to hold. But even today's atheists, he says, retain as their last ideal this will to truth. They do not realise that the will to truth is the basis of morality, and that morality inevitably rests on the assumption that God is truth. If God is truth, then ascetism in the search for truth remains the ideal; and asceticism is nothing other than a hidden will to die. Consequently a philosopher of life (as Nietzsche described himself) has one last problem: to overcome the will to truth.

Nietzsche took seriously the determinism he rightly perceived to be the common conclusion of nineteenth-century philosophy, and he applied it ruthlessly to his own life. He gave it uncompromising expression in his assertion of eternal recurrence, the theory that everything now happening will happen again and again for ever. This theory is the ultimate argument against the existence of God, for if *one* determined universe and only one came to pass, it would seem to have occurred 'from outside', as it were; but for Nietzsche there can be no 'outside', and consequently no beginning and end; this universe must eternally recur.

Nietzsche concluded that his own pain and suffering must also eternally recur, and that he must simply accept it. Integrity demanded it. 'Let us remain *hard*, us last Stoics!'[3]

The curious thing about Nietzsche, the transvaluer of all values, is that he sees himself in his sufferings as the true Christ. His life from boyhood, when his pastor father lost his reason and died, was dogged with headaches and nausea, and in his thirty-sixth year, when he was the age at which his father died, illness brought him also close to death. He

[2] *Götzen-Dämmerung, Twilight of the Idols*, ix Streifzüge eines Unzeitgemässen, 5, George Eliot.
[3] *Jenseits von Gut und Böse, Beyond Good and Evil*, 227.

accepted this suffering as fated, and also inwardly willed the pain and the solitude. The actual Christ thought the suffering was good and salvific and, in so thinking, he was completely out of touch with reality, but at least his illusion enabled him to accept suffering and to live and die without the worse illusion of theories and dogmas about Salvation. Christ on the cross remained the most sublime of symbols, even for Nietzsche; when he was sliding rapidly into insanity while staying at Turin at the end of 1888, his friends were alerted to the fact by the postcards he sent them: 'since the old God has abdicated, I shall from now on rule the world', some signed 'The Crucified'.

Nietzsche's complete rejection of both Christianity and Christ contains within it another sharp division, the division between Christ and the church. To understand the true nature of Christianity, one must first grasp that the Christianity of the church was already based on a misunderstanding.

> In reality there has been only one Christian and he died on the Cross. The 'Evangel' *died* on the Cross. What was called 'Evangel' from this moment onwards was already the opposite of what *he* had lived: '*bad* tidings', a *dysangel*.[4]

This Jesus was no genius or hero, as Renan had portrayed him. Rather, he was the Idiot. (Nietzsche once said that Dostoyevsky was the only psychologist from whom he had anything to learn.)[5] Jesus had a morbid susceptibility to the sense of touch; he shrank back in horror from every contact, every grasping of a firm object: he had 'an instinctive hatred of *every* reality'. 'The Kingdom of God is within you' (Luke 17.21). 'Resist not evil' is the key. Blessedness is in peace, gentleness, the inability for enmity. 'True life, eternal life is found – it is not promised, it is here, it is *within you*: as life lived in love, in love without deduction or exclusion, without distance'.[6] Jesus hated reality and it was reality that Nietzsche

---

[4] *Der Antichrist*, 1895, 39, *Twilight of the Idols and The Anti-Christ*, translated with an introduction and commentary, by R. J. Hollingdale (Harmondsworth, 1968), pp. 151 f.

[5] *Götzen-Dämmerung*, *Twilight of the Idols*, ix, 45.

[6] *Der Antichrist*, 29, translated by R. J. Hollingdale (Harmondsworth, 1968), pp. 140 f.

himself faced alone and in pain and so broke history into two, before him and after him; but at least Jesus did not believe anything; he practised rather than held beliefs about what was true; he acted – or rather, did not act.

The history of Judaism and the history of Christianity both followed the same pattern. In each case pure action was seized on by mean-minded men who corrupted pure action into a system of beliefs in order to enslave their dupes. Israel began as a natural religion, which correctly and instinctively lived as things are.

> The history of Israel is invaluable as a typical history of the *denaturalizing* of natural values . . . Originally, above all in the period of the Kingdom, Israel too stood in a *correct*, that is to say, natural relationship to all things. Their Yahweh was the expression of their consciousness of power, of their delight in themselves, their hopes of themselves: in him they anticipated victory and salvation, with him they trusted that nature would provide what the people needed – above all rain. Yahweh is the God of Israel and *consequently* the God of justice: the logic of every nation that is in power and has a good conscience about it.[7]

This 'natural' life was progressively corrupted by the priesthood, who forged their own self-interested versions of the ancient history and enslaved the people to themselves by turning God into a God who forgives him who repents. On this basis Christianity arose. The final corruption of Judaism in this denial of natural reality by priests and theologians and hierarchy was challenged by Jesus of Nazareth. He represented the outcasts of society; that is why he was crucified. The church, the heir and continuation of Judaism, falsified his teaching just as Judaism had earlier falsified the original religion of Israel.

Paul created Christianity out of Judaism by adding to Jesus' teaching the necessary instruments of subjection, the concepts of the Second Coming, the Last Judgement, and all temporal

---

[7] *Der Antichrist*, 25, translated by R. J. Hollingdale (Harmondsworth, 1968), pp. 135 f.

promises and expectations. In this way guilt, punishment, and sin were firmly fastened on mankind, and 'beliefs' became all important. Christianity was the vampire which sucked dry the great Roman Empire (as Bruno Bauer used to teach), and when the Renaissance was just about to triumph as the pagan Cesare Borgia became Pope, Martin Luther arose and saved Christianity.[8]

It will be clear from this summary that, although Nietzsche was heartily opposed to vulgar antisemitism, 'that does not stop it being true that, when he speaks plainly, his judgements about the Jews leave all antisemitism far behind in their severity; his anti-Christianity is chiefly based on antisemitism', to quote the words of Franz Overbeck, who had the sad task of going to Turin and bringing back the sick man to an asylum in Basel.[9]

Unfortunately, this theory of the history that resulted in the formation of the Christian Bible, both its Old Testament and its New, was not an aberration of a brilliant but isolated philosopher. The theory is lifted whole from the influential writings of Julius Wellhausen,[10] and re-expresses themes which we have encountered in Herder and Semler before him, not to mention in many scholars since Herder's day.

Although Nietzsche was an open and avowed enemy of Christianity, his person already exerted a strange fascination for Christian theologians while he was still able to talk to occasional solitary visitors – in 1888 Julius Kaftan paid him a three weeks' visit for the sake of some conversation with the master, and later confessed him 'one of the best tutors in theology'.[11] When he died the young Albert Schweitzer, living in Paris at the time, gave an admiring lecture on him at the German Institute. The picture of Jesus as the figure of

---

[8] *Der Antichrist*, 42, 58 (vampire), 61 (Luther).

[9] Franz Overbeck, 'Erinnerungen an Friedrich Nietzsche', *Die neue Rundschau*, 2. und 3. Heft (Berlin, 1906), 209–31; 320–30, at 222.

[10] F. Boschwitz, *Julius Wellhausen: Motive und Massstäbe seiner Geschichtsschreibung*, Marburg Dissertation, 1938, reprinted 1968, Appendix.

[11] Kaftan in conversation with Overbeck, 'Erinnerungen an Friedrich Nietzsche', *Die neue Rundschau* (1906), 224. Kaftan published a book *Das Christentum und Nietzsches Herrenmoral* (1896; 3rd ed., 1902), which I have not been able to see.

pure love and suffering, and the picture of the church as renewed Judaism which, through its capture of the Roman Empire, was able to enslave the world was something Nietzsche had imbibed from the best and ablest Biblical scholarship of his day. He himself rejected Christ along with Christianity, but his Christian followers were given a handle, by his own adoption of Christ-like traits, to take over his picture of Christ and make it the basis of their own continuing Christianity.

There is an old quip that the Reformation was Augustine versus Augustine; perhaps we can see the history of our own secular century as the history of Nietzsche versus Nietzsche. Nietzsche's overthrow of the authority of the Bible was met by a reaffirmation of the authority of the Bible – or rather a reaffirmation of the authority of the Bible insofar as that Bible carried within in, partly obscured, the figure of Jesus as the pure sufferer who loved without any limit at all. This is pure Nietzsche, without the venom, and it has become through Nietzsche's Christian interpreters, in scholarly circles and beyond, the dominant christology, taking various forms, from 'realized eschatology' to 'liberation theology'. It is ironic that such a determined opponent of Christianity became one of the most influential sources of a repristinated Biblical authority.

16

Wellhausen

Wellhausen gave his name to perhaps the most important and certainly the most brilliant epoch in Old Testament studies there has ever been. His disciples filled the bulk of the Old Testament chairs in the Protestant faculties of Theology in Germany and beyond, and swept all opposition before them.[1] His theory about the history of the formation of the Pentateuch (the 'Torah' or Law of the Jewish Bible, the Five Books of Moses) aroused as much public alarm and controversy when he published it in book form in 1878 as Strauss's *Life of Jesus* had aroused in 1835.[2] Popular opinion saw his theory as an attack on the authority of the Bible, and it was; but not just at the superficial level that he denied Moses wrote the books that bore his name. Wellhausen attacked the very notion that books could be sacred and inspired. The church traditionally taught that the writers of the books were inspired by God and that their writings conveyed the particular revelation of God's will. Wellhausen denied this doctrine of inspiration which led to 'Bibliolatry'. Yet, like Thomas Carlyle, he all the more passionately believed in revelation.[3] The important question is, What did

---

[1] Gunkel's judgement, the judgement of the leader of a new school who had to fight against Wellhausen's dominance; 'Wellhausen, Julius, und Wellhausensche Schule'. *Die Religion in Geschichte und Gegenwart*, v (1913), 1888–9; 2nd ed., v (1927–31), 1820–2.

[2] E. Schwartz, memorial address, *Nachrichten von der Königlichen Gesellschaft der Wissenschaften zu Göttingen*, Geschäftliche Mitteilungen aus dem Jahre 1918, pp. 43–70 at p. 58; *Gesammelte Schriften*, I (1938), pp. 326–361 at p. 344.

[3] Wellhausen's letters to William Robertson Smith, Cambridge University

Wellhausen mean by revelation?

Wellhausen was born in 1844, the son of the Lutheran pastor of Hameln on the Weser, the town the Pied Piper had once freed from rats. He loved the country people among whom he grew up for their entire lack of any sort of orthodoxy and their resignation and trust, guarantee of a rugged indestructability. They gave him faith in the German people. He thoroughly approved of the Prussian annexation of the Kingdom of Hannover and of Bismarck's aggressive policy to establish a great German nation; for his refusal to say Bismarck was a scoundrel his beloved teacher Heinrich Ewald showed him the door and never spoke to him again.[4]

As a student of theology at the University of Göttingen he had no taste for speculative theology or philosophy: 'nothing but empty striving! I always had simple aims and waited for the solution of life's problems from life itself, not from reflection'.[5] He was drawn instead to the eccentric Ewald and the study of the Old Testament. He learnt from Ewald to work first by the closest examination of the detail of an ancient text and then to move from the smallest detail out towards a natural and balanced and simple picture of the complicated whole.[6]

Wellhausen read with delight the prophetic and historical books of the Old Testament and felt guilty that he was beginning with the roof rather than the foundations, which the textbooks assured him was the Law. His guilt was gloriously lifted when, on a visit to Albrecht Ritschl in the summer of 1867, when he was just about to return to Göttingen to prepare himself for an academic career, he heard that K. H. Graf had published a book the preceding year arguing that the Prophets came first in time and the Law was

---

Library, Add 7449. An edition of these letters is to be published by Professor Rudolf Smend, Gottingen. This quotation, D768, undated [late 1881?].

[4] E. Schwartz, original address, pp. 45 f.; *GS*, I, p. 329.

[5] Schwartz, original p. 48; pp. 332 f., citing the unpublished reminiscences of Wellhausen.

[6] Julius Wellhausen, 'Heinrich Ewald', *Festschrift zur Feier des hundertfünfzigjährigen Bestehens der Königlichen Gesellschaft der Wissenschaften zu Göttingen* (Berlin, 1901), pp. 63–88 at pp. 64–66; reprinted in Julius Wellhausen: *Grundrisse zum Alten Testament*, edited by Rudolf Smend (Munich, 1965), pp. 120–138.

later. He was immediately convinced. In the next ten years, after qualifying as a university teacher and getting his first chair at the small university of Greifswald in Pomerania, he worked intensively on the new theory, profiting from the pioneering work of de Wette, the outsider J. F. L. George, Vatke the Hegelian, Eduard Reuss of Strasbourg, as well as of Graf. In a brilliant series of articles in the *Jahrbücher für Deutsche Theologie* in 1876 and 1877 he established the literary theory that made his name justly famous. His mastery of detail and clarity won acceptance for the view that still rules in Old Testament studies; he was only thirty-three years old.

His theory is beautifully simple. He argued that the first five books of the Bible, or rather the first six (Genesis to Joshua), were composed in the time of the exile, when the Jerusalem Temple was destroyed and many of the Jews and all their leaders were deported to Babylon. This complex of books of the Bible was put together by a slow amalgamation of originally independent documents. The earliest of these were the two documents J (where God was called Jahweh) and E (where God was called Elohim). J and E were combined into JE. The Deuteronomic corpus Dt was attached to JE. At the same time another independent work Wellhausen called Q because it told of four (quattuor) covenants (with Adam, Noah, Abraham and Moses) was formed. Q was enlarged to make a Priestly Codex and then this enlarged Q was united to JE + Dt to form our Hexateuch, the first six books of the Bible. Wellhausen acknowledged that J and E went through a number of recensions before being combined, and so did JE, Dt and Q, but he insisted that these complications should not obscure the fundamental simplicity of the story. Set aside Deuteronomy, and the rest of the Pentateuch could be explained as the combination of just three independent documents, J and E and Q (what is now usually called P for Priestly Source).[7]

Important as this theory is, it is only the technical and critical part of a far more significant reading not only of the

---

[7] Jahrbücher für Deutsche Theologie, 21 (1876), 392–450; 531–602; 22 (1877), 407–479; 'Die Composition des Hexateuchs und der historischen Bücher des Alten Testaments', 2nd impression of *Skizzen und Vorarbeiten*, Vol. 2 (Berlin, 1889), p. 210.

history of Israel or the history of the rise of Christianity (for Wellhausen had decided views on the New Testament as well as on the Old) but of the history of the world. Wellhausen believed he knew 'the principles that move the world'[8] and, reluctant though he was to enlarge on them, these 'principles that move the world' can be discovered clearly enough from his writings.

Wellhausen acted upon these principles, to his own great personal cost. In February 1879 his principles led him to write to Justus von Olshausen in the Minister for Education's office in Berlin asking to be transferred from the faculty of Theology to the faculty of Arts. In conscience he felt he should really resign forthwith, but his wife was ill after a miscarriage and a hysterectomy and he had no other means than his academic stipend, so he asked for a transfer. 'It strikes me as a lie,' he wrote, 'that I should be educating ministers of an Evangelical Church to which in my heart I do not belong.'[9]

It took Wellhausen nearly three years to get out of theology into a poorly-paid associate professorship in Halle, despite his constant appeals to the Ministry for a move. There was not the slightest pressure on him from the Prussian State, which was quite indifferent to the views of the pious citizens who were outraged by Wellhausen's views.[10] In fact it was probably Wellhausen's threat to resign and revert to the status of an unsalaried Privatdozent in April 1882 if he did not get a semitic language chair in Königsberg or Halle that finally made the Ministry move him.[11] Nor was there any pressure from his colleagues in the Greifswald Theological Faculty.

[8] Wellhausen to W. Robertson Smith (Summer 1882), D771.

[9] Wellhausen to Olshausen, 9.2.1879, Deutsches Zentralarchiv Hist. Abteilung II Merseburg Rep. 92 Justus von Olshausen B I Nr. 7, cited by Rudolf Smend, 'Wellhausen in Greifswald', *Zeitschrift für Theologie und Kirche* 78 (1981), 167.

[10] Schwartz, original address, p. 58; Gesammelte Scriften, p. 344. Wellhausen to W. Robertson Smith, 27 June 1881, D762; cited by Smend, *ZThK* 78 (1981), 168 f. Wellhausen to W. Robertson Smith, 9 July 1881, D763.

[11] Alfred Jepsen, 'Wellhausen in Griefswald: Ein Beitrag zur Biographie Julius Wellhausens' in *Festschrift zur 500. Jahrfeier der Universität Greifswald 17.10.1956*, Vol. II, Greifswald, 1956, pp. 47–56; reprinted in *Der Herr ist Gott* (Berlin, 1978), pp. 254–70, Anlage 5, pp. 266 f.

He had become a good friend of the leading conservative Hermann Cremer (a close collaborator of Martin Kähler's). and Cremer certainly did not put any pressure on him to go. Cremer admired him for his inward attachment to Christianity! As soon as he became convinced the church's teaching about Christ was wrong he thought he should resign from the church faculty.[12] Wellhausen's pagan aristocratic friend, the professor of classics, Ulrich von Wilamowitz-Moellendorff, thought his resignation was quite unnecessary. His judgement was that 'Wellhausen always remained a Christian; he never stopped asking the Lord Jesus to be a guest at every midday dinner ... He also remained a theologian; only that fact explains the whole cast of his history.'[13]

Why then did this Christian who always remained a theologian feel compelled to move out of the theological faculty?[14]

The simple answer is that Wellhausen no longer believed the German church had anything to do with true Christianity, except accidentally. This was not just an empirical judgement

[12] H. Cremer to M. Kähler, 14.9.1874, Neidersachs. Staats- und Universitätsbibliothek Göttingen, Cod. MS. Martin Kähler, K3, Cremer Nr 5, cited by Smend, 148; Cremer to Althoff, Deutsches Zentralarchiv Hist. Abteilung II Merseburg, Rep. 92 Althoff I. Reihe Nr. 136a, cited by Jepsen, Anlage 4, p. 266.

[13] Ulrich von Wilamowitz-Moellendorff, *Erinnerungen 1848–1914* (Leipzig, 1928), p. 188; *My Recollections 1848–1914*, translated by G. C. Richards (London, 1930), p. 226.

[14] 'And nevertheless an open question remains. How did Wellhausen come to the point of thinking that the expression of recognised truth would make [students] unfit for the service of the church, that is the preaching of the gospel? His predecessors were theologians, from de Wette by way of Vatke to Kuenan and Graf; his pupils also, who built on his theses and carried them further, would remain theologians. Why could he not remain a theologian, at the point where he simply only put the finishing stroke, as it were, under what his predecessors had already said?' Alfred Jepsen, 'Wellhausen in Greifswald', reprinted in *Der Herr is Gott* (Berlin, 1978), p. 261. See also Ernst Barnikol, 'Wellhausens Briefe aus seiner Greifswalder Zeit (1872–1879) an den anderen Heinrich Ewald-Schüler Dillmann: Ein Beitrag zum Wellhausen-Problem', *Gottes ist der Orient: Festschrift für Prof. D. Dr. Otto Eissfeldt D.D.* (Berlin, 1959), 28–39, at 29 f., and Rudolf Smend, 'Wellhausen in Greifswald', *Zeitschrift für Theologie und Kirche* 78 (1981), 141–176 at pp. 170 f. Smend rightly argues that the crux of the matter was Wellhausen's attitude to the church and his emphasis on the individual. I am deeply indebted to Smend's essay.

of the church of his day, but a judgement that the church in principle killed the true spirit of Christianity. A brilliant early book on the Pharisees and Sadducees could still be written in the hope of serving the church,[15] but by 1878 Wellhausen had come to see his opposition in principle to the church. This opposition to the church is the negative side of his view of how history was impelled forward.

Revelation for Wellhausen was 'not the books but the men – also men who had never written in a book; in short Thomas Carlyle in compendium redactus'.[16] Wellhausen is perhaps referring to a passage in Carlyle's *Sartor Resartus*: 'Great Men are the inspired (speaking and acting) Texts of that divine BOOK OF REVELATIONS, whereof a Chapter is completed from epoch to epoch, and by some named HISTORY'.[17] Neither Carlyle nor Wellhausen means by revelation the idea that the one true God makes promises and proclaims his will through chosen messengers. Wellhausen candidly admitted, 'I don't care a sausage for monotheism and the like'.[18] He agreed with the Christmas verses his friend Wilamowitz sent him in their Greifswald time together:

> We atheists? Only monotheism is atheism. Sole truth is sole lie. We both love the old gods piously and with faith . . .
>
> No god lives for ever. Christ and Antichrist brings the twilight of the gods, the monster Tryphon and Fenrer the wolf. The great Pan is dead, sounds forth the sudden news from rock to sea.
>
> Yet gods live ever in the elemental, God lives in the human breast that is striving for the beautiful and good. From this colourful reflected splendour we, his image, have our life.[19]

Wellhausen is not putting the many Great Men in place of

---

[15] Wellhausen to Dillmann, 18 (May or December) 1875, Barnikol, 32.

[16] Wellhausen to Robertson Smith, D.768, undated [late 1881?].

[17] Teufelsdrockh in *Sartor Resartus* (1833–4), chapter viii, Everyman edition, p. 134.

[18] Wellhausen to Robertson Smith, D.755, 18 August 1880, cited by Smend, 174.

[19] Wilamowitz, p. 188. Not in the English version of the book.

the One God; although the prophets are important in his scheme of history, the men who had never written a book are also important. But it is not the men themselves who move history forwards; rather it is the conjunction of the men and the circumstances in which they operated. The Great Men have the privilege, which came to them unsought, of sowing a seed in the field of Time which resulted in a play of action and reaction that brought forth fruit in Eternity. The Parable of the Seed growing Secretly, found only in Mark's Gospel, is the key to his view of history; the seed is the work of the Great Men, and the field in which the seed was sown was Time: 'Time is my possession, my field is Time' (Goethe).[20]

The right moment for the sowing of seeds in time was the open-air era when people acted in accordance with the necessity of their nature, the men of God as well as the murderers and adulterers, when they acted of their own free initiative, not according to external norms.[21] The prophets are the organs of the Spirit of Jahve, speaking spontaneously the truth which is right, which is divine and imperishable.[22] The prophets condemn the cult, but the cult itself, representing paganism, has sprung from the same conditions as prophecy itself. History is only moved forward by both the godly and the ungodly forces.[23] The cult was like a green

[20] Schwarz, original p. 48; *GS* I, pp. 332 f., citing Wellhausen's unpublished reminiscences. The reference to Goethe West-östlicher Divan, Buch der Sprüche, comes from J. Wellhausen, *Das Evangelium Marci*, 2nd ed. (Berlin, 1909), p. 35.

Mein Erbtheil wie herrlich, weit und breit!

Die Zeit ist mein Besitz, mein Acker ist die Zeit.

(How splendid, how broad and far is my inheritance! Time is my possession, my field is Time).

[21] See *Geschichte Israels: In zwei Bänden: Erster Band* (Berlin, 1878), pp. 427 f.; 442; *Prolegomena zur Geschichte Israels. Zweite Ausgabe der Geschichte Israels, Band I* (Berlin, 1883), pp. 436 f.; 451. The Prolegomena was translated as *Prolegomena to the History of Israel: with a reprint of the article Israel from the 'Encyclopaedia Britannica'* [with the further addition of section 11, 'Judaism and Christianity' from the German version of 1884]. Translated . . . under the author's supervision by J. Sutherland Black and Allan Menzies. With Preface by Professor W. Robertson Smith (Edinburgh, 1885) pp. 411 f.; 425.

[22] *Geschichte Israels*, I (1884), p. 414.

[23] *Geschichte Israels*, I (1878), p. 414: the men like the writer of Isaiah 40 ff. who

tree which grew out of the earth where it would, and the
prophets could condemn it completely.[24] The condition for
the work of the great Spirit-filled individuals was the existing
natural community with its 'real and fully profane folk-life
with its appropriate regulations and structures'.[25] The natural
community was the nation; 'the camp was, so to speak, at
once the cradle in which the nation was nursed and the
smithy in which it was welded into unity'; the camp was the
primitive sanctuary. 'War is what makes nations'.[26]

The Sermon on the Mount of Jesus, the greatest sower of a
seed in the field of Time, required the restoration of the
natural political order: 'the turn of the righteousness of the
Sermon on the Mount can only come when the civil legal
order is taken for granted'.[27]

Wellhausen's brilliant presentation of the documentary
hypothesis of the Pentateuch thus has behind it a bitter
polemic against the intellectualism of the scribes who worked
out and codified a minute written priestly law-code under
the conditions of the exile when the natural civil legal order
had disappeared. In place of the divine will proclaimed by
the prophets they put the Torah, the written Law; where
Micah needed three words – do justly, love mercy, walk
humbly (Micah 6.8) – the scribes need 613 commandments,
and even they were not sufficient. The history of David,
King and Hero, with his pagan warrior Obed Edom the
Gittite, is rewritten in the Book of Chronicles so that he
becomes a cantor and liturgist and Obed Edom a cleric
(compare 1 Chronicles 15 with 2 Samuel 6).[28] The prophets
had opposed the cult, but had never succeeded in killing it;
the scribes worked the cult into their new system and so

stood at the very end of pre-exilic history looked back at that history's 'driving
forces, godly as well as ungodly'.

[24] *Geschichte Israels*, p. 84.

[25] *Die Pharisäer und die Sadducäer: Eine Untersuchung zur inneren jüdischen Geschichte*
(Greifswald, 1874), p. 15, note 1.

[26] 'Israel', Encyclopaedia Britannia, 9th ed. xiii, reprinted in *Prolegomena to the
History of Israel* (Edinburgh, 1885), p. 434. Cf. *Israelitische und Jüdische Geschichte*
(Berlin, 1894), p. 15; cf. 4th ed. (Berlin, 1901), p. 26: 'War is what makes nations'.

[27] *Geschichte Israels*, I (1884), p. 431 f.

[28] *Die Pharisäer und die Sadducäer*, p. 15, note 1.

killed nature in it. The system became the shield to protect supernatural monotheism.

> The great pathologist of Judaism [Paul] is perfectly right: in the Mosaic theocracy the cult had become a pedagogical corrective. It is estranged from the heart; had it not been revived because it was an ancient custom, it would never have blossomed again of its own accord. It no longer had its roots in natural feelings; it is a dead work, despite all the seriousness with which it was taken – indeed because of the painstakingness and the conscientiousness. At the restoration of Judaism the old observances were patched together into a new system which served only as a form to preserve a nobler content, which could never have been saved except in armour as restrictive as this, rugged enough to ward off all foreign influences. The paganism of Israel against which the prophets protested in vain was inwardly conquered on its own ground by the Law; and the cult, after nature had been killed off in it, was made into a shield for supernatural monotheism.[29]

Monotheism was simply a false form of true individualism. The prophets saw that the religions of the nations were being destroyed by history. They were heroes whose heroism was different from that of the practical politicians.

> They absorbed into their religion that conception of the world which was destroying the religions of the nations, even before it had been fully grasped by the secular consciousness. Where others saw only the ruin of everything that is holiest, they saw the triumph of Jehovah over delusion and error. Whatever else might be overthrown, the really worthy remained unshaken. They recognised ideal powers only, right and wrong, truth and falsehood; second causes were matters of indifference to them, they were no practical politicians. But they watched the course of events attentively, nay

[29] *Geschichte Israels*, I (1878), p. 442; *Prolegomena*, German (1883), p. 451; English (1885), p. 425.

with passionate interest. The present, which was passing before them, became to them as it were the plot of a divine drama which they watched with an intelligence that anticipated the *dénouement*. Everywhere the same goal of the development, everywhere the same laws. The nations are the *dramatis personae*, Israel the hero, Jehovah the poet of the drama.[30]

What was to be done at this time of the shaking of the foundations? Amos and Hosea had made the mistake of thinking the moral personality based on an inner conviction could be the basis of a national life. Jeremiah saw through their mistake.

> The true Israel narrowed to himself. Of the truth of his conviction he never had a moment's doubt; he knew that Jehovah was on his side, that on Him depended the eternal future. But, instead of the nation, the heart and the individual conviction were to him the subject of religion. On the ruins of Jerusalem he gazed into the future filled with joyful hope, sure of this that Jehovah would one day pardon past sin and renew the relation which had been broken off – though on the basis of another covenant than that laid down in Deuteronomy. 'I will put my law upon their heart, and write it on their mind; none shall say to his neighbour, Know the Lord, for all shall have that knowledge within them'.[31]

The actual Judaism that arose in the exile could not recover the pagan cult presupposed, if opposed, by the prophets, and they could not accept Jeremiah's substitute for the cult. They patched together an artificial system by which the individual's life was drilled and regimented. They had no true 'historical life' as a nation and so created an artificial past history and an artificial future vindication when history would simply stop and they would get the fulfilment of their wishes in their

---

[30] Encyclopaedia Britannica, xiii, 410; *Prolegomena to the History of Israel*, p. 473.
[31] Encyclopaedia Britannica, xiii; *Prolegomena to the History of Israel*, p. 491.

triumph over against the Gentiles; they could do nothing of themselves to work for this Kingdom of God.

If the Jews had to wait for this artificial apocalyptic vindication, where was justice for the individual? The exilic prophet Ezekiel made an important step forward by insisting that 'the soul that sins, it shall die'. He pursued a good instinct in opposing to a fatalism that repined because of past sins the possibility of repentance and forgiveness. But his teaching of the freedom of the will was perverse because it ultimately made the difference between a pious man and a godless man turn on accident. (Wellhausen is giving the classical argument against the freedom of the will, classical yet fallacious. Determinism destroys the very distinction between willed and accidental, so that an argument that depends on the rejection of the proposition that something is possibly accidental cannot be allowed in support of a system of thought that has no room for such propositions.)

Job's answer to the problem of unmerited evil as it inflicted the individual was much better than Ezekiel's.

> Job believes more firmly in the direct testimony of his conscience than in the evidence of facts and the world's judgement about him; and against the dreadful God of reality the righteous God of faith victoriously wins acceptance.[32]

This move was a by-product of prophecy, which properly had to do with God's revelation to all, but in the failure of prophecy people like Job learnt the more potent subjective truth that the soul in its relationship to God had to dare to take its stand on itself and rely only on itself. Prophecy was turned into an inner dealing with the Deity, fully inward and self-sufficient. This is the deepest essence of the religious life.

---

[32] 'Abriss der Geschichte Israels und Juda's', *Skizze und Vorarbeiten*, i (Berlin, 1884), p. 93. The new section 11 of the 'Abriss' on Judaism and Christianity was translated and inserted into the old unrevised Encyclopaedia article 'Israel' in the appendix to *Prolegomena to the History of Israel. With a Reprint of the Article* Israel *from the 'Encyclopaedia Britannica'* (Edinburgh, 1885). In a later separate reprint of the encyclopaedia article, section 11 was put at the end: *Sketch of the History of Israel*, 3rd ed. (London & Edinburgh, 1891). This passage, p. 217.

This divine spirit of assurance rises to its boldest expression in the seventy-third Psalm: 'Nevertheless I am continually with Thee; Thou holdest me by my right hand; Thou guidest me with Thy counsel, and drawest me after Thee by the hand. If I have Thee, I desire not heaven nor earth; if my flesh and my heart fail, Thou, God, art for ever the strength of my heart, and my portion'.[33]

Wellhausen's brilliant paraphrase of Psalm 73 gives us the clue to his whole deeply religious position. To get the psalm to say what he wants, he has first adopted a conjectural emendation at the end of verse 24: 'and afterwards thou wilt receive me to glory' becomes 'and takest me by the hand, after Thee'.[34] Then the Psalmist's monotheism, by which he relies on the one God who rules heaven and earth ('Whom have I in heaven but thee? And there is nothing upon earth that I desire besides thee') becomes subtly transformed by Wellhausen into a purely inward God who is a substitute for any care about heaven and earth: 'Wenn ich dich habe, so frage ich nicht nach Himmel und Erde, If I have thee, I cease to care about heaven and earth'. Of course Wellhausen knows his conjectural emendation is doubtful, and he also knows the Psalm ends with an assertion of the objective destruction of the wicked, which will not serve his purpose, but in essence the Psalm can be made his own.[35]

Judaism could not attain to this religion; it had broken the connection between work of the hands and desire

---

[33] *Skizze*, p. 94; Appendix to English *Prolegomena*, p. 506; separate English ed., pp. 218 f. Compare Wellhausen's letter to Robertson Smith commenting on Smith's book *The Prophets of Israel*, D.770, 11 May 1882: 'The true conclusion [to the story of the prophets is not Isaiah, as Smith argued, but] lies in Psalm 73'.

[34] I am using here the translation of Paul Haupt's *Polychrome Edition of the Bible*, for which Wellhausen produced the volume on the Psalms, (Leipzig, London, and New York, 1904).

[35] *Polychrome Bible: The Psalms* (Leipzig etc., 1904), p. 194: 'The purely subjective conviction that God and man are in communion is nowhere in the Psalms more strongly felt nor more beautifully expressed [than in verse 23]. Yet this conviction does not suffice; a confirmation is needed, which is furnished by the miserable, sudden death of the wicked'.

of the heart, between the good and worldly goods.[36]

Jesus protested against the dominant tendency of Judaism. His monotheism is quite different from theirs in that it demanded the whole man. He taught the common morality that aims at the furtherance of the welfare of others. 'It is just this natural morality of self-sacrifice which he names the law of God'. 'He is most distinctly opposed to Judaism in his view of the Kingdom of God, not as merely the future reward of work, but as the present goal of effort, it being the supreme duty of man to help it to realise itself on earth, from the individual outwards. Love is the means, and the community of love the end'.[37]

If this sounds too much like an ethics of good works, Wellhausen hastens to add that self-denial, the basic demand of the gospel, enables the will to break the causal connection between its deed and their consequences: the causal nexus is broken and the inseparable interchange between God and the soul begins. We are reminded of the rapport between the prophets and God that Wellhausen emphasised in an earlier passage.[38] Jesus not only assured men of this certainty but proved it in his life. 'He had in fact lost his life and gained it; he was *able* to do what he *willed* to do.[39] He had escaped the restrictions of race and the passions of self-seeking nature; he had found freedom and personality in God, who alone is master of himself and who raises to himself those who long for him. Jesus works in the world and for the world, but with his faith he stands over the world and outside it. He can offer himself for the world because he craves nothing from the world, but, secure with God, he has attained serenity and peace of soul'.[40] He did not achieve this because he had a special nature but because he was a Man (hence his use of

---

[36] *Skizze*, p. 98; cf. Appendix to English *Prolegomena*, p. 509; the separate English ed., pp. 223 f., gives up the attempt to translate this section in full.

[37] *Skizze*, p. 99; Appendix to English *Prolegomena*, p. 510; separate English ed., p. 225.

[38] *Geschichte Israels* I, p. 414.

[39] A stoic ideal. Epictetus was Wellhausen's favourite reading as a boy. Eduard Schwartz, *GS*, I, p. 331.

[40] *Skizze*, pp. 99 f.; cf. Appendix to English *Prolegomena*, p. 511; separate English ed., p. 226.

'Son of Man' to indicate his own I); 'along with the nature of God, he discovered in himself the nature of man. Eternity for him reaches right into the present; he already lives on earth in the midst of the Kingdom of God, as well as seeing the Last Judgement already accomplished inwardly in the human soul here below'.[41] He could have dispensed with current Jewish eschatology, but probably assumed it; and we cannot trust the eschatology of the rest of the New Testament to be his, since it is so imbued with the Jewish ideas of the disciples.

Here is a statement of Wellhausen's own personal belief.

> The goal and the motive of piety cannot be anything but Egoism – otherwise the piety is self-deceit.[42] The goal of piety in the Old and New Testament as well as in the nature of things is life, the maintenance of life and of the person. Naturally in the sense that whoever saves his life loses it, and whoever loses his life for the gospel saves it. That is too little emphasised in Carlyle; he always has only the social in view. Religion is of course also that which *binds* men together; but the prior thing, it seems to me, is the completely personal and individual relationship to God. Plain self evident things, that have become theoretically difficult for me it is true. In practice this pious Egoism of losing life to gain it is naturally the most difficult thing to contemplate. Life would long ago have been sacrificed, but the cursed *affections*![43]

Wellhausen's decision to leave the Faculty of Theology and to give up training ministers for the church was founded on his refusal to live a lie, to have anything to do with the Yes and No or the Yes through No of the Jesuitism Carlyle detected in all contemporary churches.[44] The mother of the

---

[41] *Skizze*, p. 100; Appendix to English *Prolegomena*, p. 511; separate English ed., pp. 226 f.

[42] Cf. Epictetus I. xix.2: self-interest is the basis of morality.

[43] Wellhausen to W. R. Smith, D.774, undated [August? 1881].

[44] Carlyle, 'Jesuitism', *Latter-Day Pamphlets*, p. 264. Wellhausen reread this volume of Carlyle as he took his decision to resign his chair rather than remain in the Theological Faculty. Letter to W. R. Smith, D768, undated [late 1881?].

church was Judaism,[45] and Judaism was the extraordinary attempt to conserve the external trappings of the pre-exilic theocracy by imbuing these products of natural religious naivety with the inwardness and pathos and earnestness of the prophets.[46] Judaism was a pathological system that was a straightjacket on the untamed self-will of the people, something alien to their real inner life.[47] Intellectualism dominated practice.[48] All the hatred Wellhausen had for Judaism was turned on the church, for the church did for Jesus what Judaism did for Moses and Elijah and Jeremiah.

Revelation for Wellhausen is the interplay between the great individuals who sacrifice themselves and sow a seed in Time; this seed can only be sown in a period when there is fresh air, when nations are being born in war and tempered in battle, when men like Prince Bismarck act out of their own nature and dare to be great. Wellhausen knew long before the event, as so many of his contempories knew, that war between Germany and the two powers that were threatening her, Russia on the one side and the Jews who were using France to grind Germany between them, was inevitable.[49] He

---

[45] *Geschichte Israels* I, pp. 84, 439; Wellhausen to Mommsen, 15 January 1881, published by Ernst Bammel, 'Judentum, Christentum und Heidentum: Julius Wellhausens Briefe an Theodor Mommsen 1881–1902', *Zeitschrift für Kirchengeschichte*, 80 (1969), 221–254.

[46] *Die Pharisäer und die Sadducäer*, p. 13, the section pointedly referred to in Wellhausen's letter to Dillman, 18 (May or December) 1875, Barnikol, p. 32.

[47] *Geschichte Israels*, I, 442; *Prolegomena*, German, p. 451, English, p. 425.

[48] *Die Pharisäer und die Sadducäer*, pp. 16 f.

[49] Wellhausen to Robertson Smith, D.807, 19 September 1887. Kuenan had again written to Wellhausen, as he did nine years before, to protest against the annexation of Alsace Lorraine. Wellhausen is against Prussian chauvinism, but can't stand foreigners' stupidity. The annexation was justified. Wellhausen always held war with Russia was inevitable, with France stupid – but forced on Prussia because the Jews were using France to grind Germany between France and Russia. See D.772, 24 August 1882; D.791, 31 May 1884; D.809, 23 December 1887; D.825, 1 November 1891; D.826, 19 March 1892. This last letter is the one in which he pretty accurately foretells the outbreak of World War I. 'Everyone is become gradually so accustomed to the prospects of war that no one will be disturbed by it. It will easily be set off somewhere accidentally, for example in Bulgaria. Our wrath against Russia is far far greater than against France; I mean of course against the ruling circles in Russia'. See Heinz Lemmermann, *Kriegserziehung im Kaiserreich. Studien zur politischen Funktion von Schule und Schulmusik 1890–1918*, 2 vols (Lilienthal/Bremen, 1984).

welcomed the war when it came, and only regretted he did not have a son to send to the front. 'War is what makes nations', and only supreme individualists in strong nations sow a seed in Time and move history onward. Both Judaism and the church belonged to unhistorical times and stood in the way of true advance.

17

Harnack

Harnack was unshakeably convinced that world history and our own individual lives could be plotted as ascending curves, having a beginning and leading forwards to a higher and a better goal. Science itself could tell us nothing about either the curve of the world or the curve of our own individual lives, but a cool scientific examination of history would help.

A cool scientific examination of history would inevitably lead us back through the great personalities of history to the greatest of all, Jesus Christ. The cool scientific historical examination of the records of his life and the records of the effects of his life would put us in possession of his certainty of God as Father – and so in possession of certain knowledge of the significance of both world history and of our own lives.

For Harnack the Bible was no sacred revelation but simply a book to be read literally, to be taken as the moderately reliable record of what happened, and to be measured by the highest and best it itself offered. By this standard, the Old Testament was to be rejected and the New Testament to be taken in a modern sense – for the records of what occurred in Palestine are the records of what, rightly understood, produced the modern world. The cool historical understanding of the New Testament is necessary to prevent the modern world from falling back into lower stages of civilisation, and the historical study of the New Testament will alone secure to the individual the peace and certainty of progressing with the progress of history.

Harnack's father, Theodosius Harnack, was a conservative Lutheran theologian in Dorpat, in the German-speaking

University of what was then a Baltic province of the Russian Empire. His two-volume work on Luther's theology marked the beginning of a reawakened interest in Luther which has deeply marked modern Protestantism.

Already in Dorpat Adolf was learning to read Luther – and indeed the whole of the history of the early church and of Christianity – from another point of view than that of his father and his other teachers. His teacher from afar, whose lectures he never attended, was Albrecht Ritschl.

Ritschl's decisive historical work was to break the spell of the over-simple Tübingen view of the early church as a naked conflict between two opposing positions: Peter's position as a Jewish particularist expecting the triumph of the Jewish people in an earthly Kingdom of God, and Paul's position as a universalist preaching a present spiritual Kingdom. Ritschl argued that Peter and Paul were close to each other, that both had elements of both positions in their teaching and that, although Paul gave the decisive impulse towards the true view of the significance of Jesus Christ and convinced Peter and the other apostles of his correct understanding of the Gospel, he still maintained impure remnants of Jewish ideas in his system, chiefly the idea that the Gospel could be proved from the Old Testament.[1]

Ritschl's theological position, which he claimed to be based on the true kernel of Luther's teaching, decisively distinguished between religion and philosophy. True religion was the apprehension of God as Father, with Christ as the mirror of the paternal heart of God, the founder of the Kingdom of free and triumphant spirits. Ritschl thought he was replacing a philosophical view of the world with an historical view, and this became his pupil Adolf Harnack's life-long theme.

In 1872 Adolf Harnack left the University of Dorpat, full of academic honour, and went to the University of Leipzig. In Leipzig he wrote a doctoral thesis on the source-criticism of the history of Gnosticism, and a Latin study of a Gnostic

[1] A. Ritschl, *Die Entstehung der altkatholischen Kirche.* Cf. A. Harnack, *Lehrbuch der Dogmengeschichte*, Vol. I (Freiburg i.B., 1886), pp. 61 f.; *Marcion: Das Evangelium vom Fremden Gott* (2nd ed., Leipzig, 1924), pp. 11–13; 200–202.

writing as the requirement for the right to teach. In 1874 he held the first meeting of his Church History Seminar, which was to continue unbroken for over fifty years. In the early years, Martin Rade, the founder and editor of the influential monthly liberal journal *Die Christliche Welt* and Friedrich Loofs, the Church Historian, were members; Gunkel belonged for three semesters in the Giessen years; Karl Barth attended in the Winter Semester 1906–1907; and Dietrich Bonhoeffer was a member of the seminar in its last session in the Summer Semester of 1929, when Harnack turned seventy-eight.

The Leipzig years were fruitful in other ways, too. In 1876, his friend and fellow-Ritschlian Emil Schürer, founded the *Theologische Literaturzeitung* which continues to the present day (having absorbed its conservative rival, Luthardt's *Theologisches Literaturblatt*) as the leading German review of theological books; the style and format have remained the same for over a century. Harnack formally joined Schürer as editor on 1 January 1881.

In 1879, at the age of twenty-seven, he was appointed to a full chair at the University of Giessen in the Grand Duchy of Hessen, which had been incorporated against its will into the Bismarckian Reich in 1866. The theological faculty was very small, with only seventeen students in his first semester. The professors were all young – his friend Emil Schürer the oldest, aged thirty-four – but their outstanding quality soon attracted more students, and by the time Harnack left Giessen nine years later he alone had sixty students for his Church History course and one hundred and fifty for his lectures on the apostolic church.

The most important achievement of the Giessen years was the publication of the first two volumes of his textbook on the History of Dogma. He was following Ritschl's advice to his young followers, 'Trust in God, keep your powder dry, write text books and reference books' – Cromwell's advice to his troops, mediated through Carlyle, and then enlarged.

Harnack wrote with great facility – he once quipped, 'My pen is cleverer than I am'.[2] He used first to master the material

---

[2] Agnes von Zahn-Harnack [Adolf Harnack's daughter] *Adolf von Harnack* (Berlin, 1936; 2nd ed., 1951), p. 98.

(he had a tenacious memory) and then write up that section of the work at one go. He would softly read over aloud what he had written in order to get the sound right, and then make corrections. He set himself strict deadlines and almost always did better than keep them. Volume 1 of the History of Dogma, 696 close-printed pages, complete with notes and appendices, took him only thirteen months to write at a time when he was lecturing six times a week on Church History, six times a week on History of Dogma, with two hours a week for his Seminar. The children were always free to come into his study while he was writing. This was the only time in his life he broke his strict rule of not working in the evenings; the evenings were for music, whist, or patience. 'In my house no one works after 8 o'clock at night'.[3]

Volume 1 of the History of Dogma, 1866, was ready in December 1885, and the first copy was sent off to Ritschl with a fulsome letter of thanks for all Harnack owed to his intellectual father. Harnack's actual father was another matter. Theodosius Harnack was silent for a long while and then at the end of January 1886 he at last wrote a sharp and bitter rebuke to Adolf.

> Our difference is not merely theological but a profound and directly Christian difference, so that if I overlooked it I should be betraying Christ; and no one, not even someone who stands so near to me as you, my son, could demand that of me or expect it. To name only the all-decisive main issue: whoever regards the fact of the resurrection as you do is in my eyes no longer a Christian theologian. I totally fail to understand how anyone can still appeal to history after that sort of historical construction; or I understand it only if the appeal to history is meant to denigrate Christianity.
>
> So, either – or . . . For me Christianity stands or falls with the fact of the resurrection; with the fact of the resurrection the Trinity, too, stands for me rock firm.[4]

---

[3] Agnes von Zahn-Harnack, *Life*, p. 281.

[4] Theodosius Harnack to Adolf Harnack, 29 January, 1886; Agnes von Zahn-Harnack, *Adolf von Harnack*, 1st ed. p. 143; 2nd ed. p. 105.

This conflict foreshadowed the public controversies to come in Adolf Harnack's life as he applied Ritschl's teaching to the theological issues of his day. From this earlier conflict he learnt a sweet and patient tolerance of those who felt Christianity itself was threatened by his arguments – a sweet and patient tolerance, a 'contemplative calm', that must have maddened his opponents. Adolf Harnack also learnt from the conflict with his father never to force his students in any way to change their minds; consequently he never deliberately formed a 'school' around himself, and he always remained a little detached from those who thought of themselves as his followers, and so retained the power to puzzle and shock them by the unexpected positions he sometimes took up.[5]

After two years at Marburg, Harnack moved to the University of Berlin in 1888. The controversy which the conservative churchmen feared would follow Harnack's appointment soon broke, not because Harnack was looking for controversy but because the students themselves came to him for advice and he gave it, using one of his weekly lectures for the occasion, and publishing the text in *Die Christliche Welt*. A young pastor in Württemberg, Christoph Schrempf, had celebrated baptism without reading the Apostles' Creed, and he was disciplined. The students wanted to know if they should petition the church assembly to remove the Apostles' Creed from the ordination vows and from use in church services.

Harnack showed himself very sympathetic to the students' basic position, although he advised them not themselves to petition but to devote themselves to the study of the history of dogma with the resolve that they would hold fast to their ideals when they became official pastors in the church. In any case a head-on attack was the wrong way of dealing with the Apostles' Creed; most of the Creed could be reinterpreted in a satisfactory way, as had already happened when Protestants gave to the words 'the communion of saints' a different meaning from that given by Roman Catholics. All the

---

[5] See one of Harnack's rare references to the conflict with his father, in a letter to his pupil, Karl Holl, 1915, Agnes von Zahn-Harnack, *Life*, p. 238.

individual sentences which a Christian confessed were not to be taken as bare facts but as expressions of faith entertained for the sake of the invisible relationships and values they represented. There was only one clause that could not be got round in any of these ways, the clause 'conceived by the Holy Ghost, born of the Virgin Mary'. Precisely the opposite of this was the case. Nevertheless a pastor or professor who rejected this clause could in all good conscience remain at his post provided he still agreed with the basic beliefs of his church, that he never made a secret of his views, and that he did what was possible to get a change made. In general, however, he should honour the Apostles' Creed for its religious value as an old witness to his own faith, and should acknowledge that many serious and upright Christians still held to its literal meaning.[6]

In all the subsequent controversy Harnack maintained an eirenic tone, and insisted principally on the rights of historical criticism to settle the issue. If Mark, Paul, and John did not believe in the Virgin Birth, we cannot insist it is essential; belief that Jesus is the Son of God or (to use a later expression) the God-man is the foundation and corner-stone of Christianity, but this belief is independent of belief in the Virgin Birth.[7]

In 1890 Harnack became a member of the Prussian Academy of Sciences. The Academy celebrated the second century of its foundation in 1900, and Harnack prepared in the astonishingly short time of four years a four-volume history of the Academy, and he delivered the public oration on the anniversary day, in the presence of the Kaiser. The Kaiser, who had hitherto regarded Harnack as a nuisance, was impressed, and out of this encounter sprang a firm friendship between the two men. In 1905 Harnack took on the post of general director of the Royal Library in Berlin alongside his chair of Church History (although Karl Holl

---

[6] *Die Christliche Welt*, 18 August, 1892; Agnes von Zahn-Harnack, *Life*, pp. 195–201.

[7] 'Das Apostolische Glaubensbekenntnis: Ein geschichtlicher Bericht nebst einer Einleitung und einem Nachwort', *Reden und Aufsätze*, Vol. I (Gieszen, 1904), pp. 219–64, at p. 258.

was brought in to a second Church History chair to make up for Harnack's time on his new duties). In 1914, on the day the Royal Library was re-opened in its new quarters, Harnack was given an hereditary title: he was now Adolf von Harnack. In 1911 the University of Berlin celebrated its centenary, and the Kaiser used the occasion to found the Kaiser Wilhelm-Gesellschaft on lines laid down by Harnack and with Harnack as the first president. The job of the Kaiser Wilhelm-Gesellschaft, which is still continued today by the Max Planck-Gesellschaft, was to give state support to scientific, medical and industrial research. The Kaiser Wilhelm-Gesellschaft, for example, supported the institutes which developed poison gas and defences against poison gas and which found ways of recovering oil and petroleum from coal. Harnack fought hard and successfully to keep the Gesellschaft in existence in the post-war decade, and he was to die away from home in his eightieth year on an official trip for the opening of the Heidelberg Medical Clinic which was supported by the Kaiser Wilhelm-Gesellschaft (10 June 1930).

Harnack was proud of being a servant of the German Reich. He believed that Germany's power should expand. The toast proposed by his neighbour Max Delbrück (brother of his brother-in-law) at their New Year's Party to see in the new century was 'To the greater Germany and the greater Fleet'. He lived among people who believed that war was inevitable. He himself travelled and spoke at public meetings in support of peace, but began to see that the political leaders of his nation had decided on war and were taking steps that made war inevitable. He saw the threat as coming from Russia ('the Mongolian danger to Europe') and Russia's ally, France. He was shocked to learn, as he was drafting the speech the Kaiser was to use, in part, to announce the outbreak of war, that Britain had decided to come in on the side of France. He did his best, by appealing to American theologians, to keep the United States out of the war. He thought Germany should always have held firm to its defensive aims, and just before the Armistice he bemoaned the fact that the military leaders had been beguiled by advances on the eastern front and had not taken the chances available a year or even months before to conclude a compromise peace. But he believed his students on the front were dying for a sacred cause, just as British theologians, with few exceptions, believed it of their own students. He wrote a poem for them which said 'Care not for thy body nor thy limbs. What is alive in thee will return redoubled. Righteous Abel's blood abides not in the ground; of such seed, sown by God, the saying holds true: "Die and Bring Forth"'.[8]

The contributions he made to German public life and his interventions in church affairs are now almost forgotten, but his speaking and writing on theology and the Bible had an enormous influence on how educated people regard the Christian faith. Even in scholarly circles, where his name is not often mentioned, his influence lives on: C. H. Dodd in England said little that Harnack had not said before him; Bultmann can be seen as Harnack's heir; and Barth is closer to Harnack than either would have conceded at the time of their own public controversy in 1923.[9]

In the Winter Semester of 1899/1900, the forty-eight-year-old Harnack offered a course of sixteen open lectures for students of all faculties on *Das Wesen des Christentums*, the essence of Christianity. About 600 students turned up, and one of them took down the freely-delivered discourses in shorthand. Harnack had not expected this, but the existence of a transcript enabled him to publish the course pretty much as it was delivered – with a few exceptions, nothing was changed except where printed style demanded it. In the first year or so 73,000 copies were sold and by the time of his death the book had gone through fourteen German editions and had been translated into at least fourteen other languages.

---

[8] Agnes von Zahn-Harnack, *Life*, pp. 292, 439, 387, 443 f., 445, 450 f., 480 f., 449. Cf. Harnack's war speech, 'Was wir schon gewonnen haben und was wir noch gewinnen müssen' in *Deutsche Reden in schwerer Zeit: gehalten von den Professoren an der Universität Berlin, November 1914* (Berlin, 1915), p. 151 et passim.

[9] H. Martin Rumscheidt, 'Revelation and Theology: an analysis of the Barth-Harnack correspondence of 1923', *Scottish Journal of Theology*, Monograph Series (Cambridge, 1972).

The English translation was titled *What is Christianity?*

> The fact that the whole of Jesus' message may be reduced to these two heads – God as the Father, and the human soul so ennobled that it can and does unite with Him – shows us that the Gospel is in no wise a positive religion like the rest; that it contains no statutory or particularistic elements; *that it is, therefore, religion itself.* It is superior to all antithesis and tension between this world and a world to come, between reason and ecstasy, between work in the world and holding aloof from it, between Judaism and Hellenism. It can dominate them all, and to no sphere of earthly life is it confined or necessarily tied down . . .
>
> The Lord's Prayer . . . is spoken – as every one must feel who has ever given it a thought in his soul – by one who has overcome all inner unrest, or overcomes it the moment that he goes before God. The very apostrophe of the prayer, 'Father', exhibits the steady faith of the man who knows that he is safe in God, and it tells us that he is certain of being heard. Not to hurl violent desires at heaven or to obtain this or that earthly blessing does he pray, but to preserve the power which he already possesses and strengthen the union with God in which he lives. No one, then, can utter this prayer unless his heart is in profound peace and his mind wholly concentrated on the inner relation of the soul with God. All other prayers are of a lower order, for they go into particulars or are so framed that in some way or other they stir the imagination in regard to the things of sense as well; whilst this prayer leads us away from everything to the height where the soul is alone with its God. And yet the earthly element is not absent. The whole of the second half of the prayer deals with earthly relations, but they are placed in the light of the Eternal . . .[10]

---

[10] *Das Wesen des Christentums*, extracts from the fourth lecture, part 2 (Leipzig, 1900); new edition for the 50th anniversary of the first publication with an introduction by Rudolf Bultmann (Stuttgart, 1950), pp. 38–40; *What is Christianity? Sixteen lectures delivered in the University of Berlin during the Winter Term, 1899–1900,*

This popular book aside, Harnack continued to write scholarly articles and books on textual criticism, on newly-published discoveries like the Odes of Solomon, and on the literature of the New Testament. In all the upheaval of the post-war years, he produced a major study on the second-century heretic Marcion, which is still the standard book on the subject. He brought to fruition the work begun in the essay on Marcion's teaching with which he won a gold medal as a nineteen-year-old student of the University of Dorpat, the work which in his speech on taking up membership of the Berlin Academy in 1890 he said remained the real object of all his research. He argued that Marcion was as great a reformer of the church as Luther. Marcion attempted to recover the true teaching of Jesus and Paul about the God of love who was above the God of wrath of the Old Testament. Although Marcion did not succeed in persuading the church about this theology, he nevertheless gave the decisive impulse to the welding together of congregations into a catholic church. By his edition of a New Testament – a Gospel (our Luke's Gospel drastically shortened) and an Epistle (Paul's Epistles to the Romans, Corinthians, Galatians, Ephesians, Philippians and Colossians drastically shortened) – he made the church produce a New Testament canon of its own. In this way heroes move history forward.

The books on the New Testament Harnack wrote in this period were mainly detailed investigations of the language of the Gospel according to St Luke and the Acts of the Apostles to show that the author of these two books as a whole was also the author of the 'We' passages in Acts, passages written by a companion of St Paul. Harnack therefore defended, on the basis of a thorough examination of evidence, the old tradition that Luke the physician, mentioned by Paul in Colossians 4.14, 2 Timothy 4.11 and Philemon 24 was the author of the Gospel bearing his name and its continuation in the Acts of the Apostles. The German critics of his day, who were the moderate and balanced heirs of the tradition of the Tübingen school, held that the true author was a later figure

translated into English by Thomas Bailey Saunders, third and revised edition (London, 1904), pp. 65, 66 f., 67: translation slightly revised.

who at best used older traditions. Harnack's judgement is still well-represented today among New Testament scholars, and may even be said to have won a great deal of acceptance. Years before, Harnack had expressed the general judgement that the time is over 'in which one thought one had to condemn the oldest Christian literature, including the New Testament, as a tissue of deceptions and lies ... The oldest literature of the church is, from a literary point of view, truthful and reliable in the main points and in most details'.[11] He did not mean that the facts reported in this literature were reliable, only that it was written when it purported to be written, and that the authors were honest reporters of their time. His aim was to prove that 'in fact all that unfolded itself [in later church history] had come into existence and taken place in the years 30 to 70, indeed in Palestine itself, particularly in Jerusalem. Only Phrygia and Asia, where there was strong Jewish penetration, had otherwise played an important role alongside Palestine and Jerusalem. This result is becoming ever clearer and is displacing the older "critical" view that the period in which the foundations of the church were being laid was a development stretching over about a hundred years, and that to understand this development almost the whole of the Diaspora had to be taken into account, as well as the Holy Land and the earliest congregations'.[12]

The problem we have to face is why Harnack so wanted to prove that the crucial developments in the early church all happened within the first forty years (for that is the central thesis of all his historical writing about the church). This problem can also be put in the form, Why did Harnack (like Ritschl) so want to show that the Tübingen school was wrong? The Tübingen school saw the history of the foundation period as beginning with a clash between the Jewish-minded apostle Peter and the universalist apostle Paul,

[11] *Geschichte der altchristlichen Literatur bis Eusebius.* Preface to *Chronologie. 1. Band des 2. Teiles* (Leipzig, 1896); Agnes von Zahn-Harnack, *Life*, p. 258.
[12] Foreword to *Beiträge zur Einleitung in das Neue Testament*, I: *Lukas der Arzt, Der Verfasser des dritten Evangeliums und der Apostelgeschichte* (Leipzig, 1906), p. iv; English translation, *Luke, the Physician* (London, 1907).

a clash which their followers gradually overcame by bringing the two opposing positions into the harmony of early Catholic doctrine and church order.

The answer to this question bring us to the heart of Harnack's theology and to the philosophical view of the world he represents. As a pupil of Albrecht Ritschl, he thought he was a simple historian who would have no truck with philosophical defences of Christianity, but behind this facade there lay a definite philosophical view of the world and of history, a view that governed all Harnack said and did. Harnack prided himself on saying extraordinary things in ordinary words,[13] and that makes it difficult to grasp the complexity and sophistication of his philosophy; it all sounds so simple and straightforward.

Harnack, like Ritschl before him, attacked the blacks and whites of the Tübingen view of history because no 'white', no pure Christianity could exist as an actual physical entity in history. History, he believed, was a process which could be seen as leading forwards to a higher and purer resolution, but no 'right' was ever embodied in history as a discernible entity over against the 'wrong'. Paul was a decisive personality in the history of the church who solved several problems and helped the church to advance to the necessary next stage in its life, but the very contributions he made inevitably produced results that went wrong and had later to be purified by a Marcion or a Luther, other great personalities whose work also inevitably produced unwished-for and harmful effects. History as such offered no actual concrete examples of the pure religion. The Gospel is precisely this knowledge, that the essence of religion cannot be found outside of oneself in the visible world of time and space. The essence of the Gospel is that the individual comes to know himself as safe and warm in the Father's love. The individual knows that the Kingdom of God has come, and he acts securely as the fellow-worker with God in all relationships.

This gospel was discovered and established before AD 70. Church history after AD 70 is not a history of an inner-church

---

[13] Agnes von Zahn-Harnack, *Life*, p. 534.

dialectic; the new ordinances in doctrine, church order, and liturgy were only the result of compromises between the gospel preaching and the thought-world and institutions of the surrounding Graeco-Roman civilisation.[14]

Harnack's view of the Gospel is firmly based on an iron determinism. Everything that happens in the world of space and time depends on unbreakable laws, laws to which there is no exception. Outwardly the whole course of history is meaningless because everything happens exactly as it must happen. The only miracle is the miracle by which an individual comes to see an event as significant and full of worth.[15] Jesus is the one figure in history who accepted history with complete trust in the fatherly goodness of God; and through faith in him anyone can come to the same acceptance, and discover the same freedom and peace. Jesus himself was an historical man no different in nature from all other men; he had to be, because the essence of his Gospel had to be that there exists no other world than this irrevocably fixed world of space and time bound to the smallest detail by iron laws of necessity.

Harnack, like so many before and since, believed that he could logically maintain a coherent rational theory that was true and tenable alongside the view that everything (including the theory itself) was fixed and unalterable. He insisted that Christianity alone was 'religion itself', raised above all other religions because it alone denied that any religious entity existing in history had worth as such. The difficulty with Harnack's view, as with Bultmann's similar (if more sophisticated) attempt later, is that if Christianity exists as a religious entity in history it has no worth and cannot be the worthy Christianity of this new definition; but if Christianity does not exist as a religious entity in history, we cannot adhere to it. Harnack asks us to admire and value the only position that rigorously maintains that there exists no value in the actual world of space and time.

Harnack had no difficulty in admitting that Jesus' teaching

[14] See, for example, Harnack's Antrittsrede, Berlin Academy, *SB* (1890), pp. 789 f.
[15] *Das Wesen des Christentums*, pp. 16 f., English translation, *What is Christianity?*, pp. 25–9.

contained elements which were conditioned by his time and place and which we could no longer accept. Jesus did use the language of Jewish apocalyptic; he did look forward to a cosmic battle between God and the forces of evil, even though he avoided the worst excesses of crude particularist Judaism. But the essence of Jesus' teaching is that the Kingdom of God was inward and could be realised in every individual.

Similarly Harnack had no difficulty in saying that Paul still employed the Old Testament as an authoritative book when he should consistently have abandoned it. Marcion and Luther, too, produced forms of religion we should eventually have to abandon. 'In historical relationships, as soon as the sphere of pure inwardness is left behind, no progress, no success, and above all, no good comes about that does not have its shadows and that does not bring bad consequences'.[16]

Harnack had no difficulty in saying these things about Jesus and Paul, Marcion and Luther because he had the magic key to unlock the true and abiding element in all their work; they all were decisive personalities in history because they all saw that the only freedom was in the inner apprehension of the individual that he was safe in God the Father's love.

Because Harnack believed this, he could work positively in any situation that obtained. He expected no great purity in history, for history was only the unfolding of what had to be; the only progress that could be made was brought about by people who knew just this, but had come to see that they could act with perfect freedom, peace and self satisfaction because of this knowledge. People like Pastor Jatho, who trumpeted abroad that God did not objectively exist, were not in true possession of the key; they thought they could wrest history out of a false path into the true path, but they only showed they had not understood the message. Harnack did in fact say the words Jatho quoted as having learnt from him and for which he lost his pastorate, that God is only to be found in the higher moral life of personal relationships, but this was not a doctrine to be

---

[16] *Das Wesen des Christentums*, end of tenth lecture.

embodied in history. It was a way of living in the givenness of history.[17]

For all Harnack's talk about God as Father, God is not the centre of his theology, just as for all his talk about history, actual human history as the history of good and evil decisions by moral creatures is not the centre of his historical work. The problem Harnack is trying to come to terms with is not how to know and worship God or how to understand and judge rightly the actions of men in history; his problem is the dualism which the morally sensitive man who believes all is fixed sees between Spirit and Flesh, God and the World, Good and Evil, Here and Beyond, Visible and Invisible, Matter and Spirit, Instinctual Life and Freedom, Physics and Ethics. This dualism has to be resolved, and it is the Gospel's task to overcome it and reduce it to unity. We cannot do so by any world-view, for no world-view can reduce to unity our apprehensions of space and time, on the one hand, and the content of our inner life, on the other hand. The unity can only come through struggle as an endless, never-to-be-completed task. This task abides, and this task is the essence of the dramatic images belonging to the long-superseded world-view of the time when the Gospels were written; the gospel used contemporary images to express the opposition the gospel itself had to overcome. The images do not matter – Harnack has always said that they belong to a world that can never be recovered. What matters is the recognition that the dualism those images represented is in fact the dualism between a completely closed universe of space and time and the realm of human freedom and ethical responsibility. The task is to resolve the dualism into a unity and, since nothing is alterable in the world of space and time, the only thing to be worked on is the individual in his inner life.

'"From the necessity that binds all beings, the man who overcomes himself is the man who frees himself" – this

---

[17] Agnes von Zahn-Harnack, *Life*, pp. 390–400; Martin Rade (ed.), *Jatho und Harnack: Ihr Briefwechsel* (Tübingen, 1911). See also the letter to Krüger, 1 July 1911, cited in Agnes von Zahn-Harnack, *Life*, p. 398.

splendid saying of Goethe's expresses the matter at issue here.'[18]

Harnack talks endlessly of God and history, but he is really only concerned with himself and his own unremitting task of overcoming himself.

Harnack was the perfect servant of whatever comes to pass, the highly educated functionary who makes our modern world go wherever it is going. The authority of the Bible for him was the authority of the New Testament alone. In the New Testament we have records of two heroes, Jesus and Paul, who knew the secret of inwardness, and so gave history a decisive impulse to produce the present modern age.

---

[18] *Das Wesen des Christentums*, end of the eighth lecture and end of Part I of the series.

18

Gunkel

Hermann Gunkel is a most attractive man, a scholar who put himself right outside the mainstream of scholarship for the sake of his vision of history and the place of his beloved German people and church in history; and a scholar whose lonely stand has been abundantly vindicated. He appealed to the old romantic Germany over the heads of the theological technicians who seemed to have appropriated the Bible and forsaken the church. They might pride themselves on their purity of method and rigorousness of scholarship, but they were, he believed, trapped in doubtful methods and were much too narrow of vision to be true scholars. 'Would to God', he wrote in the *Christliche Welt* for 1900, 'I had a voice that could pierce the hearts and consciences of theological researchers. I should cry out day and night nothing but this message: Never forget your sacred duty to your people! Write for the educated! Speak not so much of literary criticism, text criticism, archaeology and all the other scholarly things, but speak of *religion*! Think of the main issue! Our people thirst for your words on *religion* and its *history*!'[1] He suffered for his stand. As a young man he had hoped for academic advancement in the field of New Testament studies. When that was denied him, he turned to the Old Testament and struggled all his life to get his learning and craftsmanship acknowledged, although the establishment

[1] *Christliche Welt* (1900), 60, cited by Werner Klatt, *Hermann Gunkel: Zu seiner Theologie der religionsgeschichte und zur Entstehung der formgeschichtlichen Methode*, Forschungen zur Religion und Literatur des Alten und Neuen Testaments, 100 (Göttingen, 1969), p. 85.

Old Testament scholars always sneered at his inadequate preparation, and doubted his scholarly gifts. He was stuck as an associate professor in Berlin from the age of 34 to 45, and then had to be content with a full chair at the small uninfluential university of Giessen. (But the Giessen years were the happiest years of his life.)[2] When at last he gained a chair at a major university in April 1920 after the republic had swept away the old Prussian civil service, he had to be content with Halle rather than Berlin. He was always short of money to support his large family and was glad to earn from journalism (to which he was in principle pledged in any case) something with which to supplement his stipend. He even wrote theatre criticism for the Giessener Anzeiger over the signature XYZ.[3]

His life saw the extraordinary rise and fall of the Germany he loved, but he never wavered in simple acceptance of what happened and in hope for his people. He was born in 1862, the son and grandson of Lutheran pastors in the Kingdom of Hannover. When he was four years old, Prussia annexed Hannover, and when he was ten, Bismarck exploited Prussia's victory in the Franco-Prussian war to found the German Empire (1871). By the time Gunkel was fifty (1912), Germany was producing twice the amount of steel that Britain produced and generated more electricity than Great Britain, France and Italy together; she had a large army and had just succeeded in building a modern navy to challenge Britain's.[4] That was the year Gunkel rather reluctantly accepted the task of writing a major new commentary on the Psalms. When it was finished and published (1926), things were very different, yet Gunkel showed the same equable trust in his own work and in the people for whom he wrote (for even his most scholarly writing had in view 'children and artists' who could still be enchanted by a good story or great poetry). 'When i began this book, our people were yet at the height of their power; now they lie low on the ground. In the sorrowful

[2] Baumgartner, VTS ix (1962) 8, cited Klatt, p. 194.
[3] Klatt, p. 221, note 19.
[4] Norman Stone, Europe Transformed: 1878–1919, Fontana History of Europe (Glasgow, 1983), pp. 160 f.

present circumstances it would be easy and perhaps the right thing to do from the publisher's point of view to yield to the diminished purchasing power of our exhausted people and issue this book in a greatly abridged version. I have not been able to agree to this renunciation, for I remain certain that the time will come when books are again bought and sold in Germany; and I have written on the basis of a steady faith in this future.'[5] 'Should the future ever take notice of me, would that it should say, Here was a man who in the hardest times, when all around him lay in ruins, with all tranquillity built on his own plot of land a great new house.'[6]

Two decisive loves made Gunkel the imaginative and creative scholar he became, the love for history and the love for religion. Both were kindled in the schoolboy at home, and neither was quenched – rather, both were intensified – in the student at university. As a schoolboy he had already learnt to abandon a supernaturalistic religion in favour of a view of revelation in history which he held to all his life. He devoured Gustav Freytag's *Bilder aus der deutschen Vergangenheit*, a collection of popular historical studies woven around portraits of German life to be found in extracts from old writers, first published in 1859, and so popular that, by the fifth edition of 1867, they had grown to four large volumes.[7] From Freytag Gunkel learnt that each nation had a personality which it is the duty of scholarly history to discern in the myriad of details. There is a superhuman life of a people, divided into periods, like the life of an individual growing from childhood to maturity. The greatest periods are dominated by the great individuals who impress their age with their individual spirit; 'then for a few years the whole power of the people is manifest in the service of the

---

[5] *Die Psalmen*, Göttinger Handkommentar zum Alten Testament II.2, 4th ed. (= Gunkel's 1st ed.) (Göttingen, 1926, repr. 1968), Vorwort, p. VI.

[6] Letter to his publisher, Gustav Ruprecht, 19 July 1920, cited by Klatt, p. 222.

[7] Gustav Freytag, *Bilder aus der deutschen Vergangenheit*, 5th enlarged ed. (Leipzig, 1867), Vol. 1, Aus dem Mittelalter, containing the original preface, (iv) + 559 pp. Vol. 2, part 1, Vom Mittelalter zur Neuzeit (1200–1500), viii + 464 pp; part 2, Aus dem Jahrhundert der Reformation (1500–1600), 384 pp. Vol. 3, Aus dem Jahrhundert des grossen Krieges (1600–1700), 484 pp. Vol. 4, Aus neuer Zeit (1700–1848), 496 pp.

individual, obedient to him as to a Lord – these are the great periods in the fashioning of a people.'[8]

Freytag simply assumed that the customary ways of thinking about God had now disappeared, and in their place he put what he claimed to be a far more exciting vision, of God in history.

> Whereas pious faith with ingenuous certainty sets the idea of a personal God over the life of the individual, the follower of scientific scholarship soberly seeks to recognize the divine in the great patterns which, though they powerfully tower high above individuals, yet collectively closely govern the life of the planet. But however small this planet itself might think the significance of individuals in comparison with what is inconceivable, limitless in time and space, yet in this limited sphere lies all the greatness we are able to recognise, all the beauty we can ever enjoy, and all the goodness to which our life can ever be dedicated. For that which we do not yet know and which we strive to investigate – ceaseless labour. And this labour is to search for the divine in history.[9]

The individual who devoted himself to that search, like every individual in the people who strives to develop his native powers, is never alone.

> The individual and the people! The life of a nation develops in the ceaseless influence of the individual on the people and the people on the individual. The more strongly individuals develop their human power in manifold and original ways, the more able they are to serve the highest good of the whole; and the stronger the influence that the life of the people exerts on the individuals, the more secure the foundation for the free development of man himself.[10]

The religious influence from a home where father and

[8] Vol. 1, Introduction, p. 23.
[9] Vol. 1, Introduction, p. 26.
[10] Aus neuer Zeit: Bilder (= vol. 4, Leipzig, 1867), p. 1.

234 *The Bible's Authority*

grandfather were pastors was not lost but intensified at university. After two semesters at his own state university of Göttingen, Gunkel went for three semesters to Giessen to sit at the feet of the brilliant young church historian Adolf Harnack who, together with his other hitherto unknown colleagues, had quite revived the fortunes of the theological faculty. Harnack reinforced all Gunkel's ideas about seeing history in the pattern of its successive periods of development, and delighted him with his portrait of the individuals who dominated the great ages, above all with the portrait of Augustine in his Confessions.[11]

The greatest influence of all was to come when Gunkel returned to Göttingen. At Easter 1884 the twenty-eight year old Albert Eichhorn (1856–1926) came back to Göttingen, after a few years away as a pastor, to prepare himself to write a doctorate on Athanasius, with a university career in mind. Gunkel had just turned twenty-two. Eichhorn gathered Gunkel, William Wrede, Wilhelm Bousset and Wilhelm Heitmüller into a loose society of friends devoted to history and to religion. They not only wanted to study history; they believed they would make history. They set themselves in conscious opposition to the reigning tone of theological scholarship dominated by the great Albrecht Ritschl, who had first come to Göttingen as professor in 1864 at the age of forty-two, and who at sixty-three still held sway. Ritschl thought he had made theology and religion independent of both metaphysics and history. Eichhorn and his friends laughed at his pretention and challenged his system. They scorned the cavalier way he tried to interpret scripture out of its context in history. As Eichhorn was to put the matter later, these so-called scholars used history to explain away

---

[11] Gunkel generously credits Harnack with first showing him that the history of the human spirit runs in periods against which individual figures were first to be understood, but I am sure his schoolboy reading had already taught the lesson. See Gunkel's tribute to Harnack on his 70th birthday, 'Die Lieder in der Kindheitsgeschichte Jesu bei Lukas', Festgabe für D. Dr., A. von Harnack . . . zum siebzigsten Geburtstag (Tübingen, 1921), pp. 43–60 at p. 43. See W. Baumgartner's witness to the importance of Freytag, *VTS* ix (1963), 3, cited by Klatt, p. 17 and note 1.

and apologise for the religious developments they thought had overlaid the pure rationalist's idea of religion. Eichhorn and his friends were dedicated, on the contrary, to honouring and praising the religious developments that enabled the Christian religion to conquer the world. Precisely what was unhistorical (in that it did not happen) was important as an index to the needs of the church and the historical development of the religion.[12]

Eichhorn and his friends self-consciously espoused a method of studying the Bible, and believed themselves to be inaugurating a new period in scholarship. The method and the period were soon labelled with an adjective formed out of the two words Religion and History. '. . . Perhaps the time is not far off in which the history-of-religion method will yet more decisively than ever require an interpretation of the New Testament as arising out of the time to which it belongs; this method will seek in the [Jewish apocryphal and pseudepigraphical] writings no longer this or that valuable supplement to the interpretation of the New Testament but the recognition of the very native soil of early Christianity'.[13]

In April 1885 Gunkel finished his formal theological education and for the next three years maintained himself by giving private lessons while preparing to be a university teacher. In 1888 his dissertation on the operations of the Holy Spirit according to the popular view in the apostolic age and according to the teaching of the Apostle Paul was accepted by the Göttingen faculty and he was granted the licence to teach. The dissertation was published by Vandenhoeck and Ruprecht the same year, thus beginning Gunkel's long and fruitful association with Gustav Ruprecht and the firm.[14]

[12] Albert Eichhorn, *Das Abendmahl im Neuen Testament*, Hefte zur 'Christlichen Welt' Nr. 36 (Leipzig, 1898), p. 14 et passim.

[13] Gunkel, review of Strack and Zöckler's short commentary to the Old and New Testaments with the Apocrypha, *Theologische Literaturzeitung* 17 (1892), coll. 126–130 at col. 127.

[14] *Die Wirkungen des heiligen Geistes, nach der populären Anschauung der apostolischen Zeit und nach der Lehre des Apostels Paulus: Eine biblisch-theologische Studie* (Göttingen, 1888); English translation, *The Influence of the Holy Spirit; The Popular View of the Apostolic Age and the Teaching of the Apostle Paul*, translated by Roy A. Harrisville and Philip A. Quanbeck (Philadelphia, 1979).

After a year in Göttingen Gunkel moved to Halle as a lecturer in Old Testament, the only possibility left to him for university teaching. Fortunately for him, Professor Heinrich Zimmern, an expert in cuneiform inscriptions from Babylon, was appointed to the chair of Assyriology in Halle in 1890, and Gunkel was able to draw on his knowledge in preparing the great book that both made and unmade his name, *Schöpfung und Chaos* (Creation and Chaos), published in 1895, by which time Gunkel had been promoted to an associate professorship at Halle and swiftly translated from Halle to Berlin.[15] The plan and conception of the book was simple, and the impulse that lay behind it was the old love for History and for Religion.

> This book is not written for or against any ecclesiastical or scholarly party. Neither has the author sought out the observations it contains; on the contrary, they have offered themselves to him . . . He would also wish to endorse the conviction that the saying is true, One comes to discern only as much as one has the power to love and to revere.[16]

He took Genesis 1 and Revelation 12 and showed in each case that neither chapter was the free composition of one author, and that the mythical drama each contained was derived from Babylonian religion. Revelation 12 was not of Christian origin; it was not written to relate to particular events in Jewish and Roman history of the first century AD; it was not of Jewish origin; and it was not of Greek origin. Its pictures came originally from Babylon.

Wellhausen's joke about the book – more Chaos than Creation – soon went the scholarly rounds,[17] and in 1899 Wellhausen published a new study of Revelation 12 with a measured and cold-blooded intellectual assassination of

---

[15] *Schöpfung und Chaos in Urzeit und Endzeit. Eine religions-geschichtliche Untersuchung über Gen 1 und Ap Joh 12. Mit Beiträgen von Heinrich Zimmern* (Göttingen, 1895).

[16] *Schöpfung und Chaos*, Foreword, p. VII.

[17] See Klatt, p. 70 and note 2 for a careful assessment of the evidence that Wellhausen was the originator of the crack.

Gunkel.[18] Most of what Gunkel said was not new. Everyone knew that Revelation belonged to the genre of apocalyptic, and that it reproduced a fixed dogmatic system of messianic expectations. What was new was Gunkel's assertion that Revelation was indebted not so much to the Old Testament as to Babylonian religion. That was either false or of no importance. On the contrary, Wellhausen saw a steady and historically explicable progression of thought from national and earthly restoration in the Old Testament (Daniel) to individual and transcendent spiritual restoration which finds its last and highest outcome in the gospel.

It is true, Wellhausen conceded, that some undigested remnants of ancient mythology could be discerned in Revelation, but it was a failure of method to attach any importance to these. The task of theology and exegesis is not to satisfy an antiquarian interest in these stray remnants but to focus on the author, his precise historical circumstances, and the message he wished to teach his contemporaries.

> The precise purpose of the apocalypses is a practical one and related to their actual time, meant for their contemporaries; one must date them and discern the situation in which they arose in order to uncover their heart and in order to understand them.[19]

Gunkel was devastated. He had been passed over for an established chair that very year, and now the acknowledged master of Old Testament scholarship had attached to him the label most to be feared, the label of failure in method, the label of being an antiquarian rather than a theologian or an exegete. He was stung to the quick. Method above all was what he and his friends had learnt from Albert Eichhorn, and their method must be vindicated. In October 1899 Gunkel published a spirited defence, and for the rest of his life, while never ceasing to praise Wellhausen for his irreplaceable services to Old Testament scholarship and for his superb style

[18] 'Zur apokalyptischen Literatur', *Skizzen und Vorarbeiten*, vol. 6 (Berlin, 1899), 215–249.

[19] Wellhausen, 'Zur apokalyptischen Literatur, *Skizzen und Vorarbeiten*, vol. 6 (1899), 234.

and historical sense, he kept up a steady and trenchant criticism of the weakness of the Wellhausen approach to the Bible.

Of course controversy of this sort always takes its toll, and I think Gunkel often ended up conceding more than he need have done to Wellhausen's insistence that apocalypses were directed to specific historical situations with a specific historical message – although I too must concede that the Qumran documents now provide us with abundant examples of prophecy applied to particular events in history, where 'The Wicked Priest', for example, persecuted and killed 'The Teacher of Righteousness'. More seriously, Gunkel always felt he had to justify himself and prove himself by scholarly works of a massive and detailed kind. 'Method' became a shibboleth.

Gunkel's Genesis commentary of 1901 was the last great book of his that came to fruition naturally and easily.[20] The rest of his life was devoted to unremitting hard labour. He produced one brilliant monograph on the New Testament, based on a lecture first given to the Friends of the weekly 'Christliche Welt' and entitled *Zum religionsgeschichtlichen Verständnis des Neuen Testaments* (On the History of Religion Approach to Understanding the New Testament),[21] a superb popular study on fourteen selected Psalms that laid the foundation for his great commentary,[22] a pioneering sketch of the history of Israel's literature (a task offered to him at Wellhausen's suggestion),[23] a small book on the prophets,[24] three superb 75-odd-page studies for the cheap *Popular History-of-Religion Books for the German Christian Contemporary Scene* (Elias Jahve und Baal, 1906; Esther, 1916; Das Märchen [the fairy-tale] im Alten Testament, 1917), over 320 articles

[20] *Genesis*, Handkommentar zum Alten Testament (Göttingen, 1901, 2nd ed. 1902). On the easier origin of this book see Klatt, citing a letter from Gunkel to Ruprecht, 19 July, 1920, p. 222.

[21] (Göttingen, 1903).

[22] *Ausgewählte Psalmen* (Göttingen, 1904, 4th ed. 1917).

[23] 'Die israelitische Literatur' in *Kultur der Gegenwart* ed. von Hinneberg, I, 7, (1906), pp. 51–102. See Klatt, p. 167 and note 4.

[24] *Die Propheten* (Göttingen, 1917).

for the great encyclopaedia, *Religion in Geschichte und Gegenwart*, which he founded and co-edited, over 150 articles for the second 1920s edition, together with a stream of studies and reviews and popular essays.[25]

Most of this time he felt isolated and ignored by his peers in the world of scholarship. His Psalms commentary of 1926 is rather pathetically dedicated to the arts faculty (note, not a theological faculty) of the University of Breslau for giving him an honorary degree in 1911 'which refreshed him with courage and strength at a time when he was still in the midst of the struggle'.[26]

Ignored, as he thought, by his contemporaries, the only way he could triumph was to grapple to himself up-and-coming young scholars whom he would teach his method. Walter Baumgartner was a young Swiss Old testament student studying at Marburg. He had read Gunkel and wanted to meet him. He wrote ahead and turned up in Giessen at Gunkel's house at the advertised hour for seeing students. He was received as though his visit was both unexpected and unwanted. Gunkel asked the young student what was the first question he should pose when tackling a Psalm. In all innocence Baumgartner answered, When was it written? – quite the wrong answer, which was, To what category of Psalm does it belong? Gunkel closed the interview by saying that, if Baumgartner thought it worthwhile, he could come back when the student interview time was over. Baumgartner was so put off by the brusqueness of Gunkel's manner that he thought of taking the next train to Marburg. Instead, he went back punctually to Gunkel and found the man completely changed. Gunkel had acted advisedly; he wanted to get hold of the young Swiss completely, or not at all. Baumgartner moved from Marburg to Giessen, and had to find lodgings near Gunkel's house. Every morning he called

---

[25] For Bibliography see Johannes Hempel, in *EYXAPICTHPION, Studien zur Religion und Literatur des Alten und Neuen Testaments, Herman Gunkel zum 60. Geburtstage, dem 23. Mai 1922 dargebracht von seinen Schülern und Freunden*, ed. Hans Schmidt, vol. 2 (Göttingen, 1923), pp. 214–225, and Klatt, pp. 272–274.

[26] *Die Psalmen* (Göttingen, 1926), Foreword p. XIII. See also his letter to Budde, April 1920, Klatt, p. 179.

for him to walk to the lecture Gunkel was giving; frequently he accompanied Gunkel home again after the lecture. Often Gunkel took Baumgartner for a walk in the afternoon. On the way to lectures, on the walks, sitting in a cafe, or in his study Gunkel talked about the progress of his own work or about incidents from his own life. Baumgartner marvelled at Gunkel's richness of ideas, but above all he was impressed by the painstaking way he tested his ideas, ever going back to the beginning and scrutinizing them from all sides to see if they held fast. He mistrusted himself and was always open to well-argued refutation. He wanted to teach his pupils method, not results.[27] Rudolf Bultmann received the same sort of attention from Gunkel. During the two semesters Bultmann studied in Berlin (Winter Semester 1904–5; Summer Semester 1905) he heard Gunkel lecture, and he was often with Gunkel on holiday on the North Sea before World War I. When Bousset, Gunkel's co-editor of the monograph series *Forschungen zur Religion und Literatur des Alten und Neuen Testaments* died, Gunkel declined the publisher's suggestion of Heitmüller, who was an old fellow-member of the Eichhorn circle, as a replacement, and suggested Bultmann instead, whose *History of the Synoptic Tradition* he had just read with great satisfaction.[28]

The essence of Gunkel's method was always to ask concerning sacred literature what part it played in the religious life of the people who treasured it. The trouble with Wellhausen and his school was that they were too subservient to the documents. They were inclined to date ideas and customs by their first mention in documents, to forget that they could well have been living parts of the religion of the people long before being written down, to forget that many of the most important beliefs and customs somehow escape mention in the documents.

How much there is in the life and thought of an

[27] Walter Baumgartner, 'Herman Gunkel', Neue Zürcher Zeitung, Nr. 489/499 (1932), reprinted in *Zum Alten Testament und seiner Umwelt* (Leiden, 1959), pp. 371–378 at pp. 374–376.
[28] Klatt, p. 168, note 14.

ancient people, passing from lip to lip, which never or not till quite a late period appears in the literature! All the rich content of such oral tradition must be included in our total reckoning, if that reckoning is to be accurate. The Wellhausen school follow too closely the principle, *quod non est in actis, non est in mundo* [what is not in the records does not exist], and place too much weight on the argument *ex silentio*. An element of the national faith, such as the name 'Jahveh Zebaoth', was said to be a creation of Amos; the figure of Satan was a creation of Zechariah; and the highly developed Individualism of a later age was declared to be, not the final product of a whole history of civilization and religion, but simply a conception of Ezekiel, whereas Ezekiel was only the first to formulate it clearly and dogmatically.[29]

The documents in the Bible had to be read in their historical context, not the narrow historical context of the precise historical date and circumstances at which they may have happened to be committed to writing, but the larger historical context of the whole of world history. World history was a chain of events[30] or, to change the metaphor, an organic growth in which everything was fruit and everything was seed.[31]

So are we filled with the inspiring presentiment of the endless width and fulness of the world, where one stroke cuts through a thousand connections. That is the reason why the Babylonian influence on Israel once so enraptured me, why it was for me more than a 'curiosity', more than an 'antiquarian' jotting; peoples so far distant in space, spiritually divided by a whole

[29] 'Was will die "religionsgeschichtliche" Bewegung?', *Deutsch-Evangelisch* 5 (1914), 356 ff.; English translation, 'The "Historical Movement" in the Study of Religion', *Expository Times* xxxviii (1926–27) (September 1927), 532–536 at 534.

[30] *Schöpfung und Chaos* (Göttingen, 1895), p. 117.

[31] 'Das Alte Testament im Licht der modernen Forschung' in *Beiträge zur Weiterentwicklung der christlichen Religion*, with contributions by A. Deissmann and others (Munich, 1905), pp. 40–76 at p. 55.

world, and yet in relation. Primal myths of humanity
and the Revelation of John, so far removed from each
other in time and in ideas, and yet at base the same
stuff![32]

The canon narrowed scholars' vision to the Old Testament
and the New Testament, as if these were the only two places
in which connections were to be made. The Old Testament
itself, as far back as we can go, was deeply influenced by the
myths of the heavenly battles between the gods and the
personifications of evil, battles which involved the heavenly
bodies and all of nature. However strictly in the Old
Testament these myths were made to conform to
monotheism, the old polytheistic features could still be
discerned. The Judaism of the time between the two
Testaments received another massive influx of cosmic and
gnostic ideas from the surrounding religions. Judaism before
Christ already contained not only the doctrine of the
resurrection of the dead and belief in angels and Satan, but
also had a fully worked-out Christology, an expectation of
the death and resurrection of Christ.

Think of the many mythical features that we already
find in the Christology of the New Testament. Look at
all that has been identified with Jesus: the God who can
open the seven seals of the book in Revelation 5, the
rescued son of the women clothed with the sun and the
dragon-slayer in Revelation 12, the supernaturally
conceived hero of the Infancy Narrative, the one who
descended to hell and ascended to heaven! All this is
transferred to Jesus because it already belonged before
him to Christ; and that, we insist, is the supreme secret
of New Testament Christology. The picture of a
heavenly Christ must already have arisen somewhere

[32] 'Die Religionsgeschichte und die alttestamentliche Wissenschaft', in *V. Weltkongress für freies Christentum und religiösen Fortschritt*, Protokoll der Verhandlungen (1910), pp. 169–180 at 178, cited by Klatt, p. 75. An English translation was published separately as *The History of Religion and Old Testament Criticism* (Berlin and London: Williams and Norgate), 14pp.

before the New Testament. We now know from a few traces in Jewish apocalypses that such a belief existed in Jewish circles. We have seen that already, centuries before, a similar belief came to the prophets and was in their case (to be sure) much more strongly conformed to Israelist norms. Come from afar, this picture of the heavenly King had now so possessed the men of Judaism that they could never again get free of it. Their hearts already believed in a divine revealer, in a divine-human deed, in assurance through sacraments. For the time being we cannot say in what forms such a faith consisted; here there is a great gap in our knowledge. Later Judaism, in contrast to Christianity, let most of it fall away and strongly attacked it.[33]

The intense study of Jewish literature of the two centuries BC and AD and the discovery of the Dead Sea Scrolls have vindicated Gunkel's position, I believe, although many contemporary scholars still argue that 'high' Christology is a late development in Christianity.

Gunkel did not stop at setting both the Old Testament and the New Testament in the wider context of the ancient religions of Babylon and Egypt and the later religious developments of Zoroastrianism, the mystery religions and 'gnosticism'. It was not as though individual thinkers in Israel appropriated and transformed myths from outside. He posited an organic religious life in Israel that followed discernible laws of development. Hence his test-question to the young Baumgartner, What is the first question one should pose when tackling a Psalm? The correct answer was, To what category of Psalm does it belong? Gunkel argued that, to anyone who had studied all the Psalms together, taking in Psalms that were preserved elsewhere than in the canonical collection of Psalms as well, and who had compared them with Babylonian and Egyptian Psalms, would soon see that the Psalms grouped themselves into simple classes, each class corresponding to a religious type. The main class consisted of the Hymns (e.g.

---

[33] *Zum religionsgeschichtlichen Verständnis des Neuen Testaments* (Göttingen, 1903), p. 93.

Psalms 150, 148, 147, 145), the Lament of the assembled congregation (e.g. Psalms 79, 83, 80, 44), the Lament of the individual (e.g. Psalms, 13, 54, 88, 3), and the Thanksgiving of the individual (e.g. Jonah 2, Psalms 30, 66.13–20). To the Hymns were added the related Songs at Jahve's Enthronement (e.g. Psalms 93, 97, 99), and to all these groups that had to do with the prophets' worship were added the specific Royal Psalms which deal with royal figures in Israel (e.g. Psalms 2, 18, 20, 21, 45, 72, 101, 110, 132, 141.1–11).[34] Each class was related to the needs of worship, and each class was distinguished by regular forms of speech and arrangement that followed the laws of the class. The classes were extraordinarily constant. Once a student could discern the form of a Psalm, the class to which it belonged would be obvious. Gunkel knew that his scholarly peers, if they condescended at all to try to understand his method, thought he was wasting time on mere style, manner and pattern, when he should be studying the person of the individual poet and the immediate historical circumstances in which he was writing. Gunkel defended himself by pointing out that, until one had discovered the class and the form of speech belonging to the class, one could not spot the special and the personal that (he granted) were often present.[35] 'Whoever wants to discern the heights of the individual mountains must first know how high is the whole range of mountains above which the peaks rear their heads.'[36]

Once Gunkel had insisted with all the weight of the most detailed and comprehensive scholarship on the pervasiveness and the fundamental importance of the forms, he was ready to concede to his opponents the vital and precious contribution of the individual: the individual psalmist who

---

[34] *Einleitung in die Psalmen: Die Gattungen der religiösen Lyrik Israels*, completed and edited by Joachim Begrich (Göttingen, 1933). Gunkel had already published §§ 1–5 in November 1927, but he was not able to bring the work to completion before his death in 1932.

[35] See an excellent short summary of Gunkel's approach in 'Die Lieder in der Kindheitsgeschichte Jesu bei Lukas', *Festgabe für D. Dr. A. von Harnack* (Tübingen, 1921), pp. 44–45.

[36] *Die Propheten* (Göttingen, 1917), p. 108, cited by Klatt, p. 171, note 27.

injected his own experience into the established form of the class of psalm he was writing, or the individual prophet who used the conventions of prophecy to become an individual 'hero' of religion.

Here, it seems, Gunkel conceded too much, and did so, not only because his critics demanded of him that he pay attention to the individual thinker or writer wherever he appeared, but because his own religion was intensely individual and he was personally antipathetic to the cult he had done so much to reveal as essential to the religion of Israel and Judaism.[37]

The same antipathy extended to his treatment of the New Testament and of Jesus. He had shown with masterly skill how deeply the Book of Revelation and the theology of Paul and of John were impregnated with the myths drawn from a drama spanning earth and heaven, myths that were current in the religions surrounding the Jews and which had entered into Judaism itself. But he insisted that Jesus, who had grown up in a Galilean piety based mainly on the Psalms, was immune from these influences. The secret mythical dogma had no hold on him, apart from a few commonplaces.[38]

It was this prejudice, a judgement that flies in the face of all historical probability, that Albert Eichhorn and Gunkel passed on to Bultmann and his disciples. The same position, as we have seen, was central to Wellhausen's view of Jesus, and the combined force of these scholars, otherwise so very different, convinced succeeding generations that the central problem of the history of New Testament Christology was to explain how Jesus, the proclaimer of an individual personal religion relatively free from myth, became the Christ proclaimed by the church as the heavenly pre-existent redeemer who would eventually be worshipped as Lord and finally be given a place in the three-in-one God of the doctrine of the Trinity. It seems to me that Gunkel was right

---

[37] See Klatt's very interesting remarks on Gunkel's attack on Mowinckel, pp. 248–252.

[38] *Zum religionsgeschichtlichen Verständnis des Neuen Testaments* (Göttingen, 1903), p. 86, note 1.

that the main Christological dogmas were already in existence in Judaism before Jesus was born. It is far more likely that Jesus and his disciples thought they were acting according to these dogmas during the earthly ministry of Jesus than that the dogmas were later foisted on to an entirely undogmatic story of a Galileean prophet.

Gunkel remained true to the end to the German idealistic tradition to which he always felt himself to belong, the tradition of Herder and Hegel which he had imbibed as a schoolboy through the stirring *Bilder aus der deutschen Vergangenheit* of Gustav Freytag. He never believed in a God who stood outside history to be worshipped and asked for specific help; his God was always a God to be discovered in history, in the great law-bound development of the history and religion of the peoples. Of course the individual must suffer as history rolls on. The individual must simply listen for the 'bells of eternity'[39] that sound at times in the Psalms, in the Prophets and in the New Testament. Quite other laws than the laws of individual morality must govern the affairs of the nation, but laws there must be, which would further the triumph of the 'common man'. That was why Gunkel was sympathetic to those who opposed National Socialism.[40] But, whatever happened, God was at work in history and to be discerned in history. For him there was no other God.

The belief in revelation is the necessary foundation of all religion, he held, but not a belief in 'supernaturalism', according to which children (both little children and grown-up children) believe in exceptional miraculous events. We must unfurl the banner of a higher religion which is not contradicted by history, which on the contrary is furthered by history. The historian sees order and law in history. This order is not the result of chance.

> As eternal Spirit rules in everything; it is the unity of the manifold, the building together of the contradictory; it leads the lowly to the higher existence; it draws them who follow it upwards to itself. Our dull sight does not

---

[39] *Die Psalmen* (Göttingen, 1926), VII.
[40] Klatt, pp. 265 f. and especially p. 266, note 17.

recognise it in much we see; and the heart fearfully enquires, Why? But sometimes the mist sinks and the sun of God shines. The great catastrophes in the life of the nations, when the rotten collapses and the sound triumphs, reveal to us its government. The great personalities of religion set before our eyes how Spirit itself exists and how Spirit wants to possess us. So the thought of historical development leads us on to the idea of revelation.[41]

That was Gunkel's dearest belief, and it seems to me to be groundless. The belief that history itself is controlled by Spirit derives from belief in a God who created the universe and governs it by particular interventions as well as by general providence. Once that belief in a supernatural God is surrendered, there is no basis, so far as I can see, for any optimism about a controlling Spirit. In practice such belief in a controlling Spirit has led, and still leads, to the peculiarly modern forms of tyranny, which good men like Gunkel of course did not want, but for which by their sentimental adherence to the religion they had intellectually abandoned they prepared the way.

[41] 'Das alte Testament im Licht der modernen Forschung', in *Beiträge zur Weiterentwicklung der christlichen Religion* with A. Deissmann, W. Herrmann &c. (Munich, 1905), pp. 40–76 at pp. 62–63.

19

Albert Schweitzer

Albert Schweitzer was both a preaching and an acting thinker who devoted his whole life to making clear what Jesus, as an historical hero, had achieved. He saw himself as doing the same sort of things as Jesus and Paul before him. Like Jesus, he devoted the first 30 years of his life to his private interests, and then, when he had completed his medical studies and brought out a second much enlarged edition of his book on Jesus, he took care to leave his father's manse in Günsbach on the afternoon of Good Friday 1913, the first stage of a journey to Lambaréné, French Equatorial Africa, where he was to be a medical missionary. This acted-out interpretation of the Bible has deeply influenced both the educated reading public and the churches themselves. His actual theories about Jesus and Paul are rarely explicitly discussed in academic circles – but that does not stop them being vastly influential there too.

He had an extraordinarily happy home life, and he received in Alsace a fine schooling, and a university education from some of the best young German philosophers and theologicans that were to be had.[1] As a pastor's son he was always well-fed and clothed (even if it cost his parents hard

---

[1] The details of Schweitzer's life are to be found in his two autobiographical sketches, *Aus meiner Kindheit und Jugendzeit* (Munich & Bern, 1924), reprinted in *Gesammelte Werke in fünf Bänden*, Vol. 1, pp. 253–313; English translation, *Memoirs of Childhood and Youth*, by C. T. Campion (London, 1924). 'Aus meinem Leben und Denken' (Leipzig, 1931), based on a shorter 24-page sketch in a collected volume, *Philosophie der Gegenwart in Selbstdarstellungen*, Volume VII (Leipzig, 1929), reprinted in *Gesammelte Werke*, Vol. 1, pp. 19–252; English translation, *My Life and Thought: An Autobiography*, by C. T. Campion (2nd ed., London, 1955).

work and frugality). At first he fought against his parents' unwitting efforts to make him different from his schoolfellows, but by the age of nine he gave up the struggle and began to enjoy his distinctiveness. Up till then he had been attending the village school in Günsbach, but that year, 1884, he went to the Realschule, two miles over a mountain path, in Münster. He walked there and back every day, by preference alone, to be with his own thoughts. He had private lessons in Latin to prepare him for entry into the Gymnasium (grammar school) in Mülhausen. From ten to eighteen he boarded with Uncle Louis and Aunt Sophie, childless elderly relations, in Mülhausen. He was already an accomplished organist and was now to receive first-class teaching from Eugen Münch, who died young of typhus when Schweitzer was twenty-three; a life of Münch in French was Schweitzer's first publication (1899).

He had an avid interest in politics and read the newspapers and talked politics with Uncle Louis every day. His Alsace had been French since the time of Louis XIV, who interfered with religion and language only so much as to decree that if there were as few as seven catholic families in the protestant areas, the protestant communities had to make available the choir of their church every Sunday for mass. Schweitzer could lose himself on Sundays in the Günsbach church looking at the Catholic golden altar, surmounted by large golden statues of Joseph and Mary, and through the choir windows to the trees, roofs, clouds and sky beyond. His maternal grandfather, with his keen interest in politics and the latest scientific discoveries, had lived on the best terms with his neighbouring priest; they used to do each other's pastoral visiting when one was away.

Schweitzer's family links with France were not broken by the Prussian annexation of Alsace in 1870, five years before he was born (1865). Two of his father's brothers lived in Paris, and Schweitzer visited them to take organ lessons from Widor, and spent the Winter Semester 1898–99 at the Sorbonne. But intellectually he felt more at home in the large purposeful provincial city of Berlin, which was on the way to becoming a 'world city'.

Schweitzer was named Albert, however, after his mother's older half-brother, a pastor in Strasbourg, who died young of a heart complaint in 1872, partly as a result of his heroic efforts to go to Paris for military supplies and bring them back to Strasbourg before the German siege began. He was too late. The German general allowed the medical supplies through but took the bearer prisoner. Schweitzer's mother was to be trampled to death by German cavalry in 1916, and his father, in his 70s, still cared for the Günsbach people as their pastor while they endured French shelling.

Human suffering and disease, poverty, human intolerance, anti-semitism (his wife was a Jewess), and war were the standing accompaniments of Schweitzer's happy and successful youth and young manhood.

At the age of twenty-one, during the Whitsun holiday, he decided to live for preaching,[2] scholarship, and music until he was thirty, and then, having accomplished what he had decided to do in scholarship and culture, to find a way as a man to serve directly those who suffered under the load of misery that lay on the world.

By the time he was thirty he had published a book on Kant's religious philosophy (his doctoral thesis in philosophy), a two-volume study of the Last Supper in the setting of the life of Jesus and the history of early Christianity (his doctoral thesis in theology and his thesis for the right to teach at the University of Strasbourg), and a book in French on J. S. Bach, 'the musician poet'. At thirty-one, after announcing his decision to study medicine in preparation for becoming a doctor in tropical Africa, he published a 418-page book on the history of research into the life of Jesus. By the time he had finished his medical studies and made practical provision for founding a tropical hospital and got himself a wife, he had bought out a much larger German book on Bach, written a brilliant history of research into the thought of the Apostle Paul, produced a slight but interesting psychological estimate of Jesus (for his Doctorate in medicine), published a second

[2] The preaching office appears with scholarship and music in the list of things to be given up in Schweitzer's first account of his life, *Gesammelte Werke* 1.300; cf. 1.99.

edition, much revised and enlarged, of his book on research into the life of Jesus, and begun to bring out (with Widor) a critical annotated edition of Bach's organ preludes and figures. He was just thirty-eight when he set out for Lambaréné.

Although he himself made this somewhat dramatic division of his life into two parts, the preaching, intellectual and cultural part and the serving medical part, it would be a mistake to exaggerate the change of course. He still continued to publish books after he began his work as a medical missionary. He published a large two-volume study of the philosophy of culture in 1923, and completed his study of Paul with *Die Mystik des Apostels Paulus (The Mysticism of Paul the Apostle)*, published in 1930. But, at a deeper level, his decision to turn to direct practical service of suffering humanity followed directly from his scholarly work. He believed the unresolved problems of philosophy could only be solved by action.

Schweitzer's scholarly method was always historical. The history of the study of a subject would always show to the sharp eyes of the historical investigator the unresolved problems in the subject, and the way to resolve them. The solution, however, was never abstract; it was always an acted-out achievement of the will. Consequently his own intellectual work could only reach a successful conclusion if it was acted out in an achievement of the will. Jesus, Paul, and Bach each completely embodied and resolved and brought to an end the problems unresolved by their predecessors. They achieved something because they committed their whole being to the realisation of their ideals. Schweitzer's historical investigation of ethical thought, of thought about Jesus, and thought about Paul in the last century or so showed that we were as far away from a solution as were the best eighteenth-century thinkers. Schweitzer believed he could see the solution to each of these problems, but the solution in each case was the discovery that his contemporaries overlooked the fact that Jesus, Paul, and Bach embodied dogmatic ideals in action. The embodiment of dogmatic ideals in action was the solution to the problems their predecessors could not crack. Schweitzer would hardly remain an honest man if he did not himself also resolve his predecessors' problems in the only way he had found they could be resolved, by embodying dogmatic ideals in action. Schweitzer's life and thought belong closely together because he found that the problems of thought could not be resolved without action, without deeds of the will. Schweitzer held that the speculative system-builders had failed and necessarily had to fail – Kant, Fichte, and Hegel. But there was another tradition, represented by the men of affairs who gave themselves up to the world of nature – the Stoics, Spinoza, and Goethe. This tradition could now succeed, but it would only succeed in the action of the will of individuals. Schweitzer saw himself as the great pioneer of a new age of peace; the climax of his intellectual work was to be the practical exercise of his will in the direct service of others.

It is no wonder, then, that Schweitzer's books are themselves exciting historical dramas. The great figures of the past who grappled in vain with the central problems of life are paraded before us, and each is shown to be right or wrong in an interestingly one-sided way. Each tendency is, however, part of a law-bound historical development, and a proper exposure of the law governing the discussion of the subject will inevitably show how the problem is to be resolved.

The history of research into the life of Jesus is not just the demonstration that all researchers have seen themselves in Jesus – have looked down the deep wall and seen their own faces reflected – but is the demonstration of the true solution to the problem. Nor is Schweitzer's history the story of a gradual progress ever upwards to the final achievement of a solution; on the contrary, the eighteenth century saw the outlines of an answer much more clearly than their successors. The subject is in a worse state by 1900 then it was at the end of the eighteenth century. The title of the first edition of Schweitzer's book on Jesus tells of a decline: Reimarus, the eighteenth-century high-school professor, fragments of whose work on Jesus were published by Lessing, saw much more clearly than the brilliant young scholar William Wrede the facts about Jesus. So the book was called *From Reimarus to*

Wrede. The drama of this book of Schweitzer's, like all his others, lies in the cool assumption that the author, who had already taken the decision to devote his life to serving suffering humanity to make restitution for his own personal good fortune is cleverer than the most sophisticated scholars of his day, whom he shows to be epigoni.

I myself think that Schweitzer's historical conclusions about Jesus and Paul are much more valuable than those of most of his contemporaries, so I cannot dismiss this seemingly arrogant claim of his out of hand. I propose to treat in turn his study of Jesus and his study of Paul, and then to conclude by showing how his historical conclusions and his philosophy of life fit together to make a unity.

Schweitzer began his university studies as both a theological student and an arts student at the University of Strasbourg in the Winter Semester of 1883–84. He heard lectures on the history of philosophy from Wilhelm Windelband (1848–1915), a Kantian, and Theobald Ziegler (1804–1918), whose passion was social ethics. But he also heard Heinrich Julius Holtzmann (1832–1910) on the Synoptic Gospels. On April Fool's Day 1894 he began his compulsory military service, but his commanding officer let him off pretty regularly to get to Windleband's Summer Semester course at 11 o'clock.

In the autumn he packed his Greek New Testament in his duffel-bag in order to prepare for a scholarship examination at the beginning of the Winter Semester in the Synoptic Gospels. He had already worked through Holtzmann's great commentary on the Synoptics in the *Hand-Commentar zum Neuen Testament*, 1889. Now he wanted to test his grasp of the subject using just the New Testament itself, working in the evenings and on the rest days.

Holtzmann had finally established that Mark's Gospel was the source of Matthew and Luke, and he assumed that Jesus' career could be understood from Mark's gospel alone. Schweitzer disagreed. With a natural historian's grasp of the importance of all the available evidence, he believed Matthew and Luke, apart from the birth narratives, to be subsquentially reliable. He also had the natural historian's eye for the main problems.

There were two main problems. The first was Jesus' evident reluctance to say who he was, to identify himself openly with any of the mythical figures who were to appear at the end of world history according to current Jewish apocalyptic expectations: Elijah, the prophet who was to return to prepare the way of the Lord, or the Messiah himself.

The second was Jesus' evident expectation that world history was about to end with the coming in power of the Kingdom of God.

As Schweitzer read Matthew 10 and 11, everything seemed to fall into place. There Jesus was reported as sending out his disciples with the promise that they would not have completed their mission to the cities of Israel before the supernatural Son of Man should come, and the supernatural messianic Kingdom break into history (Matt. 10.23). When the disciples returned, Jesus had to rethink his ideas. Not only had the Kingdom of God failed to come, but the disciples had not been persecuted in the way Jesus expected, for he shared the current Jewish apocalyptic view that God's people would have to suffer great persecution before the great deliverance arrived.

The fruit of Jesus' reassessment was his discovery that he himself, as the Messiah-designate, had to suffer persecution alone in the place of his disciples. That was Jesus' messianiac secret which he entrusted first to Peter, who betrayed him by refusing to accept that his master must suffer violent death, and then to all the disciples, to be betrayed by Judas to the Jewish religious authorities. Jesus believed that at his death or after three days the Kingdom of God would supernaturally break in and end all the injustice, war, and suffering of human history.

This was the Ariadne's thread which guided Schweitzer triumphantly through the labyrinth of nineteenth century New Testament scholarship. He first published his theory in the two volumes of a book on *The Last Supper in relation to the Life of Jesus and the history of primitive Christianity*.[3] In the

---

[3] *Das Abendmahl in Zusammenhang mit dem Leben Jesu und der Geschichte des Urchristentums. Heft 1: Das Abendmahlproblem auf Grund der wissenschaftlichen Forschung des 19. Jahrhunderts und der historischen Berichte.* (Preface dated August 1901).

Last Supper Jesus set forth his death in a secret parable as the event which was to conclude world history and bring in the Kingdom of God. He did not command the Last Supper to be repeated because there would be no more earthly time in which to repeat it.

Jesus believed that his coming suffering and death would be an expiation for the guilt of others. This was a secret between him and God which could not be understood by the others until his coming glorification. Then they would realise that he had suffered for them. When the Kingdom did not come, Jesus' world view was in fact destroyed, finished, brought to an end. The disciples could not see this because they never understood the connection Jesus made between his suffering and the immediate coming of the Kingdom of God. They found Jesus' tomb empty and in their enthusiastic expectation of their master's coming glory they saw him in visions as risen from the dead; so they were certain that he was with God in heaven and would soon come as Messiah and bring in the Kingdom. But this was only to fall back into the eschatological expectations of John the Baptist, where one had to repent and achieve moral renewal in expectation of the coming Kingdom. The idea that moral repentance and suffering for others actually *brings* the Kingdom was lost. The early church rightly focused attention on Jesus, and saw that his death had something to do with forgiveness of sins, but they could not understand Jesus' thought and intention in dying. But the failure of Jesus' expectations to materialise really destroyed the possibility of that world-view – and the modern theologians have in fact given up any such beliefs.

When, however, we understand the inner connection Jesus believed there to be between his death and the coming of the Kingdom of God, when all guilt will have been borne by his suffering and all sins forgiven, then we are in a position to see why the eschatological world view is at an end, and what remains over. The eschatological world view entailed a God who would intervene supernaturally in history, from outside. Schweitzer clearly did not believe in such a God, and held that the fact that Jesus, who did believe in such a God, was proved wrong on the point (because his God did not bring in the Kingdom at or soon after his death) closes the issue for him.

What is left over is Jesus' supernatural personality. Subsequent generations are now free to allow his spirit to penetrate their world-views.

What, then, is left over? There is no doubt Schweitzer believed this timeless ingredient to be the heroic will of the individual which by affirming life will create life. He expresses his view poetically in a picture of Jesus' crucifixion that appeared in the first edition of his Life of Jesus and was omitted from the revision.

> The Baptist and Jesus are not ... borne upon the current of a general eschatolagial movement ... They themselves set the times in motion by acting, by creating eschatological facts. It is this mighty creative force which constitutes the difficulty in grasping historically the eschatology of Jesus and the Baptist. Instead of literary artifice speaking out of a distant imaginary past, there now enter into the field of eschatology men, living, acting men. It was the only time when that ever happened in Jewish eschatology.
>
> There is silence all around. The Baptist appears, and cries: 'Repent, for the Kingdom of Heaven is at hand'. Soon after that comes Jesus, and in the knowledge that He is the coming Son of man lays hold of the wheel of the world to set it moving on that last revolution which is to bring all ordinary history to a close. It refuses to turn, and He throws Himself upon it. Then it does turn; and crushes Him. Instead of bringing in the eschatological conditions, He has destroyed them. The wheel rolls onward, and the mangled body of the one immeasurably great Man, who was strong enough to think of himself as the spiritual ruler of mankind and to

bend history to His purpose, is hanging upon it still.
That is His victory and His reign.[4]

This first edition of Schweitzer's survey of the attempts in
the previous century or so to write a life of Jesus was to keep
him busy from 1901 to 1905. Schweitzer believed that the
secret of the universe could only be read off nature and
history, and was not to be discovered by thought which
believed it could stand over against the process itself. The
history of the attempts to solve a problem – for example, the
problem posed by the enormous historical importance of Jesus
– could itself be the best way to solve the problem. The
contemporary failure to make sense of the fact Jesus was so
quickly and naturally called Messiah though he kept secret
his private beliefs during his ministry, and the contemporary
failure to understand the central importance of Jewish
apocalyptic ideas in Jesus' thought were failures which a
historian of the failed histories could make plain. Schweitzer
set himself to master the entire history of the study of the
Jesus' life since Reimarus, with the express intention of
bringing the whole debate to a triumphant close.

The University Library at Strasbourg provided him with
an almost complete collection of all the books on the subject,
including the pile of large and small scale reactions to David
Friedrich Strauss's first *Life of Jesus*, and to Renan's *Life of
Jesus* of 1863 (Ernest Renan, 1823–1892). These books came
from the library of Eduard Reuss, an early advocate of the
priority of Mark's Gospel, and from the libraries of other
Strasbourg teachers; nowhere else in the world could
Schweitzer have so easily collected the materials necessary for
writing his great book.

Here is his description of the final stages of writing.

When I had worked through the numerous Lives of
Jesus, I found it very difficult to group them in chapters.
After attempting in vain to do this on paper, I piled all
the 'Lives' in one big heap in the middle of my room,

---

[4] *Von Reimarus zu Wrede. Geschichte der Leben – Jesu – Forschung* (Tübingen, 1906),
p. 367; English translation: *The Quest of the Historical Jesus: A Critical Study of its
Progress from Reimarus to Wrede* (1st ed., London, 1910; 3rd ed., 1954), pp. 368 f.

picked out for each chapter I had planned a place of its own in a corner or between the pieces of furniture, and then, after thorough consideration, heaped up the volumes in the piles to which they belonged, pledging myself to find room for all the books belonging to each pile, and to leave each heap undisturbed in its own place, till the corresponding chapter in the sketch should be finished. And I carried out my plan to the very end. For many a month all the people who visited me had to thread their way across the room along paths which ran between the heaps of books. I had also to fight hard to ensure that the tidying zeal of Frau Wolpert the trusty Württemberg widow who kept house for me, came to a halt before the piles of books.[5]

Notice how Schweitzer has compared his own room to a landscape covered with small paths which visitors have to thread their way through. The landlady would like to tidy all the books away, but Schweitzer himself is busy ordering them, putting them into piles, placing them so that others can see them for what they are. His piles leave negotiable paths. Eventually that passable negotiable landscape will be securely mapped in Schweitzer's book, and then the great heap of books and pamphlets can be cleared off the floor and returned to the University Library.

The one who cleared the books away is not going to stay in rooms as a University professor. He not only orders the books and clears them away; he himself goes away, too, to act out the same drama in his age that Jesus acted out long ago. Jesus' world picture was false – but Jesus' deed was so masterful and heroic that it could afford to prove the world view wrong and still remain there as a heroic timeless deed which overarched history.

During the years Schweitzer studied medicine he found time to do for the study of Paul what he had done for the study of Jesus. *Paul and his Interpreters* was a survey of a

[5] *My Life and Thought*, translated by C. T. Campion (2nd ed., Longon, 1955), p. 58; *Aus meinem Leben und Denken* (Leipzig, 1931); *Gesammelte Werke in fünf Bänden*, Vol. I, pp. 61 f.

century of attempts to understand the thought of the Apostle Paul.[6] Schweitzer discovered that a remarkably similar mistake ran through the history of all these attempts: just as the central importance of Jewish eschatological expectations was overlooked in the lives of Jesus, so was it overlooked in the descriptions of the thought of Paul. Schweitzer conceded that many scholars had granted Paul shared current apocalyptic expectations in his earlier writings, but they thought that he soon abandoned such crude Jewish ideas and moved across to a Hellenistic spiritualised religion which taught freedom from the law and mystical identification with Christ's dying and rising again. They tried to explain Paul's thought out of the Greek and Oriental mystery religions.

Schweitzer the historian saw with great clarity that this supposed shift in Paul's thought from Jewish ideas to Hellenistic ideas could not be maintained. Its *reductio ad absurdum* was the Dutch school's theory that the supposedly later Hellenistic writings of Paul were not genuine but belonged to the second century; they asserted that no Jewish rabbi could have argued in the way this later Paul was supposed to have argued.

Schweitzer had no time to do more than hint at his own solution. He started from the assumption that Paul, like Jesus before him, belonged completely to the world of Jewish apocalyptic thought. He then argued that the later stage in Paul's thought, where he was supposed to have moved across to mystical Hellenistic ideas, was really Jewish apocalyptic thought raised to its 'highest degree of intensity'. Greek Mysticism took its devotees on a journey of the mind away from this world into the mystical world. Paul's mysticism was quite different because it was based on Jewish eschatology which envisaged the transformation of this world into the Kingdom of God. Paul's Christ-mysticism inserts the coming Kingdom of God into this world in the person of the predestined members of the future Kingdom. The cosmic catastrophe of the consummation of history became actual

[6] *Geschichte der paulinischen Forschung von der Reformation bis auf die Gegenwart* (Tübingen, 1911); English translation: *Paul and His Interpreters*, translated by W. Montgomery (London, 1912).

for Paul in Jesus' death and resurrection and can become actual also in the lives of believers who die and rise with Christ. Those are the only places in which it becomes actual. These believers are actually transformed into Christ's risen bodily nature and so will share his blessedness in the supernatural Kingdom for a great period of time before the final resurrection and the last judgement[7].

Schweitzer's interpretation of the Bible has led him to the point where he claims to have found the eternally valid secret of life. The historian of ideas, whose work on the history of nineteenth-century study of the life of Jesus and the theology of Paul will remain as permanent monuments to his greatness as an historian, claims to have used his historical work to solve not just the problem of Jesus' life and Paul's thought, but the central problem of life itself. Jesus and Paul each said something permanent, and each said the same sort of thing. What could it be, this idea that was not itself subject to the historical forces that made all other ideas appear temporally conditioned and doomed to lose their once proud pretensions to truth with the passing of time? Why was Schweitzer's reading of Paul and Jesus right, and permanently right, while all the other readings were defective?

His answer was simple, and appears in scarcely-varying terms in every book he wrote, from the book on Kant in 1899 to the book on Paul's mysticism in 1930, and he continued to preach the same message until the day of his death in 1965 at the age of ninety. The heroic will is timeless.

> The last and deepest knowledge of things comes from the will. It follows that what governs the direction of the thought which seeks to bring together the final syntheses of observations and insights in order to achieve a world-view is the will; it is the will that represents the primary essence of the relevant personalities and times, an essence of which no further explanation is possible.[8]

[7] *Die Mystik des Apostels Paulus* (Tübingen, 1930); English translation: *The Mysticism of Paul the Apostle* (London, 1931), by W. Montgomery who died suddenly a few days after finishing the work.

[8] This quotation and the paraphrase that follows come from the last chapter of the 1913 edition of *Geschichte der Leben–Jesu–Forschung*. See Henry Clark, *The Ethical*

Schweitzer's contemporaries failed to understand Jesus not just because they could make nothing of the bizarre eschatology, but because their willing and hoping was not strongly determined towards achieving the moral consummation of the world. They had no equivalent to the thought of Jesus. The only way to understand Jesus was 'from will to will'. Only from will to will could there be any direct unmediated communication between one world-view and another.

The only way to understand the permanent in other world-views was to understand the will that determined the direction of that world-view. The only way to escape the temporary and the time-conditioned in one's own age was to work on one's own will, for only the will is permanent and timeless. History cannot teach us the content of the will, for we only discover the timeless in history when we recognize the will there which we will in ourselves. Fortunately, the idea of the moral world order 'lies in us and is given with the moral will',[9] as Kant said long ago. All we have to do is to work on ourselves, to free ourselves from the world and from ourselves. Then we will find power and peace and the will to life.

The only victory that is important in the world is the victory of the individual over himself.

The maturity towards which we have to develop is that we must work on ourselves to become ever more simple, ever more genuine, ever more honourable, ever more peaceable, ever meeker, ever more generous to others, ever more ready to share their sorrows. We have to devote ourselves to nothing other than this sober process. In this process the soft iron of youthful idealism is hardened to the steel of an imperishable idealism for life. The great wisdom is: to be done with disappointment. All events are the working of spiritual power – the successful, the working of power that is

Mysticism of Albert Schweitzer (1962), *The Philosophy of Albert Schweitzer* (London, 1964), Appendix II.

[9] *Gesammelte Werke*, Vol. 5, p. 885; cf. *Die Religionsphilosophie Kant's* (Freiburg i.B., 1899).

strong enough; the failures, the working of power that is not strong enough. My offer of love achieves nothing. The reason is, because there is still too little love in me. I am powerless against the falsehood and the lies that have their existence all around me. The reason for that is I myself am not yet truthful enough. I have to observe how mistrust and ill-will ply their sorry trade more and more. That means that I have not yet divested myself of littleness and envy. My peaceableness is misunderstood and reviled. That means that there is not yet enough readiness to make peace in me. The great secret is to go through life as someone ever full of power. This is possible for the one who takes no account of men and events but who, in all that happens, is thrown back on himself, who seeks the final ground of things in himself . . .

We live in a world where sheer force, clothed in lies, force more powerful than ever before sits on the throne of the world. Yet I remain convinced that truth, love, peaceableness, meekness and generosity are the force above all force. The world would belong to these things if only enough people thought and lived purely and strongly and steadily enough the thoughts of love, of truth, of peacemaking and of meekness. All ordinary power limits itself. For force engenders an opposite force that sooner or later will equal it or overcome it. But generosity works simply and steadily. Generosity engenders no tensions that hamper it. Generosity relaxes existing tensions, it disperses mistrust and misunderstandings, it strengthens itself in that it calls forth generosity [in others]. That is why it is the most purposeful and the most intensive power ... An immeasurably deep truth lies in the fanciful words of Jesus, 'Blessed are the meek, for they shall inherit the earth'.[10]

The reason why the will of the individual who works on

[10] *Aus meiner Kindheit und Jugendzeit* (Munich, 1924); *Gesammelte Werke in fünf Bänden*, Vol. 1, pp. 311–313.

himself alone to achieve the perfection of the world is so
powerful is that he 'finds unity with the eternal moral world-
will'.[11] Schweitzer never uses the word God except to
indicate this mysterious life-force before which we have to
bow. 'We live in the world and the world lives in us . . .God
is the power that everything contains [or that contains
everything].'[12] There is no other way to be in touch with
this God than through working on one's own will. This God
cannot give anything to anyone who asks, or change a
hopeless situation so as to deliver the righteous. Nothing
outside of us can be changed; all we have power over is our
own wills.

All this reminds us very strongly of Nietzsche and
Schopenhauer and Wagner, and these are the immediate
sources of Albert Schweitzer's thought. He himself claimed
to be combining Schopenhauer's world-denying philosophy
with Nietzsche's world-affirming philosophy,[13] and he was
always spell-bound by Wagner's musical presentation of
heroism. But the line of thought goes back to the Stoics, as
he himself was fully aware.

It is maddeningly difficult to come to terms with
Schweitzer's ideas. If we should dare to oppose him and say
that his philosophy is false, he first of all silently accuses us of
dilettantism: we have not acted on our ideals and gone out to
Africa to serve and suffer with the downtrodden and diseased.
But worse still. He does not have to meet our arguments at
all. Our very opposition to him is a sign that he himself has
not been loving enough and generous enough and peaceable
enough towards us. He does not have to take account of our
arguments or of facts about the world. That cannot be
changed. All he can work upon is himself. Nevertheless, he is
sure we are not capable of understanding him or Jesus or

[11] Chapter 25, Schlussbetrachtung, *Geschichte der Leben – Jesu – Forschung*
(Tübingen, 1913); Siebenstern Taschenbuch ed. (Munich & Hamburg, 1966), vol. 2,
p. 628; *Gesammelte Werke* 3.885.
[12] *Strassburger Predigten über die Ehrfurcht vor dem Leben*, edited by U.
Neuenschwander (Munich, 1966), 23 February 1919, *Gesammelte Werke* 5.130.
[13] *Civilization and Ethics. Philosophy of Civilization*, Part II (London, 1923; 2nd ed.,
1929), p. 180.

Paul because we are not heroic enough; we lack the heroic energy. Without will one cannot understand will.

Schweitzer destroys the possibility by his theory that I or anyone else can do him any good, just as he has destroyed the possibility that Jesus can do him any good. The only good that can come to him is from himself. He perhaps dimly saw that there are really no exceptions in a world-view that denies free people can help other free people; there is no exception in the case of oneself. If no one else can really affect me then neither can I affect myself. But Schweitzer was ready for this final disappointment, for behind all his wonder at life and creativity he had a limitless sad resignation to whatever had to be. He himself is in the end 'merely the brain in which the philosophical ideas and problems of his day [came] to fruition' (to quote what he said about Kant, but which he applied to Bach, and must have applied to himself).[14] He spoke of hearts in which there is 'an unquenchable yearning for the Kingdom of God, but also consolation for the fact that we do not see its fulfilment'.[15] He knew that if anything happened as a result of his work on his own will, it would be a miracle – but he did not think there was a God who could work miracles, so that he had to do with resignation in the face of necessity. Recall his verdict on Jesus cited above. 'The wheel [of the world] rolls onward and the mangled body of the one immeasurably great Man, who was strong enough to think of himself as the spiritual ruler of mankind and to bend history to His purpose, is handing upon it still. That is His victory and His reign'.[16]

Schweitzer's remains the greatest attempt to force the Bible into a Stoic mould. He got very many facts about Jesus and Paul right – above all their eschatology; but he would not let their eschatology be ordinarily Jewish. He could not see that Jesus may have meant there to be a time between his resurrection and the coming Kingdom of God when all people would be able to receive actual gifts of grace from the

---

[14] *J. S. Bach*, English translation by Ernest Newman, 2 Vols. (London, 1911); Vol. 1, p. 2.

[15] *The Mysticism of Paul the Apostle*, English translation, p. 396.

[16] *The Quest for the Historical Jesus* (London, 1910), p. 369.

Father and from him. Stoicism cannot allow anyone to be anyone else's helper or saviour, and Stoicism cannot allow that God is a person who answers prayers.

Schweitzer the Stoic, fed in his youth on Schopenhauer and Nietzsche and Wagner, tried to extract a philosophy of will and a practice of will from Jesus and Paul. His was a brilliant failure – his books on Jesus and Paul are still the best starting point for studying Jesus and Paul. But it was a failure, both historically and philosophically. Historically, Jesus cannot have thought he could force God's hand. Philosophically, we are free to ask for and receive gifts from one another, and from God. Unless we are, there is no point in arguing.[17]

---

[17] Nicholas Denyer, *Time, Action and Necessity: A proof of free will* (London, 1981).

20

Barth

Karl Barth is not easy to understand. He has thrown great boulders of books in the path of anyone chasing after him, and once stated explicitly that no one could interpret him properly unless he had read everything he wrote.[1] The Church Dogmatics is just over nine thousand pages long — long pages, and one page in ten more closely printed as an excursus to the text proper. And he wrote other major books besides the Church Dogmatics — a book on Anselm and a history of Protestant thought in the nineteenth century, for example — and published countless lectures and pamphlets as well.

At a simple obvious level we can say that Barth saved the honour of theology in the twentieth century. He refused to apologise for theology any more, asserting theology's sovereign rights in the world of politics and of thought; and he unswervingly opposed Hitler from the very first as a false god.

He belongs in the history of Biblical criticism because his first book was a commentary on Paul's Epistle to the Romans, and because his theology was emphatically Biblical. Once again we find that a new attempt to understand the Bible is part of a great cultural, social and political upheaval, as it was with Kant and Herder and Hegel, with David Friedrich Strauss, Bruno Bauer and Heinrich Ewald. The Reformation

---

[1] Barth's preface to Otto Weber's summary of the Church Dogmatics. Otto Weber, *Karl Barth's Kirchliche Dogmatik: Ein einführender Bericht* (Neukirchen Kreis Moers, 1950), Geleitwort, p. 5; English translation by Arthur C. Cochrane (London, 1953), p. 9.

was by no means the last time that a world crisis seemed to
hinge on how one read the Bible.

Yet what a difference this time! Barth's theology, it is true,
is still studied – but that is not surprising; there is so much of
it, it is so learned, and it is so hard to understand, it could
have been designed for the benefit of doctoral students. As a
living theology it has failed to catch the imagination of the
church at large. Barth's political influence, it is true, did help
inspire many pastors and congregations to retain their
integrity in the face of the overwhelmingly sudden and
complete National Socialist revolution, and helped save the
lives of many German Jews, but even here there are
reservations to be made. It was not until 1944 that men like
Bonhoeffer, partly inspired by Barth, made any serious
attempt to overthrow Hitler, and ten years does seem a long
time for opposition to organise itself. And we must ask why
such a magnetic personality as Barth, with a following of
devoted students from as early as 1920 onwards, did not
produce in German public life a clear understanding of the
basic moral and political law that murder is forbidden, for
whatever reason.[2] Barth in fact helped to foster general public
doubt that there were any unalterable absolute moral and
political laws like the law against murder by his reiterated
insistence that any discussion of such moral rules was a
subsidiary matter when the only question was the question
about God. He may even have helped feed the general
German bourgeois scorn for the Weimar Republic and
hindered the formation of a solid democratic centre party.[3]

Barth constantly presented himself as the one perfectly
serious theologian who was talking only about God, while
other theologians were missing the point by concerning

[2] See Ludwig Marcuse, *Mein zwanzigstes Jahrhundert: Auf dem Weg zu einer
Autobiographie* (Munich, 1960), p. 155 et passim for a picture of German intellectual
life at the time and its impotence against National Socialism.

[3] Klaus Scholder, 'Neuere deutsche Geschichte und protestantische Theologie:
Aspekte und Fragen', *Evangelische Theologie* 23 (1963), pp. 510–36. For the general
educated scorn, see Wolfgang Trillhaas, *Aufgehobene Vergangenheit: Aus meinem Leben*
(Göttingen, 1976), Chapter 5: Ebert, the Social Democratic President of the
Republic, was a figure of fun and the Republic was even blamed for the collapse of
Germany in November 1918!

themselves with human religious preoccupations of various sorts. He also presented himself as the only perfectly serious opponent of Hitler with the only effective answer to him, while others imagined he could be fought with human principles of justice and goodness.[4]

These claims for himself seem to be in a plain straightforward sense doubtful. He always said he was swimming against the stream, but in fact he is a highly representative man of the 1920s. He always said he was confronting man with God, but the essence of his theology is that we can never know anything of God's plan in order to follow it out.[5] He always said he was uncompromisingly against Hitler, but that opposition was to take the form of public pronouncements, the advocacy of oaths against Hitler and the like, means hardly calculated to make an impression in a police state.

One claim of his is fully justified. He always said that his thought was simple, even though it also required devoted and lengthy study to master. That seems right. In all Barth's writings we find the same basic simple pattern of thought.[6] In this chapter I hope to show the simple mechanism that works Barth's thought, to produce the effect he wanted. When I say that every one of his major claims for himself was straightforwardly doubtful, I do not mean that he acted in bad faith or concealed what he was doing: he always said he was taking the only line possible for a modern theologian, and I have to agree that anyone who was deceived into thinking he was any different from the man he was had

---

[4] For example, *A Letter to Great Britain from Switzerland*, Introduction by A. R. Vidler, translated by Ernest L. H. Gordon & George Hill (London, 1941). The British talk about 'Western civilization', 'the liberty of the individual', 'freedom of knowledge', 'the infinite value of the human personality', 'the brotherhood of men', 'social justice'. These have a positive value for him, and he would not stop anyone saying them. 'But I doubt whether I can admit that those concepts do really describe the grounds upon which we Christians must decide on our Christian attitude to the war'. They are too weak to make an impression on Hitler (pp. 16 f.). The German is in Barth's *Eine Schweizer Stimme 1938–1945* (Zollikon, 1945), pp. 179–200.

[5] E.g. *Die kirchliche Dogmatik* III/3 (Zurich, 1950), §49.3, pp. 224, 266 f.; *Church Dogmatics* III/3 (Edinburgh, 1961), pp. 198, 234 f.

[6] The Rev Principal J. M. Owen of Perth first drew my attention to the basic simplicity of Barth's thought. See his dissertation on Barth and Elert, Heidelberg.

simply not paid close enough attention to what he actually said and did.

Barth was born in Basel on the 10th May 1886. His father and his father's father were ministers, and his mother's father and *her* mother's father were ministers.[7] All were Swiss Calvinists, but all had studied at one time or another in Germany and had come under the influence of the orthodox-sounding Biblical pietism of Johann Tobias Beck (1804–1878) and Richard Rothe (1799–1867). Barth's father moved to Bern just before Barth's third birthday and, after a short time as a lecturer in the university, he was promoted to Professor of Early and Medieval Church History, but with a strong leaning towards New Testament. He was decidedly 'positive' in his theology rather than 'liberal', but he lost calls from the conservative German Universities of Halle and Greifswald because of his denial of the Virgin Birth.

Karl Barth began his theological studies with four semesters at Bern, in every one of which he attended his father's lectures. In the Winter Semester of 1906–1907 he went to Berlin for Harnack, and there he fell under the spell of the writings of Wilhelm Herrmann (1846–1922), who was teaching at Marburg. The Summer Semester 1907 he spent back in Bern as president of his student brotherhood. He then wanted to go go Marburg for Herrmann, but his father would not let him – just as he was not to let him marry the girl he had fallen in love with at this time. He spent a hard-working but otherwise desolate time in Tübingen (Winter Semester 1907–1908), but was able to prevail on his father to let him go to Marburg in the summer. He was just twenty-two. He stayed in Marburg until late summer 1909 and for the greater part of the time worked as editorial assistant to Martin Rade on *Die Christliche Welt*, the weekly organ of German liberal Protestantism. He even edited two issues in the summer of 1909 when the Rades were on holiday.[8] In

---

[7] See Eberhard Busch, *Karl Barths Lebenslauf: Nach seinen Briefen und autobiographischen Texten* (Munich, 1976); English translation *Karl Barth: His life from letters and autobiographical texts*, by John Bowden (London, 1976).

[8] *Die Christliche Welt*, 23 (1909), nos. 33 and 34, 12th and 19th August. The second issue contained three short reviews by Rudolf Bultmann, then 25 years old.

September 1909, he entered the ministry of his Church as an assistant in Geneva. In May 1910 his family made him break off with Rösy Munger and at Pentecost he confirmed the members of his first confirmation class, among whom was Nelly Hoffmann, sixteen at the time. In May the next year he began to take an interest in her; they were engaged shortly afterwards, and were to marry two years later, in March 1913, by which time Barth had been pastor of Safenwil, a small industrial town, for nearly two years. Barth was already an active member of the Swiss Social Democratic Party, much to the horror of the factory owners in his congregation. Shortly after the marriage Barth's old friend Eduard Thurneysen became pastor of the neighbouring parish and they began to visit each other frequently – even though the road lay over mountain passes and valleys – and to take seriously the fact that 'God is, God counts, God wills'.[9] In spring 1915 Barth went back to Marburg for his brother Peter's marriage with Martin Rade's daughter, and took the opportunity to visit Bad Boll to sit at the feet of Christoph Blumhardt the younger (1842-1919), the pietistic prophet of the Kingdom of God, who was also an active member of the Social Democratic Party.

In the summer of 1916 the thirty-year-old Barth began to write in prophetic style a commentary on Paul's Epistle to the *Romans*. The book was finished in the summer of 1918, as the war drew to a close, and printed by December with financial help from Barth's friend whom he had met through Thurneysen, the left-wing businessman Rudolf Pestalozzi. The book was little noticed outside Switzerland until Barth became famous in Germany for a 51-page pamphlet on 'The Christian in Society' which was the text of an address at a conference on religion and society in Tambach, Thuringia. Barth was already hard at work on an entirely rewritten second edition of his *Romans*. While he was writing it, in January 1921, he received a call to a new chair for Reformed Theology which was being established with the help of American Presbyterian money on the edge of the theological

[9] Busch, p. 85; English translation, p. 73 ('God is, God counts, God wants').

faculty in Göttingen. The family moved to Göttingen in the autumn of that same year, a few days after Barth had sent the manuscript of the second edition of *Romans* to press.

Barth's lectures appeared only 'below the line' in the lecture-list, outside the lectures by members of the faculty, and he was not supposed to lecture in systematic theology proper. These things did not stop him either from attracting a devoted band of student followers or from lecturing on systematic theology. In the Summer Semester of 1924 he offered the first of a series, which was to continue for two more semesters, devoted to Instruction in the Christian Religion (the title of Calvin's *Institute*). These were the days of student 'claques' and Barth was accompanied by his 'claque' when he went away to lecture, just as Bultmann was surrounded by his 'claque' when he visited Göttingen.[10] Barth's *Romans* was being read eagerly by high school boys in Bible study groups – Wolfgang Trillhaas, the Lutheran theologian, and Gerhard von Rad, the Old Testament scholar, neither of whom had thought of becoming pastors, were decisively turned in that direction at such a reading of Barth's *Romans*[11] – and Bonhoeffer's cousin Hans-Christoph von Hase who was studying mathematics at Göttingen, changed to theology because of Barth's lectures.

Barth was called to Münster and began to teach there at the beginning of the Winter Semester 1925–26. All professors are civil servants in Germany and so Barth took on German citizenship alongside his Swiss citizenship. In 1927 he published the prolegomena to a Christian Dogmatics, *The Doctrine of the Word of God*. In 1930 he moved to a chair in Bonn, and started his dogmatics again with lectures in the Summer Semester 1931 under the overall heading of *Church Dogmatics* rather than *Christian Dogmatics*, in which he tried to eliminate all philosophical basis for his system and to speak

[10] Wolfgang Trillhaas, 'Karl Barth in Göttingen', *Perspektiven und Gestalten des neuzeitlichen Christentums* (Göttingen, 1975), pp. 171–84. See also Trillhaas's autobiography, *Aufgehobene Vergangenheit: Aus meinem Leben* (Göttingen, 1976), especially Chapter 9. Gogarten, Karl Ludwig Schmidt and George Merz also had their admiring circles.

[11] Trillhaas, *Aufgehobene Vergangenheit*, pp. 58 f.

only about the grace of Jesus Christ from a position in the church alone. Barth thought he was driven to this standpoint by a study of Anselm of Canterbury, one of the greatest philosophical theologians of all time.[12]

Barth was a member of the German Social Democratic party. When the party itself advised members to resign and go underground, Barth decided to clear his membership with the Government Minister with responsibility for the University. This man, who also had read Barth's *Romans* in his youth, gave permission, and when the SDP was finally banned in June 1933, Barth was able to claim that his own membership was entirely in the clear, as he had permission from the Minister to be a member.[13] Barth actively helped form the Confessing Church, a tightly organised brotherhood of pastors in the various regional churches of Germany, drawn together at first more by opposition to the German Christians than by opposition to the National Socialist Workers' Party (Nazi Party) as such. Barth largely wrote the Barmen Declaration of 1934, which began with a stirring pledge of complete and absolute loyalty to Jesus Christ, which in Barth's mind excluded the sort of complete obedience to Hitler which Hitler was demanding in the personal oath all civil servants and officers in the armed forces had to take. In July 1935 Barth was relieved of his teaching post, and a few days later moved to Basel to a professorship which atheist sympathisers with his political stand had fixed up for him at short notice. It was not until 1938 that he was made a member of the faculty. Apart from two semesters back in Bonn at the invitation of the British Control Commission, he remained at Basel for the rest of his life. During the war he made his only explicit attempt to alter the traditional structure and content of the Christian faith in its Reformed Church form by advocating the abandonment of infant baptism.[14] He

[12] *Fides quaerens intellectum* (Munich, 1931); English translation, *Anselm: Fides quaerens intellectum* (London, 1960).

[13] Busch, pp. 237 f.; English translation, p. 225.

[14] 'Die kirchliche Lehre von der Taufe', *Theologische Studien* 14 (Zollikon-Zurich, 1943); English translation by Ernest A. Payne, *The Teaching of the Church regarding Baptism* (London, 1948).

characteristically claimed that this was the true church position. His other great explicit departure from Reformed theology was his insistence that all are saved (as well as damned – but salvation is the first thing that is to be said about everyone).

What, then, was this great theologian's attitude to the Bible, on which he claimed to be basing all his theology?

Barth begins from the starting-point that none of the miracles in the Bible actually happened, in the sense that none of them is the interference of God in the regular occurrence of events. Opponents of Barth like Bultmann were infuriated by Barth's seeming to say that he believed that the resurrection happened (in the normal sense, by which the grave became empty and the transformed body of Jesus left this universe) when he did not believe anything of the sort – but Barth never really concealed his actual position from those who took care to read carefully what he wrote. All Barth insisted on was that the forty days between the resurrection and ascension were a dialogue, not a monologue of the disciples with themselves; that means that the disciples were more like an audience that had arranged to be present at a performance than like individuals sharing a common interior experience. But Barth is perfectly explicit that the history of the forty days is not part of the facts of history to which the life of Jesus from his birth to his death belong.[15]

Barth said at times that a historical decision about these matters was unimportant – 'This grave might be proved to be finally closed or open; it is really all the same; what use is a grave proved closed or open near Jerusalem in the year 30?'[16] From his point of view he was quite right. He knew that great historians like H. J. Holtzmann and Albert Schweitzer believed the grave to be empty; he also knew that they, no more than he, thought this account of the historical events did anything to increase the possibility that Jesus' body

---

[15] *Kirchliche Dogmatic* III/2 (Zurich, 1948), pp. 534 f.; *Church Dogmatics* III/2 (Edinburgh, 1960), p. 446.

[16] *Die Auferstehung der Toten: Eine akademische Vorlesung über 1. Kor. 15.* (Munich, 1925, 2nd ed., 1926), p. 78; English translation, *The Resurrection of the Dead* (London, 1933).

had been changed into a risen body. Barth thought that no historical judgement on the truth or falsehood of events alleged to have happened could in principle show that special revelation from God had been made by those events – or could even raise the probability that special revelation was conveyed by the events. He therefore welcomed sceptical judgements because they made it even more unlikely that the historical investigation of an event could appear to support a claim that God had revealed something in the event; if the grave remained closed and if Jesus' body was still there, no one would be tempted to raise the question whether or not the historical fact of an open and an empty tomb increased the probability that God had raised Jesus from the dead. Barth is shrewd enough not to state this argument as clearly as I have done, because, had he done so, he would have laid himself open to the charge that he was using an historical event, namely the closed tomb, to change people's view of the possible nature of revelation – and he wants to say that revelation is entirely independent of history. But it is clear to me that Barth did accept the view of the theologians who taught him and influenced him – above all, Harnack and Herrmann, – that the tomb was closed. 'Critical-historical study means the deserved and necessary end of the "foundations" of this [reliable and shared] knowledge [of the person of Jesus Christ]; these "foundations" are no foundations, because they are not laid by God himself', Barth wrote in answer to Harnack's charge that only scientific historical investigation of the life of Jesus could guarantee us against thinking of a dreamed-up Jesus rather than the true Jesus. 'Whoever does not yet understand', Barth continued, '. . . that we know Christ no longer according to the flesh [2 Cor. 5.16], he could well let critical Biblical scholarship tell him so: the more fundamentally shocked he is, the better for him and for the matter in hand. And *that* might then perhaps be the service that "historical knowledge" is able to perform for the real task of theology'.[17] Of course Barth has

---

[17] An exchange of letters between Harnack and Barth begun by Harnack's fifteen questions to those theologians who despise scholarly theology, *Die Christliche Welt* (1923), issues 1/2, 5/6, 9/10, 16/17, 20/21, January to May reprinted as 'Ein

avoided the issue, which is, How can we tell we are talking about the same person when we both talk about Jesus? Barth has an answer to this difficulty, to which we must return, but here he is insisting on his principle that historical investigation can make no difference to belief.

In history itself there is nothing, so far as the eye can see, that could provide a foundation for belief ... In history itself everything could always also have been regarded as quite different. One should unequivocally hold that faith is based on revelation – on historical revelation to be sure, but on revelation; and one should get accustomed to thinking of revelation as a special category, as that unresolvable unity of happening, speaking and listening which is actually witnessed to in the Bible. Whoever wants to find revelation must find revelation and not something else, not something that revelation is as well. Otherwise he does not find revelation at all.[18]

Barth comes closest to revealing his own position in the casual remark, 'The more clearly the biblical witnesses of Jesus Christ speak, the more what they say gets lost in what we should today call the realm of pure legend'.[19] In other words, the more clearly the Bible claims a revelation has occurred, the less reliable that passage is as history.

Barth, it seems, fully shared the historical judgement of liberal Biblical scholars and theologians that the events supposed in the Bible to reveal God's power did not actually occur, and that what did occur was capable of a non-

Briefwechsel mit Adolf von Harnack' in Karl Barth, *Theologische Fragen und Antworten, Gesammelte Vorträge*, Volume 3, (Zollikon, 1957), p. 7–31. English translation and commentary in H. Martin Rumscheidt, *Revelation and Theology: An Analysis of the Barth-Harnack Correspondence of 1923* (Cambridge, 1972). ◆

[18] *Die christliche Dogmatik im Entwurf, Volume 1, Die Lehre vom Worte Gottes, Prolegomena zur christlichen Dogmatik* (Munich, 1927), p. 237.

[19] 'Das christliche Verständnis der Offenbarung: Eine Vorlesung', *Theologische Existenz Heute*, New Series, No. 12 (Munich, 1948), p. 18. A course of Open Lectures in Bonn, Summer Semester 1947. English translation by R. & K. Gregor Smith, 'The Christian Understanding of Revelation' in *Against the Stream* (London, 1954), p. 222.

supernatural explanation. But he did not follow the liberal theologians in disregarding these events and concentrating on something else. Rather he affirmed that the whole complex event of the Bible, which patently as a book did centre around these alleged revelations of God's power in creation, the exodus, and the giving of the Law, in the incarnation, death and resurrection of the Messiah, was an indispensable part of a larger pattern of revelation.

Even quite conservative theologians (like his father) expressed doubt about the Virgin Birth. Not him. Given a choice between two theologians, both of whom earnestly wish to affirm the mystery of Christmas, one of whom acknowledges and confesses the Virgin Birth as the sign of the mystery and the other of whom denies the Virgin Birth as mere externality or leaves the matter of the Virgin Birth open, Barth is in no doubt he wants to be the first sort. Those who deny the Virgin Birth willy-nilly go looking for points of contact with natural reason; this fatal tendency makes them blind to the miracle of the Virgin Birth.[20] 'Virgin Birth affirms: birth without preceeding sexual union of man and woman.'[21] Barth uses this uncompromising statement to underline his theology of God's sheer grace: 'willing, accomplishing, creative, sovereign humanity as such is here not in view, is not to be used for this work'.[22] The unwary reader might think that Barth actually believes the Virgin Birth; he certainly wants to look like the first sort of theologian and not like the second. A few pages later all is made clear. Most theologians of the first type unfortunately believe the Virgin Birth as a 'Mirakel' not as a 'Wunder', a distinction hard to render in English but firmly established in German theological vocabulary by Barth's teacher Herrmann. A 'Mirakel', according to Barth, is an extraordinary occurrence within this our world and consequently also a component of our human world view. A 'Wunder', on the other hand, is a sign of God that sets a boundary to this our

[20] *Die kirchliche Dogmatik* I/2 (Zurich, 1938), pp. 196–7; *Church Dogmatics* I/2 (Edinburgh, 1956), pp. 179–80.

[21] *Die kirchliche Dogmatik* I/2, p. 207; *Church Dogmatics* I/2, p. 190.

[22] *Die kirchliche Dogmatik* I/2, p. 210; *Church Dogmatics* I/2, p. 192.

world as simply a created world, a sign of God who is the Lord of the world.[23] Barth very carefully affirms the Virgin Birth as 'Wunder' and not as 'Mirakel'. If we return a few pages to his uncompromising statements about the Virgin Birth, we find the same distinction: the Virgin Birth is a 'Wunder' that cannot be understood from the continuity of other events in this world and it is not factually grounded in this continuity; in other words, it didn't happen.[24] The Virgin Birth is on all fours with the empty tomb.[25]

To understand what Barth was getting at we have to remember that he was very much a member of a generation, a generation that received its formation in the years before World War I and then had to try to cope with the disillusion and cynicism produced by the futility of the suffering during the war itself. The characteristic books produced by Barth's generation were Oswald Spengler's *Decline of the West* and Ernst Bloch's *Geist der Utopie* (1918), Karl Jaspers' *Psychologie der Weltanschauungen*, Graf Keyserling's *Reise-Tagebuch eines Philosophen* and Theodor Lessing's *Geschichte als Sinngebung des Sinnlosen* (History as giving meaning to the meaningless) (1919); Leopold Ziegler's *Gestaltwandel der Götter* (1920), Max Brod's, *Heidentum, Judentum, Christentum* (1921), Ludwig

---

[23] *Die kirchliche Dogmatik* I/2, p. 216; *Church Dogmatics* I/2, p. 197.

[24] *Die kirchliche Dogmatik* I/2, p. 198; *Church Dogmatics* I/2, p. 181.

[25] *Die kirchliche Dogmatik* I/2, p. 199; *Church Dogmatics* I/2, p. 182. One can only note with sadness the attempt of a perceptive and sympathetic Barthian to supply his hero with what he calls a 'secondary extratextual referent of the "empty tomb"'. 'The extratextual referent of the "empty tomb" is therefore not a factual empty tomb, as hermeneutical literalism would suppose, but rather the risen Christ himself. However, since the risen Christ did not, according to Barth's interpretation, rise without his body, it would appear as if some further, though secondary, extratextual referent were implied. For although Barth never developed the point, would not his interpretation seem to entail as a referent, if not a factual empty tomb (whose story might well be a legend), at least something analogous to it, in effect its virtual equivalent? [For example, if Jesus' body had been thrown into a common grave, presumably it would no longer be there.] Otherwise, would it not be hard to see how Barth's insistence on the physicality of Christ's resurrection could remain intelligible?' George Hunsinger, 'Beyond Literalism and Expressivism: Karl Barth's Hermeneutical Realism. (To Hans Frei on the occasion of his 65th birthday, 29 April 1987)', *Modern Theology* 3 (1986–7), 209–223 at 211 with note 4, 211 taken into the text.

Klages' *Vom kosmogenischen Eros* (1922), Sigmund Freud's *The I and the Id*, Fritz Mauthner's *Der Atheismus und seine Geschichte im Abendlande* (1923). Barth's *Romans* belongs in this list, and neither his *Romans* nor his theology can be understood properly outside this context.[26]

This was a generation that saw through every pretension yet believed that by relentless and unremitting cynicism they could discover the secret of the whole universe that would bring utopia. They were philosophically sophisticated and well-schooled, these expressionists, but they despised the university schools of philosophy. Their characteristic mode of discourse was not argument but prophecy; 'the cry drowned the word'.[27] They thought that they were on the edge of a new way of understanding, a break-through of the eternal. The philosophy behind this was a flourishing idealism: the Kantians held annual conferences, and the followers of Schopenhauer met in the boardroom of the Deutsche Bank.[28] The dominant interpretation of Kant was that he preached we must behave *as if* God existed, *as if* the natural laws held, *as if* we have freedom, and *as if* we were eternal beings. The generation that saw through everything was yet able to affirm everything and to find paradise again. Bloch said that 'not only things but in the end even God is still the bushel over the light [Matthew 5.15]; so the longing soul has to penetrate behind God himself'. He ended his book on the *Spirit of Utopia* with these quasi-religious words.

> For only the wicked exist because of their God, but as for the righteous – there, God exists because of them, and in their hands is the hallowing of the name; the very naming of God is given to them: God who stirs in us and moves us, as dimly-discerned portal, darkest question, exalted inwardness; in the hands of philosophy devoted to God, in the hands of truth as prayer.[29]

[26] The list comes from Ludwig Marcuse, *Mein zwanzigstes Jahrhundert: Auf dem Weg zu einer Autobiographie* (Munich, 1960), p. 66. Professor Wilfried Barner of Tübingen first drew my attention to the affinity of Barth's *Romans* with Ernst Bloch's *Geist der Utopie*.

[27] Marcuse, p. 70.   [28] Marcuse, p. 63.

[29] *Geist der Utopie*, 2nd ed. (Berlin, 1923), pp. 305 and 365.

Barth, of course, could not talk of getting behind God, but he certainly did talk of getting behind every other way of naming God besides his own. He explicitly compared his own non-systematic system to Kant's, and lined himself up with Kant as popularly interpreted in his day.[30] And Barth's only way of naming God was to will hollowness, the cavity, the negation, where others had named God.[31]

It is *as if* revelation were taking place, and only the one who has the will to endure a God who was the negative outside the brackets could receive the revelation. This is the heart of the matter, and anyone who distracts us with lesser matters (important as they are) is betraying the cause.

Having establishing his main point, Barth then goes on to draw on the rich resources of the dialectical movement which Hegel had deeply implanted in philosophy. The journey of the mind, a journey full of peril and excitement, is everything. In Barth's case the starting point was man as addressed personally in preaching. Revelation is the matter in hand, so the place of revelation must be now, as one is addressed. Barth's main enemy in discussing the Bible is the liberal theologian who tries to test the historical accuracy of the claim to revelation, but here his main enemy is Roman Catholicism that claims to provide official credentials for the clergyman. As far as I can see, there are two actual authorities and only two: the authority of established facts and the authority of a properly authorized person, but Barth, like the Kantians of his age, could only acknowledge these authorities *as if* they existed. The liberal theologians and the Roman Catholics thought these authorities might or might not be genuine. For Barth, the only way to experience authority was to put oneself under it, not to ask questions about its genuineness. Consequently one had to put oneself under the preacher as speaking God's revelation to oneself. That is stage one of the dialectic. Stage two comes when we consider the preacher. He too

[30] 'Der Christ in der Gesellschaft: Eine Tambacher Rede' (Würzburg or Munich, 1920), p. 16.
[31] '... der Wille zum Hohlraum, das bewegte Verharren in der Negation', *Der Römerbrief*, (2nd ed., 1922), p. 17.

must be under authority. His authority and the authority which he uses in preaching is the Bible. Barth quite rightly saw the Bible as a phenomenon that all Christians depended on, consciously or unconsciously.

But we cannot rest in either stage one or stage two, because although the preacher appeals to the Bible, he appeals to it as pointing beyond itself to revelation itself, to God who reveals himself. Beyond the Bible is the inexpressible revelation with which the Bible and the preacher must agree if they too are to be worthy of being witnesses to the Word of God. This is stage three.

The undialectical thinker might imagine that stage three is a sort of final goal and resting place. But he would be mistaken. The only way to understand stage three is from the Bible, and when one asks the Bible for an answer to the question about God, one receives a revelation of the lordship of the triune God in the incarnate Word witnessed to by the Holy Spirit. But that answer, of course, is simply a summary of the three stages of the movement of thought, for the incarnate Word is the centre of the Bible and the witness of the Holy Spirit occurs only in the church.[32]

His exegesis of individual passages in the Bible is governed more by the need to preserve this self-sufficient dialectical movement than by the force of the passages themselves. The Prodigal Son is a story about a repentant sinner, but Barth makes it into a drama of the procession of the Son away from the Father into a far country and his return to the Father. The 'light that lightens everyone' in the Prologue of John's Gospel, with its suggestion of a general revelation, is not congenial to Barth's theology, so he asserts that 'light' refers to the eternal life of special revelation.[33]

Barth's complex and fascinating theology is a constant journey from the church to the Bible to the unutterable revelation, and back through the Bible to the church.

For all Barth's talk about the church we should be clear

---

[32] *Kirchliche Dogmatik* I/2 (Zollikon, 1938), pp. 505 f. English translation (Edinburgh, 1956), pp. 457 f.

[33] *Gesamtausgabe II: Akademische Werke 1925/1926: Erklärung des Johannes-Evangeliums* (Kapitel 1–8), edited by Walther Furst (Zurich, 1976), pp. 75 f.

that he does not mean any of the organized established churches. Barth claims (and had to claim) that his movement of thought puts anyone who follows it in the position of being (by the grace of God) completely master of the world. The meeting of the gracious God with sinful man 'is God's pronouncement of judgement, his will for his creation, the meaning of all being in time'.[34] The Bible speaks to the church and through the church to the world in order to *rule* the world.[35] Barth claims to have the secret of all human existence. It follows that the church is the natural home of all people who understand themselves as ineluctably caught up in the dialectic in which revelation occurs. Barth logically drew the correct conclusion from his own system that any definition of the church which put any condition whatever on membership except the condition of surrendering oneself to this process of revelation was a false condition, a condition which denied the validity of the system. The system only got going when people acknowledged themselves as having no meaning unless the revelation that alone gave them meaning was received by taking part in the only movement in which meaning was bestowed. It follows that conscious thinking beings alone could receive revelation and grace. Consequently the church should abandon infant baptism. Infant baptism sprang from a false understanding of the church, as though the church had ministers who were authorised to transmit messages or to bestow grace from God: as though God who revealed himself were an existent being. Anyone, according to Barth, who even wondered whether or not God existed was not talking about God.[36] This means that God is only encountered in the movement of the system.

God, according to Barth, affirmed the salvation of everyone, and everyone could simply accept that God had chosen him or her.[37] That was the only condition for entering

[34] 'Die Schrift und die Kirche', *Theologische Studien*, No. 22 (Zurich, 1947), p. 6.

[35] 'Die Schrift und die Kirche', p. 14.

[36] *Kirchliche Dogmatik* II/1 (Zollikon, 1940), pp. 42 ff., 46 f. English translation (Edinburgh, 1957), pp. 40 f., 43 f.

[37] The classic statement of Barth's position was in the pamphlet *Evangelium und Gesetz*, Theologische Existenz Heute, Heft 32 (Munich, 1935).

Barth's completely human church, the church of humanity without any restrictions. Then, in the movement of the dialectic into which the member was drawn, demands and responsibilities followed, but in a paradisal existence where all was safe and assured. The member received the preaching which assured him of God's grace; he lived out of the Bible interpreted with sovereign freedom as the witness to this grace; and could be assured that this dramatic encounter with preacher and Bible agreed with the primal revelation on which the whole universe depended.

To be a Christian is to be involved in a continuous theatrical performance in which oneself in contact with sheer revelation is the subject of the play: everything is connected together as a marvellously meant play. In the Göttingen years Barth delighted to act and take off himself in end-of-term gatherings with members of his evening seminars, and his whole theology was a great performance with himself as the centre, which he invites us to share.[38]

Barth's eclipse as a theologian is partly undeserved. He is probably right that the only way the church can survive (if the universe is as he thought it was) is by means of a theology something like his. The difficulty is that the decision to enter his world is just as arbitrary as the decision to enter any other world where total demands are made on the participants. If no claims can be tested on moral or factual grounds by a detached observer, then one cannot either approve or disapprove of Barth's system or of any part of it. Barth condemned the very attempt to ask whether any events reveal God or whether God exists or whether God gave some people authority to speak or act for him. It follows, then, that Barth's system is a pure humanism which believes that the salvation of humanity lies in the acceptance of the irrational. These are labels which Barth himself could not use because he perfectly correctly saw that such labelling presupposes a standpoint outside the system which, according to the system, does not

<hr/>

[38] W. Trillhaas, *Aufgehobene Vergangenheit* (Göttingen, 1976), p. 93. Barth invited a young theologian who visited him in Basel in the 50s to inspect the portraits of great theologians mounted beside the stairs. In the last frame at the top of the stairs was a mirror.

exist, because no judgement of value or of meaning can be truly made except in the system. But Barth could not be completely consistent, and he in fact thinks the system is meaningful; he assumes he can make a judgement that his system will not allow him to make. His work is one of the great self-defeating failures of our age. He rescued the authority of the Bible at the expense of making it a work of art, the text of a theatrical performance.

21

Bultmann

At the beginning of his university days Rudolf Bultmann wrote to his mother that he wanted to be at home in four other disciplines as well as theology: law, history, medicine and philosophy. If he did not quite accomplish this heroic task, he made himself master of the Greek and Latin classical tradition and became the close friend and collaborator of the philosopher Martin Heidegger (1889–1976). In the 1920s young philosophers like Hans-Georg Gadamer, Gerhard Krüger, Karl Löwith and Hans Jonas attended his classes – for Hans Jonas the Jew, Bultmann's teaching was the impulse that launched him on his life's work. In his own field of theology he was not only an accomplished New Testament scholar but also a systematic theologian with a light touch and a rare mastery of the history of the key theological debates.

He was a shy man who did not like to express his deep emotions, but all observers mention his eyes as giving the clue to his inner life; even in photographs his large fine hooded eyes are remarkable and fascinating. He never directly and actively took part in political activity as Barth had done,[1] but it was his fate to live in Germany when the internal politics of that nation had a devastating effect on the life of millions of innocent people in that and other lands. Bultmann suffered from a hip complaint from birth and so was not

[1] E.g., Karl Barth-Rudolf Bultmann Briefwechsel 1922–66, edited by Bernd Jaspert, *Karl Barth Gesamtausgabe* v: *Briefe*, volume 1, (Zurich, 1971), p. 316 = Bultmann's autobiographical note, S. Ogden, *Existence and Faith* (New York, 1960); C. W. Kegley, *Theology of Rudolf Bultmann* (New York, 1966), pp. xix–xxv.

called up into the army in World War I (he turned 30 the month war broke out), but one brother was killed in France in 1917 and during World War II his sole surviving brother died in a concentration camp. He abhorred the racialism and the lies of the national socialist regime in Germany (1933–1945) and was a member of the Confessing Church, but he also saw national socialism as a distortion of something good, a movement in German life and thought which he welcomed and to which he belonged. His sustained life-long preaching of the Bible and of belief in Jesus Christ as the only way for humanity to understand itself has to be set against a very dark backdrop.

Rudolf Bultmann came from a clerical family in Oldenburg. His father was a pastor, son of a missionary and born on the mission field in Freetown, Sierra Leone.[2] His mother was daughter of a pastor in Baden. Bultmann was the oldest son, born on the 20th August 1884, the same year as C. H. Dodd and two years before Karl Barth and Paul Tillich. These four were to dominate theology in the mid-twentieth century; they were members of the last theological generation to come to maturity before the outbreak of World War I.

At twelve Bultmann entered the humanistic Gymnasium (grammar school) in Oldenburg and received there a thorough old-fashioned grounding in Hebrew, Greek and Latin. He particularly enjoyed religious instruction, Greek, and German literature. He enjoyed visits to concerts and the theatre. While he was preparing for his first theological exams, after four years at university, he spent a year back teaching in his old school (1906–7), and during World War II when there was a danger that religious instruction for the senior classes in the Marburg Gymnasium might have to cease, he volunteered to help out (1942–5, when he had already turned fifty-eight).

[2] Bultmann's grandfather, the Rev. F. Bultmann, missionary to Sierra Leone, made an English version of the picture book called the 'Herzbuch', the 'Ghostly Mirror' (originally French, translated into German in 1732) for use on the Western Africa mission field. *The Heart of Man shewn in Ten Pictures as either the Abode of Satan or the Temple of God*, 4th ed. (Reutlingen, 1865). There is a copy in the New College Library, University of Edinburgh.

He prepared himself for the work of a Lutheran pastor by attending three Universities, Tübingen for three semesters (Summer Semester 1903 to Summer Semester 1904), Berlin for two semesters (Winter Semester 1904–5, Summer Semester 1905) and Marburg for the last two semesters before his exams (Winter Semester 1905–6, Summer Semester 1906). In Tübingen he laid the foundation for his profound grasp of German philosophy, and was particularly influenced by the church historian Karl Müller, who showed him that the Catholic church represented the survival of paganism. In Berlin he heard the great Old Testament scholar Hermann Gunkel (1862–1932) who took him under his wing, as we have seen. He consciously sided with the spiritual master of the Berlin theological faculty, Friedrich Schleiermacher (1768–1834), the one who lifted old traditions to a new level, against Adolf Harnack, the mere scholar. He was later to defend Schleiermacher against Barth's earlier attacks on him as a liberal – a point Barth took.[3] Schleiermacher said that no one could report on the origin of his own religion except as a miracle – an idea that remained fundamental in Bultmann's own thought.

If Tübingen and Berlin were important for Bultmann, Marburg was decisive. Already as a seventeen-year-old he had heard Wilhelm Herrmann give a lecture, and in Marburg he was able to follow his courses. Herrmann was a liberal theologian who had seen through liberalism, and he was to provide the decisive impulse to Bultmann, as he did to Barth. The old orthodox faith as a set of dogmas to be believed (fides quae creditur) was shown to be impossible by the enlightenment, but the faith that came to be put in place of this old faith, faith as that by which one believed (fides qua creditur), was bankrupt. This faith, faith in faith, had no object.

The other great influence on Bultmann in Marburg was

---

[3] Antje Bultmann Lemke, 'Der Unveröffentliche Nachlass von Rudolf Bultmann: Ausschnitte aus dem biographischen Quellenmaterial' in Bernd Jaspert (ed.) *Rudolf Bultmanns Werk und Wirkung* (Darmstadt, 1984), pp. 194–207, at p. 200; *Karl Barth – Rudolf Bultmann. Briefwechsel 1922–66*, letter of 31 December 1922, pp. 12 f.; English translation, *Karl Barth – Rudolf Bultmann: Letters 1922–66* (Edinburgh, 1982).

Johannes Weiss (1863–1914). Weiss had begun his scholarly career by laying bare the simple historical fact (still disputed) that Jesus taught the future coming of the Kingdom of God, and that under critical scrutiny none of Jesus' sayings spoke of the present Kingdom.[4] This was the point taken up by Albert Schweitzer and made the key to his reconstruction of Jesus' life. Schweitzer, however, did not follow Weiss's later view, that Jesus proclaimed not himself but another as the coming Messiah. Bultmann did. What Bultmann the historian believed he had discovered about Jesus remained central to his thought and his faith. Although Jesus himself proclaimed a coming Kingdom that did not come, and although the early church turned Jesus the proclaimer into the person proclaimed, by giving him the exalted title and position of 'Lord', a title and position Jesus himself did not think was his, both false moves still rightly belonged to the heart of the Christian faith. The future eschatology of Jesus was proved wrong by its failure to transpire, but the eschatology, the pressure of the end of history on the normal course of history, remained. The high mythological titles and status of Jesus were foisted on to him from another world-view than his, a world-view we moderns can accept no more than we can accept Jesus', but the point of these titles remained. The point lies in the force of the rhetoric. That Jesus had preached with such power, that Jesus made such direct, compelling, and all-embracing demands on those who heard him justified the eschatology and justified the titles – provided they were not taken literally but as rhetoric.[5]

Johannes Weiss suggested that Bultmann should prepare himself for a career as a university teacher of New Testament

---

[4] *Die Predigt Jesu vom Reiche Gottes* (Göttingen, 1892, 2nd ed. 1900). Bultmann listed the second edition as one of his choices in the series 'Milestones in Books', *The Expository Times*, 70 (1958–9), 125. The other five books were Carl Weizsäcker, *Das Apostolische Zeitalter der christlichen Kirche* (1886); William Wrede, *Das Messiasgeheimnis in den Evangelien* (1901); Wilhelm Herrmann, *Ethik* (3rd ed., 1904); Karl Barth, *Der Römerbrief* (new ed., 1922); Martin Heidegger, *Sein und Zeit*, Vol. 1 (1927).

[5] 'Die Christologie des Neuen Testaments', a previously unpublished essay in *Glauben und Verstehen: Gesammelte Aufsätze* (= volume one) (Tübingen, 1933), pp. 245–67; English translation, *Faith and Understanding* I, (London, 1969).

studies and proposed the subject for his doctoral dissertation, the style of the Pauline preaching and the Cynic-Stoic diatribe. Johannes Weiss himself moved to Heidelberg in 1908 and so it was Wilhelm Heitmüller (1869–1925), who showed Bultmann how to get to the heart of a complicated matter and express it simply, who supervised the thesis. The work on stoicism posed to Bultmann the problem to which he was to devote his life, which he expressed in an early article in the leading New Testament Journal, *Zeitschrift für die neutestamentliche Wissenschaft*.[6] The article was published in two parts the year Bultmann turned twenty-eight; it was on the New Testament and the religious moment in the ethical teaching of Epictetus.[7] Epictetus was a determinist who preached that freedom could only be attained by inward withdrawal from the rewards and the pain and punishment of the world; nothing could either elate or harm the inwardly indifferent. Epictetus' statement that the servant of God was free was, said Bultmann, merely talk,

> for this freedom consists not at all in the free act of the
> will but in the eschewal of acts of the will. Man is not
> free in the sense that he is able to master and form
> nature, but only in so far as he cuts himself off from
> nature and is not touched by nature ... For Epictetus

[6] The valuable letters Bultmann wrote to his friend Walther Fischer, now in the possession of Professor Rudolf Smend of Göttingen, Fischer's nephew, show the centrality of this theme in Bultmann's formative years. Not only Johannes Weiss, but also Adolf Jülicher and Johannes Bauer, each wanted Bultmann to do a doctorate under their direction, but it was Weiss who won. 'Weiss has already given me the area of work: the relation of Paul's theology to Stoicism' (3.ix.1906). Next year he wrote to Fischer, 'Epictetus ... is disappointing. The "freedom" of man is ... essentially a negative ideal for the Stoic, and scarcely anything of the πάντα μοι ἔξεστιν ["all things are lawful for me", 1 Cor.6.12; 10.23] is detectable. I find it often very questionable whether much power really belongs to such stoic resignation, whether monkish asceticism is really anything very remarkable. I almost think that all it needs is a *salto mortale* [a fatal leap] of the spirit, to which belongs to be sure not nothing, but yet not very much' (26.iii.1907). I cite these letters with the gracious permission of Mrs Antje Bultmann Lemke. See Martin Evang, *Rudolf Bultmann in seiner Frühzeit*, Beiträge zur historischen Theologie 74 (Tübingen, 1988), p. 35.

[7] 'Das religiöse Moment in der ethischen Unterweisung Epiktets und das Neue Testament', *ZNW*, xiii (1912), 97–110; 177–91.

only knows what happens, not what God's will is. God's will is not recognised on the basis of God's revelation, so that the event which is not able to be understood might be given meaning. Rather Epictetus works on the assumption that the event is understandable . . . Nature is not meant to serve to some end; rather God wills precisely nothing other than what happens in nature.[8]

Bultmann naturally fully accepted Epictetus' and the Stoics' basic assumption, for he belonged heart and soul to the circle that went regularly to the weekly open evenings held by Martin Rade, the editor of *Die christliche Welt*, who was professor of pastoral theology at Marburg. Bultmann and his father used regularly to attend the annual conferences of the 'Friends of *Die christliche Welt*' before and immediately after World War I. The weekly journal was devoted to espousing the latest modern knowledge and in making the Christian faith understandable and believable to modern man. All miracles and all myths were to be rejected or reinterpreted, and Rade's characteristic solution to the problem of faith was to argue that, just as the natural sciences rested on a leap of faith (since the basic premise, that nature was law-bound could not be proved, only assumed), so Christianity depended on a similar leap of faith.[9] Yet Bultmann as early as 1912 stood out as a distinctive different thinker in this circle. He already shows signs he would abandon both the reductionism – he preached all the doctrines of old-fashioned Lutheran orthodoxy – and the putting of Christian faith on a level with other faiths, whether the faith on which science rested or the faith necessary for a nation to fulfil its destiny. The Christian faith for Bultmann was *sui generis*. His teacher Herrmann had already made that plain to him, and by 1912 Bultmann knew that everything depended on 'revelation', as

---

[8] *ZNW*, xiii (1912), 180 f.

[9] See Bultmann's discussion of this move in 'Wahrheit und Gewissheit', a lecture to the autumn conference of the Bund für Gegenwartschristentum in 1929, published as an appendix to *Theologische Enzyklopädie*, edited by E. Jüngel and K. W. Müller (Tübingen, 1984), pp. 183–205 at p. 197.

the citation from his article on Epictetus I have just given shows. Gogarten and Barth may have helped him to greater clarity and Heidegger may have given him added philosophical sophistication in making his case, but the outlines of his problem and his characteristic solution were already present before he turned thirty.

In the year his article on Epictetus appeared he completed the further dissertation required by German universities of all who are allowed the right to teach. This was on Theodore of Mopsuetsia, the Church Father who most consistently pursued the plain literal meaning of the text of the New Testament in his exegesis.[10]

His extraordinary gifts as a teacher soon showed themselves. In his third semester as a Privatdozent (unsalaried lecturer) he attracted twenty-eight students to lectures on the Pastoral Epistles at a time which clashed with Martin Rade, and sixty-one students came to his seminars (Übungen).[11]

In 1915 he became engaged to Helene Feldmann, in 1916 he was appointed to an associate professorship in Breslau and in August 1917, shortly before his thirty-third birthday, he was married. In 1920 he completed the manuscript of a small but masterly book on the history of the traditions about Jesus preserved in the Synoptic Gospels: the whole Synoptic tradition in under 250 pages. That summer he moved to Giessen to a full chair in New Testament Studies and the following summer to his old University, Marburg, to succeed Heitmüller. He remained at Marburg to the end of his days, retiring from the chair in 1951 at the age of sixty-seven.

The book on the history of the Synoptic tradition was revised and enlarged in a second edition, 1930, and its results were gathered up in a tract on Jesus for a popular series of lives of 'the imperishable', 1926. Bultmann, following Gunkel's method, argued that the basic units of the Synoptic Gospels belonged to the various styles of folk-literature: miracle stories, disputes of a great teacher with his opponents,

---

[10] *Die Exegese des Theodor von Mopsuestia*, only printed on the centenary of his birth (Stuttgart, 1984). The theme was suggested and the thesis supervised by A. Jülicher.

[11] Bultmann to Walther Fischer, 2.xi.1913.

wise sayings of the teacher, parables and so forth, all formed and passed on as part of preaching of the church. He tried to show that many of the themes were commonplaces of the time, and not necessarily part of Jesus' teaching. Jesus did not hold himself to be the Messiah, though the tradition assumed he was (a point he had learnt most clearly from William Wrede), but Jesus certainly did call men to decide decisively to follow him; 'Let the dead bury their dead' was fundamental to his mission, for all the world was otherwise dead (Matthew 8.21 f.; Luke 9.59 f.).

In July 1923 Bultmann was asked to write the new commentary on St John's Gospel for the old Meyer series. He rightly saw that the Mandaean religious writings that were being published by the great Göttingen orientalist Mark Lidzbarski offered important parallels to the language of the characteristic discourses of Jesus in the Fourth Gospel, and he began to offer St John's Gospel in lectures, which culminated in the 560-page commentary published in seven fascicles, beginning in 1937 and completed in 1941.[12] His work on John was a characteristic combination of painstakingly detailed literary criticism with a passionate re-presentation of the Gospel as timeless and ever-relevant preaching. He argued that the Gospel contained many layers of tradition – pre-Christian discourses which originally applied to John the Baptist and were now applied to Jesus, a 'signs' source of Jesus' miracles, and the folk-literature similar to the folk-literature in the Synoptic Gospels. All the source material had been rearranged and added to by the evangelist, who was a great theologian, the greatest in the New Testament. He had eliminated all the future eschatology from Jesus' teaching and had clearly shown that faith in Jesus could not be based on the historical facts about Jesus, but only on an encounter with the living word spoken to the believer out of the community of believers.

[12] Professor Nikolaus Walter, formerly Professor of New Testament Studies, Katechetisches Oberseminar of the Evangelican Church of Saxony, Naumburg (Saale) and now Professor, University of Jena, gave me the publication details: fascicle 1 (pp. 1–80), 1937; fascicle 2 (pp. 81–160), 1938; fascicle 3 (pp. 161–240), 1939; fascicle 4 (pp. 241–320), 1939; fascicle 5 (pp. 321–400), 1940; fascicle 6 (pp. 401–80), 1940; fascicle 7 (pp. 481–563), 1941.

In mythological language we are told [in John 16.7b] that the revelation, which took place in Jesus' work, only retains its significance as the real, absolute revelation, when it retains the element of futurity . . . and the presupposition for its contribution must be made clear: the historical Jesus must depart, so that his significance, the significance of being the Revealer, can be grasped purely by itself. He is only the Revealer, if he *remains* such. But he remains it only by sending the Spirit; and he can only send the Spirit when he has himself gone . . .

The revelation is always only indirect; but because it occurs within the sphere of human history, it gives rise to the misunderstanding that it is direct. In order to destroy this misunderstanding the Revealer must take his leave; he must leave his own in their λύπη [grief], in temptation, for it is in this λύπη that the disciple is freed from the things that are directly given (which are always slipping away into the past) and turned towards that which is only indirectly attainable and always in the future (cf. Loisy) . . .

. . . what was misleading for the first disciples was the illusion of a false certainty which thought that it possessed the revelation in what was directly given, in immediate experience and gifts, and which therefore was bound to hope that it would never have an end. But the fact that everything that is given and experienced in time is essentially transient is brought home to the disciples by the circumstance that the Giver himself goes away. Otherwise he would be misunderstood about his gift. He can only be the Revealer as the one who is always breaking the given in pieces, always destroying every certainty, always breaking in from the beyond and calling into the future . . .

The intention of the revelation is to set the believer free; the certainty which it gives is not the continuation of the present – of something that has in fact already gone by – but the eternity of the future . . .

But this is what is meant by saying that the revelation is the word, and indeed the word in its being spoken: that is, the word which does not mediate a subject-matter to be appropriated once and for all, but which is always spoken into the world's situation, and which thereby calls the hearer out of the world . . .

The word is very far from being a closed doctrine, or complex of statements, nor on the other hand is it the historical account of Jesus' life. It is the living word; that is, paradoxically, the word which is spoken by the community itself; for the Paraclete is the Spirit that is at work in the community. And to ensure that we do not think of this word as the human spirit aroused to self-awareness in the believers (Hegel), it is made quite clear that the Paraclete is the Spirit who is to be sent by Jesus to continue his work.[13]

This is the evangelist's theology, according to Bultmann, but the evangelist's work had finally been subjected to editing by an 'ecclesiastical' redactor who rearranged the material and added a few characteristic sentences to make Jesus refer to the church's sacraments, for example.

In the Summer Semester of 1926 Bultmann offered a course which was a guide to tackling theological studies. He and the existentialist atheist philosopher Heidegger had been attending one another's classes since Heidegger came to Marburg in 1923. The friendship and collaboration reached a high-point in the Summer Semeester of 1927 when they together offered a seminar on Luther's commentary on Galatians, just before Heidegger left Marburg to return to Freiburg as a full

---

[13] *Das Evangelium des Johannes. Meyer Kommentar* (Göttingen, 1941), pp. 430–2 (from the sixth fascicle, published in 1940). *The Gospel of John: A Commentary*, translated by G. R. Beasley-Murray (General Editor), R. W. N. Hoare, and J. K. Riches (Oxford, 1971 (= 1964 German)), pp. 558–61. In the note that mentions Loisy, Bultmann also quoted with approval Hölderlin:

He through whom the Spirit has spoken must betimes away

and R. M. Rilke:

Could you but feel his passing's needfulness!
Though he himself may dread that he must go.
In that his word passes beyond the here and now,
Is he already there, where you cannot follow it.

professor. Heidegger helped Bultmann put his ideas into philosophical shape, and sharpened up for him his old conclusion that Christian faith had to be a step beyond the best that a philosophical analysis of the world could offer. All this is put succinctly into the lectures on theology, which he offered under the new title 'Theologische Enzyklopädie' in 1928, 1930, 1933 and 1936. He resisted his publisher's urgent pleas for publication, but all the moves are repeated in various forms in articles, lectures, sermons and talks, and are distilled in his commentary on John's Gospel and in the programmatic call for the demythologization of the New Testament, first made in those words in 1941.

In the Summer Semester of 1931, just before he turned forty-six, Bultmann joined with other Marburg professors of all disciplines in a series of public lectures on the present crisis. Bultmann's theme was 'The Crisis of Belief'.[14] With hindsight we can see that the actual crisis in Germany in 1931 was the final failure of the German middle-class to believe that democracy and the rule of law were the essential requirements for political stability and a solution of the mass unemployment caused by the world-wide depression. The solid citizens of Germany in the twenties despised their republic and longed for strong leadership and a restoration of the old values of obedience and hard work. They believed Germany had been wrongly repressed from without by the harsh terms of the Treaty of Versailles which gave the Saar to the French, and they believed Germany was sapped from within by Jewish intellectuals.

Bultmann shared the common feeling that Germany was facing a crisis, but his lecture was a stirring plea to his audience to relegate the crisis in morals, the crisis in standards of trustworthiness in social life, the crisis in views about the nature of the state, the crisis in respect for the laws, or even the crisis in religion to a subordinate and unimportant position. All these crises might be resolved. What was

[14] *Krisis des Glaubens – Krisis der Kirche – Krisis der Religion: Drei Marburger Vorträge von Rudolf Bultmann, Hans Frhr. von Soden, Heinrich Frick* (Giessen, 1931). Bultmann's lecture, pp. 3–21. *Glauben und Verstehen*, vol ii (Tübingen, 1952), pp. 1–19; English translation *Essays: Philosophical Theological* (London, 1955), pp. 1–21.

important for belief was to recognise that true belief entailed a perpetual crisis. He closed with a long quotation from the dialogue between father and son in Dostoyevsky's 'Jüngling' (The Disciple). The son asks in terrible fear of a coming world catastrophe,

> 'Yes, but what then should I do?'
>
> 'O God, don't be in so much of a hurry; all that won't be so quick in coming. But in general the best thing to do is to do nothing – at least then you preserve a quiet conscience and can say to yourself that you had nothing to do with it'.
>
> 'No, enough; say something to the point. I want to know what I should do in practice and how I should live'.
>
> 'What you should do, my dear boy? Be honourable, don't lie, don't covet your neighbour's house – in a word, read the Ten Commandments – there is all that written down for ever'.

In January 1933 Adolf Hitler was sworn in as Chancellor, and he banned the Social Democratic and Communist Parties, arrested and beat up their leaders, and removed all Jews ('non Arians') from government posts – and that included university professorships. Selected young university teachers were sent to special training camps to be toughened up physically and mentally. On the 27th May 1933 Martin Heidegger delivered the rectorial address at the University of Freiburg on 'The Self-Assertion of the German University'. He gloried in the fact that knowledge now had to bow to necessity, and proclaimed a new principle of knowledge. 'Questioning is consequently (as a consequence of Nietzsche's discovery that God is dead) no longer the preliminary stage which is to be overcome on the way to an answer as attained knowledge; rather, questioning now itself becomes the highest form of knowledge'. 'Struggle (der Kampf) alone keeps the dialectic (Gegensatz) open. Struggle alone plants in the whole body of teachers and students that basic impulse out of which the self-assertion that sets itself bounds empowers determined self-confidence to reach genuine self-mastery'. 'We will it, that our people fulfill its historical task. We will our very selves. For the vital and recently expressed power of the people, which already is straining forward to its goal over us, has already taken the decision that that is to be'. He concluded with Plato's words, 'All that is great stands fast in the storm'.[15]

Bultmann defended Heidegger's address in his Enzyklopädie course later in the semester. Heidegger had not meant to back the racial and biological theories of the Nationalist Socialist Party. His view of the people, nationhood, could not be based on anything so observable, anything so determined by what lay in the past. When he said we must put ourselves under the power of our origins as a people, he meant historical origins, not biological origins. And when he said that these origins lay not behind us as by-gone, but before us in the future as a trust, he meant that nationhood (Volkstum) was nothing that was simply given, but only something that develops itself in determined taking of the initiative. The National Socialist movement was right to turn away from Idealism, Rationalism, Liberalism and Democracy insofar as these timeless general ideas try to give life a purpose and a reality, for they measure the individual by general rules. This movement follows the direction of the attacks on Idealism and Romanticism made at first by Kirkegaard and Nietzsche and followed up by Jakob Burckhardt on history, and brought to clarity by the 'philosophy of life' of Dilthey and the Graf Paul Yorck von Wartenburg.[16] These attacks are made currently valid by Heidegger's phenomenology and by dialectical theology. The danger of the National Socialist movement is that in reaction to Idealism and Rationalism it will fall into Romanticism and a materialist biology. 'The historical moment and its demand is always concurrently determined by the concretely 'given'. But as what is historically given it is never

[15] *Die Selbstbehauptung der deutschen Universität: Rede, gehalten bei der feierlichen Übernahme des Rektorats der Universität Freiburg i. Br. am 27.5.1933* (Breslau, 1933), pp. 9, 12, 21 f.

[16] *Briefwechsel zwischen Wilhelm Dilthey und dem Grafen Paul Yorck von Wartenburg 1877–97* (Halle, 1923).

umambiguously determinable in its approaching actuality. That also applied to the meaning of nationhood'.[17]

Of course Bultmann had to be careful what he said. In August 1934 his close friend Hans Freiherr von Soden was summarily retired from his chair in Marburg; fortunately his aristocratic fearlessness in challenging the authorities led to his reinstatement on the 24th October, just in time to begin his new semester's lectures. The students at the first lecture received him as a hero, and he remained at his post, an active member of the Confessing Church, like his fellow-member Bultmann, on the liberal wing.

In the summer of 1933 Bultmann had the young Jewish scholar Hans Jonas to a farewell midday meal before Jonas went into exile. This is how Jonas described that meal in his memorial speech on Bultmann's death.

> It was in summer 1933, here in Marburg. We sat around the table with his lovely so richly sympathetic wife and the three schoolgirl daughters, and I related what I had just read in the paper, but what Bultmann had not yet seen. The German Association of the Blind had just decided to expel their Jewish members. In my horror I launched into a rather unseemly tirade: in the face of eternal night, I cried out, in the face of the one most awful thing that can happen to oppressed mankind, this betrayal of solidarity in a shared loss . . .! and I stopped short, for my eye fell on Bultmann, and I saw that a deadly pallor had come over his face; I saw in his eyes such a pain that my words died away in my mouth. In that moment I knew that one could simply trust oneself to Bultmann on basic human issues; that here words, explanations, arguments, above all rhetoric were out of place; that no madness of that time could dim the steadiness of his inner light. He himself had not said a word. For me that has ever since belonged to the picture of this inwardly moved but outwardly so completely unemotional man.[18]

---

[17] Bultmann, *Theologische Enzyklopädie* (1933) (Tübingen, 1984), pp. 64 f.

[18] Hans Jonas, 'Im Kampf um die Möglichkeit des Glaubens: Erinnerungen an

The next year Jonas's book, the first volume of a large work on Gnosis, appeared, and Bultmann was courageous enough to write a foreword.

In 1934, when the church authorities tried to bring into the church the regulations which governed other civil servants so that pastors who were Jews would be retired, Bultmann and Hans von Soden rallied the Marburg Faculty to protest and Bultmann took part in the war of words that followed. He was careful to make it perfectly plain, however, that he was not addressing himself to the question of the 'Arian Paragraph' in the sphere of the state, only in the sphere of the church.[19]

In 1938 von Soden helped persuade the Confessing Church not to object to all ministers' giving their personal oath to Hitler; what was the point in resisting?

In 1941 Bultmann published as one issue of Ernst Wolf's *Beiträge zur Evangelischen Theologie* two essays, the first on the question of natural revelation (the idea that God revealed himself in the events of nature and history) and the second on the New Testament and Mythology.[20] The real discussion of the second of these two essays hardly got going until after the war; in the English-speaking countries it was little noticed, I think, until the late 50s.

In 1948 Bultmann published the first part of his *Theology of the New Testament*, which was completed by two further parts in 1951 and 1953. In this he distilled all his work on the New Testament in dead-pan epigrammatic form. His excurses, printed in smaller type, scattered through the book, usually contain more exact information and argument than

Rudolf Bultmann und Betrachtungen zum philosophischen Aspekt seines Werkes' in *Gedenken an Rudolf Bultmann*, edited by Otto Kaiser (Tübingen, 1977), pp. 41–70 at pp. 43 f.; 'Is Faith Still Possible? Memories of Rudolf Bultmann and Reflections on the Philosophical Aspects of His Work', *Harvard Theological Review*, 75 (1982), 1–23, at 2 f.

[19] Hans Liebing, *Die Marburger Theologen und die Arierparagraph in der Kirche* (Marburg, 1977); see p. 32.

[20] *Offenbarung und Heilsgeschehen* containing 'Die Frage der natürlichen Offenbarung' (pp. 3–26) and 'Neues Testament und Mythologie' (pp. 27–69). Reprinted in *Glauben und Verstehen*, vol. ii (Tubingen, 1952), pp. 79–104; *Kerygma und Mythos*, ed. H. W. Bartsch (Hamburg, 1948), pp. 15–53; English translation, *Kerygma and Myth* (London, 1953), pp. 1–44.

most learned articles, not to say books. Bultmann was already sixty-three or sixty-four when the first part appeared, and had lived through the two wars and the terrible deprivation that went with being on the losing side both times. But he never gave up, inwardly and spiritually.

The confidence that sustained Bultmann, the key to his understanding of the Bible is summed up in some words of poetry with which he concluded his important article on 'Christ, the End of the Law'.

> The deed of a man, the only one he knows, is to feel himself in the ranks of the chosen (Karl Immermann, *Merlin*).[21]

Bultmann's central problem was the uniqueness and absolute superiority of Christianity to all other religions or world-views. His earlier published scholarly article on the religious moment in the ethical teaching of Epictetus and the New Testament ended by arguing that the religion of the New Testament could give exactly what was lacking in Stoicism: a living religion, a primal belief in God, a new valuation of the individual, the awakening of the human soul to its own proper life. He asked, 'Doesn't that shed light on the historical situation; . . . and doesn't that help us to explain the victory of the religion of the New Testament?'[22]

In the debate over his programme for the consistent demythologization of the New Testament he was attacked on the grounds that he had failed to give up the one last remnant of mythology in his own thinking, the claim that the Christian revelation is exclusive of all so-called revelations, that forgiveness of sins is proclaimed only by the one word of Christ.[23] 'God has achieved the world's forgiveness

---

[21] *Christus des Gesetzes Ende*, Theologische Aufsätze by R. Bultmann and H. Schlier (Munich, 1940). Bultmann's gives the title to the collection, pp. 3–27, at p. 27.

[22] 'Das religiöse Moment in der ethischen Unterweisung des Epiktet und das Neue Testament' *Zeitschrift für die neutestamentliche Wissenschaft und die Kunde des Urchristentums* xiii (1912), 92–110; 177–91, at 191.

[23] See the notable sympathetic exposition of Bultmann's thought, which nevertheless concludes that there is this structural inconsistency in his solution:

through the cross of Christ' is not, according to Bultmann, a
mythological idea to be eliminated with the other
mythological ideas that seem, to the superficial eye, to be so
similar; 'God is only accessible in Jesus Christ' is not
mythology at all, according to his claim.[24]

It follows that anyone who thinks Bultmann is inconsistent
has not succeeded in grasping his point. The alleged
inconsistency of a thinker who asserts on the one hand that
all attempts to speak of the other-worldly in terms of this
world are strictly impossible and on the other hand that the
Christian faith, which is the only true religion, stands or falls
with the forgiveness of God proclaimed to the concrete
individual man by the preaching of Christ is no accidental
inconsistency: this alleged inconsistency is the main
preoccupation of every single book and article and review
that Bultmann ever published.

The point can be put in terms of Bultmann's belief in the
authority of the Bible, which is our central concern.
Bultmann the critic systematically eliminated as impossible
for belief all statements in the Bible, from Genesis to
Revelation, that might be claimed today as reports of natural
or historical events that provide evidence to support anyone's
belief in God. Yet he can assert the Bible's authority in words
that would seem to satisfy the strictest orthodox Lutheran:
'In truth, does the Christian proclamation appeal to anything
else than the printed book fallen straight from heaven?'[25]

Bultmann began with two assumptions. The first, learnt
from Johannes Weiss as we have seen, that Jesus did not
himself believe he was the Messiah, gave Bultmann an
impregnable case for arguing that Christianity's uniqueness
rested on no such comfort as could be derived from the Son
of God's knowing who he was. If anyone wished to say Jesus

Schubert M. Ogden, *Christ without Myth: A Study Based on the Theology of Rudolf
Bultmann* (1961; London: Collins, 1962).

[24] 'Die Bedeutung des Alten Testaments für den christlichen Glauben', *Glauben
und Verstehen*, Volume 1 (Tübingen, 1933), pp. 315–6; 'The Significance of the Old
Testament for the Christian Faith' in *The Old Testament and Christian Faith*, edited
by B. W. Anderson (London, 1964), p. 11.

[25] *Glauben und Verstehen* i.99; *Faith and Understanding* 1 (1969), p. 130.

was the Son of God, he would have to do so entirely on his own responsibility, without any support from the historical Jesus. The Jesus of John's Gospel makes clear to his disciples that only if he goes away can the Spirit come. The Jesus of the Synoptic Gospels likewise teaches that no signs are to be given, that there is no evidence to be relied upon; his call to decision is sheer summons. Jesus as teacher belongs to Judaism and his teaching is not the gospel and does not belong to the theology of the New Testament; only when the proclaimer becomes the proclaimed do we have gospel and the possibility of theology of the New Testament. Jesus' call to decision alone remains; here alone is christology implied.[26] Even Paul did not think his own theology through as clearly as he could have done and it is our responsibility to do his work for him properly.[27] Perhaps John was the most consistent of all about the matter; but even he has to be freed from the distortions introduced by his ecclesiastical editor.

Bultmann's second assumption was about the structure of human thought, and this he learned from Herrmann.[28]

---

[26] *Kerygma und Mythos*, ed. H. W. Barsch (Hamburg, 1948), pp. 133–4; English translation *Kerygma and Myth* (London, 1953), p. 117. *Glauben und Verstehen* i.266; *Faith and Understanding I*, pp. 283–5. Cf. F. C. Baur, *Vorlesungen über neutestamentliche Theologie*, ed. F. F. Baur (Leipzig, 1864; repr. Darmstadt, 1973), p. 128. *Theologie des Neuen Testaments* (Tübingen, 1953), pp. 7–8; English translation, vol i (London, 1952), p. 9. 'Die Christologie des Neuen Testaments', *Glauben und Verstehen*, i.265–6; *Faith and Understanding I*, ed. R. W. Funk, translated by Louise Pettibone Smith (London, 1969), pp. 281–3. The preaching of Jesus belongs to the presuppositions of New Testament theology and is not a part of this theology itself: *Theologie des Neuen Testaments* (Tübingen, 1953), first sentence; English translation, vol. i (London, 1952), p. 3. The proclaimer proclaimed: *Theologie*, p. 34; *Theology*, i p. 33.

[27] Review of the 2nd ed. of Barth's *Romans*, *Christliche Welt* 36 (1922), 372; reprinted, J. Moltmann, ed., *Anfänge der dialektischen Theologie*, Part I (Munich, 1962), p. 140. 'Die Christologie des Neuen Testaments', *Glauben und Verstehen*, i.262–3; *Faith and Understanding I*, pp. 262–3. *Neues Testament und Mythologie*, Beiträge zur Evangelische Theologie (Munich, 1941); reprinted in *Kerygma und Mythos*, ed., H. W. Bartsch (Hamburg, 1948); English translation (London, 1954), pp. 1–44.

[28] W. Herrmann, 'Der Christ und das Wunder' (1908), reprinted in *Schriften zur Grundlegung der Theologie*, part II (Munich, 1967), pp. 170–205. Bultmann, 'Zur Frage des Wunders', Glauben und Verstehen, i 214–28 at 215; 'The Question of Wonder', *Faith and Understanding I*, pp. 247–61. Shorter version, Sermon on Luke 15.1–11, 13 July, 1941, *Marburger Predigten* (Tübingen, 1956), pp. 137–47; English translation by H. Knight, *This World and Beyond: Marburg Sermons* (London, 1960), pp. 155–66.

According to this picture (which Bultmann had grasped and made the basis of his life work by 1912,[29] and which every reader of Bultmann must keep firmly in view whenever reading Bultmann from whatever period of his work), human beings live in two worlds. In the first world, which for clarity's sake I will call World A, mankind is completely bound by the regular laws of nature. Nature is a closed, endless system. This is not something that needs arguing. The very fact that we explore nature entails the acceptance that nature is law-abiding; that is simply given. However, we also live in World B, the world of spirit. This is the world of the beyond where we penetrate to what lies behind World A, behind 'Diesseits'. In World B we create laws, ideas, values; this it the world of science, art, morality. Its creativity relies on the standing tension between World B and World A. The temptation is to think that by discovering World B behind World A we have discovered a justification for religion, for God. This World B is indeed the world of the noblest humanity, but it is the world of humanity and God is not there.[30] It is the world of work, indeed the world of works, viewed with all the horror Lutheranism attaches to any reliance on works. The religious temptation for those who live only in World A is to try to find God there by exploiting the as-yet-unexplained, by trying to make room for miracles; the label for this sort of false religious faith is *fides quae creditur*, the faith which is believed as consisting of objective observable facts about the world. The religious temptation for those who know about World B is to exploit the human capacity for shaping ideas; the label for this sort of false religious faith is *fides qua creditur*, the faith by which one believes, and its

[29] 'Das religiöse Moment in der ethischen Unterweisung des Epiktets und das Neue Testament', *ZNW*, 13 (1912), 97–110; 177–91. Sermon of 12 July, 1914, *Das verkündigte Wort: Predigten – Andachten – Ansprachen 1906–1941*, ed. E. Grässer with M. Evang (Tübingen, 1984), pp. 257–62. 'Das Problem der Ethik bei Paulus', *ZNW*, 23 (1924), 123–40. 'Zur Frage des Wunders', *Glauben und Verstehen* i.214–28; 'The Question of Wonder', *Faith and Understanding I*, pp. 247–61.

[30] Sermon, 12 July, 1914, *Das verkündigte Wort* (Tübingen, 1984), p. 109. Epictetus is sharply criticized for making fellowship with God part of human nature: 'Das religiöse Moment in der ethischen Unterweisung Epiktets und das Neue Testament', *ZNW*, 13 (1912), 177–8.

outcome faith in faith, faith without an object or faith with an idol of human creating as its object. If we truly understand the nature of World A and World B, according to Bultmann, we realize that World A is actually without meaning, and that this meaninglessness must also overwhelm us in World B. All our human effort is in vain. Without God all we have left in World B is an inward and painful longing, a yearning. Only when we come to the point where we realize we are guilty of past and present and future and all endeavour is pointless and hopeless can we escape. We have to receive redemption as a gift, or not at all. Only if freedom and purity comes to us as sheer grace, as gift, as revelation can it come at all. This is World C which cannot be developed by us and cannot be taught. This world simply happens to us; this is the only miracle, the true miracle.[31] The only way is to receive this world, to do nothing, to become as a child, to obey. Only when we recognize that we are without God does God reveal himself to us. This preaching of forgiveness

---

[31] W. Herrmann, 'Faith is a miracle or it is not faith': cf. *Dogmatik*, (Gotha and Stuttgart, 1925), English translation by N. Micklem *Systematic Theology* (London, 1927), § 31. Bultmann, Sermon, 12 July, 1914, *Das verkündigte Wort* (Tübingen, 1984), p. 260. *ZNW*, 13 (1912), 177–9. 'Zur Frage der Christologie', *Glauben und Verstehen*, i.88–9; 'On the Question of Christology', *Faith and Understanding I*, pp. 119–20. Letter to Jochen Niemöller, 2 March, 1943, Antje Bultmann Lemke, 'Der unveröffentlichte Nachlass von Rudolf Bultmann'. Ausschnitte aus dem biographischen Quellenmaterial', *Rudolf Bultmanns Werk und Wirkung* (Darmstadt, 1984), p. 204. *History and Eschatology*, The Gifford Lectures 1955 (Edinburgh 1957), pp. 150–2, 155. No basis of faith: only the proclamation of faith with the demand to believe: 'Welchen Sinn hat es, von Gott zu reden?' (1925), *Glauben und Verstehen*, i.26–37 at 37; 'What does it mean to speak of God?', *Faith and Understanding I*, pp. 53–65 at pp. 64–5. R. Bultmann, H. Frhr. von Soden, H. Frick, *Krisis des Glaubens: Krisis der Kirche: Krisis der Religion. Drei Marburger Vorträge* (Giessen, 1931), pp. 5–21; reprinted in *Glauben und Verstehen*, vol. ii (Tübingen, 1952), pp. 1–19; 'The Crisis of Belief', *Essays: Philosophical and Theological*, translated by J. C. G. Greig (London, 1955), pp. 1–21. To stand in a new world: R. Bultmann, 'Die Christologie des Neuen Testaments', *Glauben und Verstehen*, i.258; *Faith and Understanding I*, p. 275. 'Die Bedeutung des Alten Testaments für den christlichen Glauben' *Glauben und Verstehen*, i. 313–36; 'The Significance of the Old Testament for the Christian Faith', *The Old Testament and Christian Faith: Essays by Rudolf Bultmann and others*, edited by B. W. Anderson (London, 1964), pp. 8–35. *History and Eschatology*, The Gifford Lectures 1955 (Edinburgh, 1957), pp. 150–52.

brings no new thing, no knowledge, no sight, evokes no mystical experiences. 'The proclamation introduces nothing new into our life.' Preachers have only the *fides quae creditur* to proclaim; their task is not to produce faith nor to talk about people of great faith and love.[32]

Once we understand the structure of Bultmann's thought we can see why Christianity is *the* religion and Christ's redemption not a mythical story that must be eliminated. All other religions and all false forms of the Christian religion try to establish themselves in World A or in World B, as though there were room for religion in either of those Worlds. Only Christ preached is the end of all such endeavours, for only the preaching of Christ eliminates completely all human endeavour, all pretext of human ability to do anything at all for salvation. Only Christianity leaves human beings completely without God. There is literally nothing on which to rely.[33]

The one great central temptation of humanity is to want to put something, some value, some safe standing-place there, where there is really only nothingness, only the insoluble problem. All human hatred and lack of love springs from the self-assertiveness that tries to establish some value or some positive power that can be depended on. The basic sin, the only sin, is self-assertiveness. Immoral acts are unimportant in comparison with this sin, for even a good man is self-assertive. To know oneself loved is the only way to love; only the lucky one can give luck to others.[34]

This view of Bultmann's might appear to the casual reader as a particular world-view, but that is why he has been so persistently misunderstood. World-views belong to the anxious who try to impose a pattern on events. The true believer knows the world-views are a part of the basic sin

[32] 'Welchen Sinn hat es, von Gott zu reden', *Glauben und Verstehen* i.37.

[33] 'Zum Problem der Entmythologisierung', *Kerygma und Mythos*, vol. 2 (Hamburg, 1952), pp. 179–208 at p. 207; 'Bultmann Replies to his Critics', *Kerygma and Myth* (London, 1954), pp. 191–211 at p. 210. 'It is precisely its immunity from proof which secures the Christian proclamation against the charge of being mythological': *Kerygma und Mythos*, i.51; *Kerygma and Myth*, p. 42.

[34] 'Krisis des Glaubens' (1931), pp. 14–15; *Glauben und Verstehen*, ii.10–12; *Essays*, pp. 12–14.

of humanity. The liberating truth actually entered history with the actual specific man, Jesus Christ. Casual readers think that Bultmann is describing a particular way his theology happened to get going, taking his theology to be a world-view. They then object that Jesus Christ is not the only particular person who could trigger this world-view. They miss Bultmann's point that what Jesus Christ began is not another world-view but an end to the human pretension that constructs world-views.[35] Therefore, for Bultmann, Jesus Christ as preached is indispensable and unique; he is the only way to human freedom. The historical Jesus and the historical church are both parts of human history which are from outside subject to the determined laws of history. But that is not what is preached; what is preached is the end of any view of history or of any philosophy as a way to freedom. 'Revelation' is what is meant by this self-understanding, the self-understanding that knows that the world of nature and history is closed, determined, and godless. The person who knows this is freed from any possible sort of anxiety about what to do or what to think, and knows himself as one of the elect. He is free to love, and only he is free to love. Anyone who objects to this game is automatically self-judged: he is branded as someone who is anxious and fearful and ready to accept any comforting illusion.

Bultmann is able to draw on a long tradition of theology that condemned all attempts to set up some interpretation of the world in defiance of God, interpretations that measured God and judged him for all the evil and suffering in the world. Augustine had argued that humanity was incurably wicked by the first disobedience of Adam; if God chose to save some and damn others, that was his merciful decision and no one was in a position to argue. The same theme was repeated by Luther and Calvin. Bultmann simply took up the story and argued from Paul, as his predecessors had done, that man could do nothing but obey. Bultmann claimed to carry

---

[35] 'Zur Frage des Wunders', *Glauben und Verstehen*, i.228; *Faith and Understanding* I, p. 261.

through Paul's principle more clearly than Paul did himself, and by that principle all attempts to justify oneself were condemned. All man could do was to accept the gift of being justified while remaining continually also a sinner.[36] No actual specified deeds followed this justification, for that would be to contradict the gift; all that man could do was to obey.

It followed that all attempts to give God existence, to name his qualities, or to establish his being were faithless as well as impossible. God is only known as he acts to justify the godless sinner and free that sinner for absolute obedience.[37] Only that sort of obedience is love. Any attempt to deduce a political or social programme from this obedience shows lack of faith and is to fall back into self-assertiveness from which the word of the cross frees the concrete individual man.

Christianity's uniqueness consists then, according to Bultmann, in its preaching a God who has no existence and in promulgating an ethics with no content save obedience.

Bultmann is a master of rhetoric and sometimes when reading his urgent and beautiful prose, full of pleading and shrewd argument, we can almost believe he brings it off. The fatal defect is that Bultmann cannot possibly show what he has to show: that his position is not a system at all, and that it alone is immune from any sort of examination (for that is what he actually means when he says it is no world-view and unprovable). If he insists (as he does) on this unprovability as proof of the absolute truth of what he says, we have no other weapon to use against him than to walk away. There is no arguing with someone who says that what they say is immune against argument; but that does not prove they are right.

Nevertheless Bultmann has vigorously drawn correct conclusions from his premises. If God's justification of sinners is sheer gift, then there is nothing at all the sinner can do to be justified. If the universe is completely governed by laws in every respect, there is no sense in doing anything to gain

---

[36] 'Das Problem der Ethik bei Paulus', *ZNW*, 23 (1924), 140.
[37] *ZNW*, 23 (1924), 135.

one's freedom. If that is the nature of the universe there is no possibility of serving God, in any natural or historical event. If Christianity is the only religion that knows these things, then the word of Christ preached, which confronts every specific individual who comes to know himself subject to these constraints, is the only forgiveness of sins and freedom there is. Furthermore, anyone who argues for another sort of God or tries to substitute a better world-view for this one simply shows he has not submitted to the only set of constraints there are.

The Bible reigns supreme, for only the Bible relentlessly hunts every man out of every hiding-place of self-assertion and confronts every man with the only conditions under which freedom from sin can be appropriated. But the Bible is not for Bultmann the record of what God has done or of what God has promised, in the sense of offering information to an enquirer; to such an enquirer Bultmann returns a dusty answer indeed. For Bultmann the Bible is the specific offer of forgiveness which can be appropriated by sheer undifferentiated obedience. On Bultmann's terms, Bultmann's position is the only possible conclusion. Bultmann cannot be allowed his terms because they are terms which preclude not only argument with him but argument with anyone at all.

Bultmann lived under the authority of the Bible, as a man and as a scholar, yet anyone who reads the Bible in its straightforward obvious sense as about God's creating and sustaining the universe and as about God's promises and gifts to humanity, would find Bultmann's reading of the Bible and the human situation passing strange. Why should the Bible itself be made to require the elimination of the more characteristic notes of the Bible? How he came to think it did, that is the theme of this book. Bultmann was steeped in the tradition we have been exploring, and all the architects of that tradition had worked out their contributions by reading the Bible – even Kant and Bruno Bauer and Overbeck and Nietzsche, the most antipathetic to Christianity. The key to their work was always provided by the Bible as read in the light of the theological systems under which they had been educated. We need only recall the importance of faith for

Kant and spirit for Hegel, but each chapter in the story has offered us fresh examples of the same thing. The power of the Bible led all these thinkers to despise crass rationalism just as much as superstitious religiosity. Above all they valued dialectical thinking, the ability to put thesis against thesis in order to rise to a higher truth which comprehended the value in each of the positions that were superseded. But this was the logic of the Bible, which moved from slavery to freedom, from death to life; this was the inner logic of a God who was Father, Son and Holy Spirit, a God who become God by going out from himself into his opposite and returning to himself.

I hope this book has made the reader entranced with the beauty and perceptiveness of the systems each of the twenty-one thinkers espoused. But I hope also that it has provided enough examples of theories that can scarcely be maintained in the face of calm and reflective thought to make the reader thoroughly dissatisfied with the way the Bible has been widely and influentially read – a way that continues to flourish today. My aim as historian has been to give lots of examples of perceptive thinking that, too often, suffered from a fatal flaw. I aim to do philosophy a service by providing these examples because philosophy that does not study closely and accurately lots of cases of thought on the subject under scrutiny runs a very great danger of espousing an old or new set of oversimplifications. I have directed attention to the constant dismissal of the notion that God could be discerned and his existence proved by reflection on the nature of the universe of which thinking human beings are part, a dismissal magisterially advocated by Kant. I have also directed attention to the constant assumption that the world must be regarded as a fixed, closed, and endless system, a position again regarded by Kant as one half of the truth. The first of these positions has recently been again challenged by a philosopher who cannot be brushed aside, David Braine of Aberdeen.[38]

---

[38] David Braine, *The Reality of Time and the Existence of God: The project of proving God's existence* (Oxford, 1988); cf. J. C. O'Neill, 'Can we avoid the conclusion that God exists?', *The Philosopher*, 18 (1980), 15–20. Clement Dore, *God, Suffering and Solipsism* (Basingstoke, 1989).

The second has been persistently challenged by many solid and patient philosophers, the prince of whom was A. E. Taylor of Edinburgh.[39] We cannot as theologians regard these matters as settled or boring. Nothing less is at stake than the very ability to argue at all. The history of how the study of the Bible fixed the authority of the Bible at the heart of European consciousness while neutralising the God of the Bible is a history to make us stop and think again. It is our history, and it's deeply flawed.

[39] A. E. Taylor, 'The Freedom of Man', *Contemporary British Philosophy: Personal Statements*, Second Series, ed. J. H. Muirhead (London, 1925), pp. 270–304.

Index

This book is due for return on or before the last date shown below.